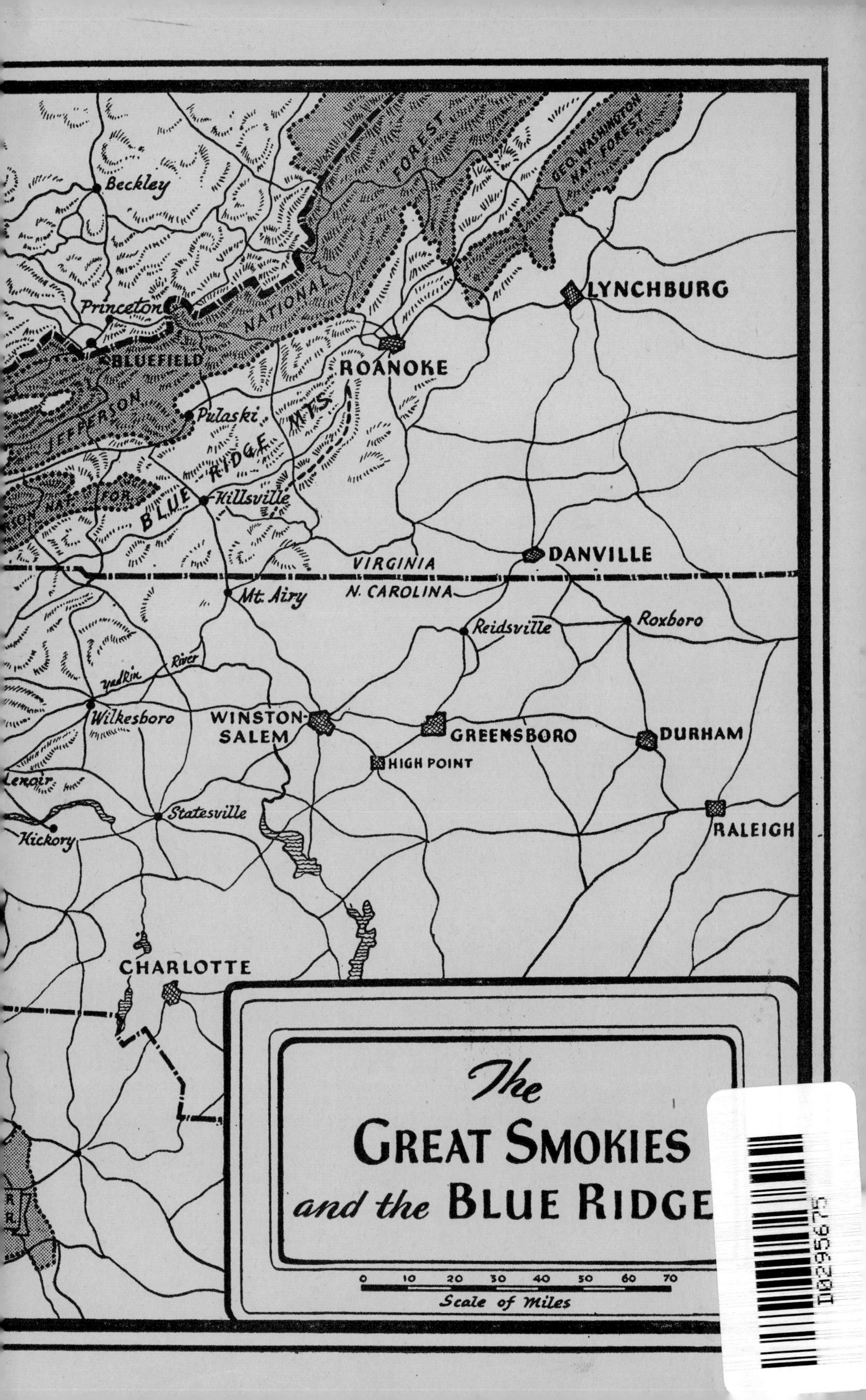
The
GREAT SMOKIES
and the BLUE RIDGE
Beckley
Princeton
BLUEFIELD
NATIONAL
FOREST
GEO. WASHINGTON NAT. FOREST
LYNCHBURG
ROANOKE
JEFFERSON
Pulaski
BLUE RIDGE MTS
NAT. FOR.
Hillsville
VIRGINIA
N. CAROLINA
DANVILLE
Mt. Airy
Reidsville
Roxboro
Yadkin River
Wilkesboro
WINSTON-SALEM
GREENSBORO
DURHAM
HIGH POINT
Lenoir
Statesville
Hickory
RALEIGH
CHARLOTTE
0 10 20 30 40 50 60 70
Scale of Miles

To Ralph C. Pickens, Jr.
to read and pass along—

Ralph C. Pickens
Tryon N.C. Feb. 8, 1944

THE GREAT SMOKIES

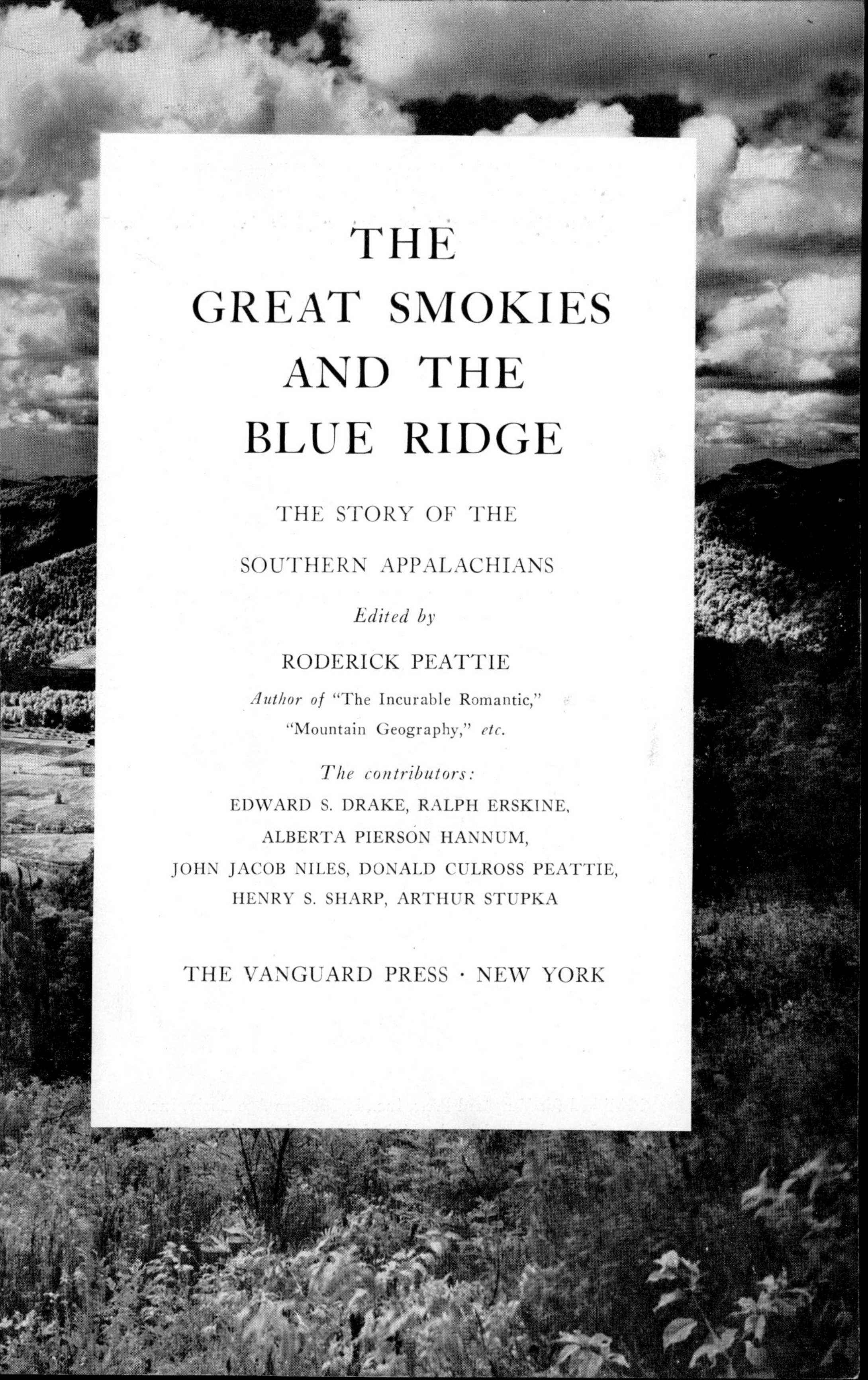

THE GREAT SMOKIES AND THE BLUE RIDGE

THE STORY OF THE

SOUTHERN APPALACHIANS

Edited by

RODERICK PEATTIE

Author of "The Incurable Romantic," "Mountain Geography," *etc.*

The contributors:

EDWARD S. DRAKE, RALPH ERSKINE,

ALBERTA PIERSON HANNUM,

JOHN JACOB NILES, DONALD CULROSS PEATTIE,

HENRY S. SHARP, ARTHUR STUPKA

THE VANGUARD PRESS · NEW YORK

This book has been produced in full compliance with all government regulations for the conservation of paper, metal, and other essential materials.

Published for Vanguard Press, Inc., by Modern Age Books, Inc.
Manufactured in the United States of America
by H. Wolff, New York, N. Y.

CONTENTS

ILLUSTRATIONS

Acknowledgment: Photographs number 1, 5, 6, 21, 26, and 28 are printed by courtesy of Bayard Wootten, Chapel Hill, N. C.; numbers 2, 3, 8, and 9, courtesy of the U. S. Forest Service; numbers 4 and 12, courtesy of Elliot Lyman Fisher, Asheville, N. C.; numbers 7, 10, and 11, courtesy of the National Park Service; number 13, courtesy of the Wildflower Preservation; numbers 15, 16, 23, 24, and 25, courtesy of Carlos C. Campbell, Knoxville, Tenn.; number 14, courtesy of Wylie Bowmaster, Norris, Tenn.; numbers 17 and 18, by Hansel Mieth, courtesy of *Life Magazine,* copyright, Time, Inc., 1943; numbers 20, 22, and 29, courtesy of the North Carolina Department of Conservation and Development, Raleigh, N. C.; number 19, courtesy of Ralph Erskine.

THE GREAT SMOKIES

AN INTRODUCTION AND A STATEMENT OF PHILOSOPHY

by Roderick Peattie

I offer this volume with enthusiasm and excitement, for I know the region of the Southern Appalachians well enough to have a deep attachment to those uplands, and yet I know it so incompletely and imperfectly as to enjoy the offerings of the contributors with keen interest. Thus this volume is for those who still have the pleasant discovery of this mountain area before them, as well as for those who, like myself, know it only in part. My love for the Southern Appalachians began early, for, indeed, my first and still my favorite mountain stands there. Let me record its name and, I am sure inadequately, give my youthful impressions. It is Tryon Mountain, in the North Carolina Blue Ridge, and it is more of a mountain than many because it rises boldly above the low-lying Piedmont. Actually it is a long plateau-like mass with a peak symmetrically midway of its length.

I must have been ten years old when I journeyed from the flat Midwest, where I had been raised, and by chance passed through the mountain zone by night train to breakfast in a mountain inn. The morning was misty, and then suddenly, dramatically, through a cleft in the valley fog appeared Tryon Mountain, clean, washed by the air of the winter morning. I remember feeling that the mountain might fall over on me. I had never looked up before to see the Earth. I have read many first impressions of mountains, Ruskin and Whymper and the rest of them. I have not the pen skill of these masters. But they were men and somehow their writings are academic. I had a naïve advantage over them. After my first fear of the mountain mass I capered a dance about the floor to show my delight.

Tryon is one of the more pleasant towns of the world. It is among mountains and claims a number as its own but it was Tryon Peak that I selected for my first adventures. I came to know it in every season. I explored its surface on foot and on pony back. I pushed aside heavy foliage to enter glens misty with the spray of cascades. I knew where old man Tiger's deserted cabin was hidden away in a clearing of the forest. I have idled away hours by the fords along the road. One summer I lived in a cabin on the tableland that flanked the peak. At the margin of the platform was an overhanging ledge. From here could be seen on one hand a chaos of peaks beyond peaks and on the other an expanse of half a state of rolling hills. In sunlight and in moonlight I have stretched myself as near the edge as I dared and dreamed. My sister was more verbal than I. The view inspired her poem wherein are the lines:

> "Here falls your darkling mountain wall and there
> Blue swims in blue and silence holds the world."

I am the boy who lay on that ledge. The dreams I dreamed are now forgotten but the view is as vivid as the first sight of one's love. I can remember sunrises when the hills would slowly emerge from the morning fog and, finally, the red fields glistening with dew. It was these first impressions of those personalities in rock we call mountains that started me on journeys through ranges of two continents.

My peak is but typical of a thousand that this book will describe.

They are so many that few men will know them all. The area which we are describing is that oval-shaped mass of uplands culminating in the Great Smokies and the Blue Ridge. The whole has a charm born of a disordered, tumbled ruggedness. The very confusion has the advantage of hiding secrets from those whose enthusiasm and perseverance is insufficient and not worthy of rewards. The drainage, the V-shaped valleys that make road-building difficult, isolates coves and communities. The head o' hollow, aflame with redbud, is not for the casual auto traveler. It must be searched out and its discovery then becomes a personal victory. Many of the delights of this land of peaks are accessible only to nag travel or afoot. Few of the peaks have auto roads and seldom are they conquered with ease. The winding trails are full of surprises. Always the achievement of a summit gives one a fine sense of conquest. Yet we would be wrong if we said that the automobile does not serve one well. Today there are magnificent highways to the very heart of the mountain areas. They are, to say the least, what the guide book refers to as "scenic."

But all the pleasures and novelty of these mountains are not in the natural beauty, the breathtaking view from the peak, or the sudden coming upon the unexpected glade white with dogwood blossoms. These mountains are peopled with a folk almost unique among mountain men. In spite of their feuds (of which too much has been made), these people are as gracious to the visitor as could be wished. They are as interesting as the mountains. The inhabitants of the Great Smokies and the Blue Ridge are so in tune and in tone with the topography and the climate that their character seems verily to be born of the mountainous milieu. As many of the clearings are hidden in the laurel, so the true nature of the cabin dwellers is not easy to discover. These people are shy, never forward. One must not barge in upon their privacy, for they resent the blatant visitor, even militantly. *They* are not queer, but we are "quare" to them. To learn to know them calls for a sympathetic understanding of their codes. To gain confidence and friendship one must understand the mountain folkways. One must never hurry them and there are certain amenities which are important.

I remember when a nervous Northerner with whom we were traveling abruptly asked a mountain man the direction to a town. The mountain man did not know. My mother saw the hurt the Northerner had made by his discourtesy. Mother looked about the cabin clearing and said, "This is a very pretty place you have."

"Right pretty," was the reply.

"It's been a fine ride up this road. You certainly are fortunate to live where you can see Hogback Mountain."

"We always like that mountain."

"When we get to the fork should we bear north or south?"

The mountaineer grinned. "Take the north fork and it's been sure a pleasure to have you stop."

A gentleness of manner has been enforced upon them by the mildness of the elements.

To get the most out of mountain or man you should attune yourself to the peace you will find there. You should take your pleasures leisurely. Let beauty ease your soul. Drink it as slowly as you would take a rich, fine wine. Contentment rains down upon the beautiful land like a mist. One chance view from a peak is not the whole story. Return again and again to learn the moods of nature. Clear days in winter are one thing; the haze of summer another. The valley in mottled sunlight is not the valley under the threat of the approaching storm. Learn to know the round of the season, the winter morning with its vivid clarity and the red earth glistening with hoarfrost, the succession of spring flowers, dogwood, laurel, rhododendron and azalea, the luxuriant foliage of summer and the magnolias growing in the spray of some cascade. Come to know the beauty of autumn in your favorite valley. Drink deep of your mountain experiences but drink slowly and you will perhaps return to live out your old age.

Not only in the matter of time sequence but philosophically it is right that this volume should have a chapter on geology. The study of geology everywhere, but particularly in this region, is fundamental, not only in understanding character of slope and trend of valley but it is preface to human history. These southern highlands are born of a geologic parent known to geologists as Appalachia. Let us call it Appalachia, *primus*, lest we confuse it with *secundus*, our highlands as we know them. *Primus* was never seen by man nor did land animals roam its naked, treeless slopes. Before the Paleozoic era and up to the end of that era it stood a gray-pink mass somewhere to the east of the present ranges. Now of alpine grandeur, then eroded to low mature hills, its elevations were again and again heightened as if to compensate for the erosion. Thus it furnished sediments to the continental seas on the west. Great thickness of sediments accumulated. It is these, indurated by time and pressure, plus volcanic rocks, that make up the mountains. The story of intrusion and thrust which made the mountains is worth a volume alone. If but a single chapter is given to the millions of years from the Cambrian period to the beginning of human history and many chapters given to the culture of man, lay it to our greater knowledge of the details of human history, or charge it, if you will, to our egocentric point of view.

It was during the Paleozoic era that land animals and plants came into being. The tale is long to tell. Suffice it that we discuss the complex end result. Our concept of the Southern Appalachians is formed as much by the character of the forest as by the topography. It is not a relatively simple forest like the fine spruce stands of the Laurentides. It is intricate in detail and its varieties are legion. Moreover, the area is, much to our pleasure, in a flower and bush-blossom zone. There is variety partly because of altitudinal differences and partly because of exposure and slope. The whole is a botanical delight.

In the last few minutes in the day of its geologic history, came man. First the Indian, little disturbing nature, stealthily infiltrated the beautiful wilderness. But history, human written history, does not antedate the coming of the white man. Now the invasion was discordant. The white man did not fit into the environment. Rather he slashed the forests for his cabin clearing and his precipitous fields, he permitted soil to erode in a manner offensive to the law of nature and in places begrimed the scene with the smoke of factories. Lumbering made gashes in the mountainsides and carefree streams were dammed and harnessed for his purpose. He did not adapt himself so much to Appalachian nature as he altered it to his purpose. He imposed an Old World culture upon the serenity of American wilderness. This is what geographers call an impact of culture.

Yet the rock was and still is basic in our philosophy. It is like a gray-green boulder and the uncontinuous veneer of humans is like a lichen. Lichens furnish infinitesimal amounts of humic acid which etch the surface of the boulder, but the lichen does not destroy the boulder. The forces which alter Appalachia significantly are the diastrophic forces of nature, the strains of the earth's interior, the stresses of tides and the passing stars and the elements of weather, ice and stream. The ax and the plow do not fundamentally change the mountain. The quarry and the mine are but tiny pittings of the surface.

Appalachia *secundus* has been passive in its relation to us. And yet directly or indirectly it has limited human activity. Men in days of colonial culture were not always forceful enough to overcome certain conditions of life resulting from the character of the rock. Little groups passing up the valleys into hidden hollows in the rock became so isolated as to be out of the stream of civilization. They were by-passed by the flow of more modern ideas. True, the settlers brought with them the culture of the historical moment. But it is a biologic principle that any life group, lowly or human, that becomes isolated from the main body of that form of life, undergoes a divergent evolution. Thus, an indigenous culture was imposed upon the culture which the mountain pioneers introduced in the region. The two cultures, the Old World and the purely mountain culture, went to make up Appalachian life until the turn of the century. Since then modernization has greatly altered modes and habits of the mountain people. Good roads and fine schools are now common throughout the area. Previous to this modern period there was such meagerness of resources that the indigenous culture advanced only to its narrowly potential limits. It gave what is known as cultural stability. It preserved for us colonial life.

To know these stages of development we offer a description of the stability of culture in a chapter on the unique mountain folk-ways. This is not presented as an example of quaintness but rather as an explanation of how these people evolved as they did. It is a serious study in one important phase of our national life, a form more purely American than the Puritanism of New England or the Lockian Democracy of the Tidewater Country. The chapter on changing ways of the mountain folk at once describes them today and gives details of the road system to enable the visitor to find his way about. The exceedingly interesting crafts and the mountain music deserve and here have special attention.

This volume is then a guide to the understanding of a mountain area and the people who live therein. To understand a mountain one must appreciate the process of mountain-making, the forces which created its surprising bulk. One must understand the living forces of degradation which have made and are making the val-leys or the mountain slopes. A delight of every mountain trail is the zonal successions of plants. What kind are the trees, the flowers, the birds? Scientific knowledge of nature is always exciting in a green laboratory. A special chapter on the Great Smoky Moun-tains National Park is found at the end of the book. Moreover this volume is a sympathetic guide to mountain cultures. You are to take your journey along the mountain ways or vicariously in an armchair in a goodly company of experts. Each is a specialist.

Because of his desire to be known as a lover of these mountains, Donald Culross Peattie contributes three chapters to this volume. On that day I first saw Tryon Mountain Donald was beside me in a high chair. Though he has traveled far since, in a sense he has never left those mountains. After studies in botany at Chicago and Harvard he made North Carolina his first collecting ground. Chimney Rock to Caesars Head, the "Shortia" country and the summit of Mt. Mitchell were his conquests.

Dr. Henry Sharp is Professor of Geology at Barnard College, Columbia University. He is one of a half-dozen men in the country competent to write upon the complicated geologic history of the Great Smokies and the Blue Ridge. He has skillfully reduced the detail for the layman.

Alberta Pierson Hannum is the most sympathetic of creative writers who has turned to the mountain folkways for material—sympathetic and distinguished. *Thursday April*, *The Gods and One*, and *The Hills Step Lightly* are among her outstanding works. Born on the plains of Ohio, she has taught and lived in the mountains, returning again and again. Though a "fotched-on" woman, one who came from the outside, there are few better qualified through understanding and artistry to tell the tale of mountain ways.

Ralph Erskine, though of Wisconsin extraction, annually visited his father's winter home in North Carolina. Gradually those visits have lengthened until now he lives in Pacolet Valley and seldom leaves it. His especial interest in the mountains has extended from the days of horseback to those of the auto. His sense of the artistic has led him to a fine appreciation of the mountain crafts. He has been a sportsman and when he tells of the hunt it is from first hand.

John Jacob Niles has a farm, Boot Hill, in Kentucky. But his passion has been the mountain ballad and carol. As a child he learned and sang and later years found him a most distinguished and most understanding student of the music of the mountain folk. He is well known to this country for his lecturing and his records, but your editor has the pleasure of being the first to persuade him to put pen to paper in other than musical script. No one could write on the ballad and carol more authoritatively than he.

Edward S. Drake, the one-time friend of the Grand Old Man of the Mountains, Horace Kephart, is seized with an irrepressible madness about twelve times a year. The cure is once again to return to the Appalachians. I know of no one who has sent more visitors on to the region and sent them with more exact road directions. He can provide the traveler with the exact distance by highway and the exact depth of mudholes in the byways.

Arthur Stupka is park naturalist of the Great Smoky Mountains National Park. His reputation as a scientist is well founded. He has a rare quality of popularizing his science. In addition, he likes people and at his headquarters in Gatlinburg is at your disposal. He writes, "I am doubly fortunate, for my outdoors laboratory is not only a naturalist's paradise, but the sort of people with whom I come in contact are the finest in the world"; and so writing confesses his own character.

One apology for the volume must be made. The terminology of the mountain ranges is not consistent because the ranges themselves are confused and disordered and because new practices are coming into vogue. This is particularly true of the term Unakas. Such will offend only the pedantic and they are seldom pleased. If your pleasure in this volume is comparable to mine in composing it, this book will well serve its purpose.

CHAPTER ONE

INDIAN DAYS AND THE COMING OF THE WHITE MAN

by Donald Culross Peattie

SPANISH EXPLORATIONS

The first part of the great Appalachian chain which white men ever beheld was that farthest from the sea, distant from it some three hundred miles. This is the southern end of the great continental chain; here are the highest mountains in eastern North America, the most rugged, heavily timbered, and the most beautiful.

It must have been a fair day when, after monotonous piedmont travel, the first explorers in 1540 saw the Blue Ridge rising before them. There was promise in its peaks that seem to be higher and more distant than they are, in its shadowy gorges and intricate spurs, its gaps leading to adventure farther on. And beautiful were the mountains when the travelers entered them, for the month was May, the most flowery of all the year in the richest of mountain floras. It is the season when the thrush is singing, and the redbird swoops from one blossoming bough to another, calling "pretty-pretty-pretty, quick-quick-quick."

But the chroniclers of these Spanish adventurers were deaf to birds, to the hypnotic chant of Appalachian streams, and the sound, so ancient and still so strong, of a wind threshing some high grove of hardwoods, laden with the smell of balsam from knobs higher still. The reader of those old accounts hears darker echoes—the blows of swords, the whistling of arrows, the groans of the wounded, clanking of armor, frightened neighing of horses, song of the lash and the splash of it on red skins. He hears the deep baying of the greyhounds hunting Indians for the chain gangs, and the chanting of the friars, bringing the word of Christ to the Devil's wilderness.

For this party, under the renowned Hernando de Soto, came well equipped for a conqueror's purpose. De Soto had been with Pizarro at the sack of Peru. He knew not only the possible rewards of boldness and firmness on the part of a few determined and sufficiently ruthless Europeans when dealing with the simple savage; he also recognized from experience the needs of a conquistador. For those savages the chains had been linked, the iron collars for ankles, wrists and throats had been forged, the lashes braided, and the greyhounds trained and starved. "Florida"—the Spaniard's word for about the same country that we mean by "Dixie"—was to place De Soto, he hoped, with Cortez and Pizarro. Its fabled riches were to repay these six hundred gentlemen of Spain and Portugal for selling their patrimonies, their moldering keeps and maternal jewels, to invest in this dazzling speculation.

That was how De Soto came, marching through Georgia only forty-eight years after Columbus had discovered America. The Spaniards were always successful conquerors, and their demands included, always, slaves and guides and revelation of the whereabouts of those cities with walls of gold which Spanish daring so confidently expected. The Indians who told the truth were tortured; so of course they pointed always to the next tribe beyond, and the Spaniards had no recourse but to believe the lies they wrung from the natives. The only time for doubt would have been before setting out.

De Soto put his weary columns in march again. His route is debatable; Georgians believe his mountain route was all in Georgia, and have marked his conjectured footsteps with monuments. Tennesseans think he reached their state, but North Carolinians think not. He could have taken as many ways over the Southern Appalachians as Hannibal across the Alps. The difficulty in following his course, no matter how logically you read his compass directions and estimates of distance traveled in Spanish leagues, is that his place names are Spanish renditions of Indian words that have vanished.

I shall simply follow James Mooney, widely recognized as the foremost authority on the Cherokees, whose mountain stronghold De Soto is approaching. Mooney's reasons for the itinerary he gives De Soto, the reader may search out and judge.

All authorities, I think, agree that De Soto's country of Chalaque is a Spanish attempt at the word Cherokee. Mooney thinks De Soto marched from Cofitachiqui (Silver Bluff, Georgia) to the headwaters of the Keowee, where the Valley Cherokee had their farms and towns in the foothills of the South Carolina Blue Ridge. From there the Spaniard seems to have turned northeastward, crossing the Saluda, the Tyger, the Pacolet, along an old Indian path, till he came to the Broad River, where it emerges from the mountains. He calls this country Xuala (in English rendered Sualla), which is probably the Indian word Suwali, one of the names for the Cheraw Indians.

He found the Indians' town situated on a small stream, close under a high mountain range. This has been interpreted as the neighborhood of Chimney Rock. The long pass up the mountains is known as Hickory Nut Gap, and it is an easy one, just as the Spanish chroniclers report. Once across, they came to a westward-flowing river (the French Broad), which they rightly took to be a tributary of the Mississippi. From here on De Soto seems to be lost, as he illogically turns south to ascend the river to its headwaters, and then presses on over an intricate system of high ridges and deep defiles, of which the chroniclers make complaint. De Soto is plainly tangled up in the wild Toxaway country (he even calls it the country of Tocax), and it is reasonable to think that he was being deliberately misled by his guide. This was an Indian "queen," who had met him with presents and loving words, and had remained as his prisoner and a hostage for the submissive behavior of her people. Now, having thoroughly lost him in the mountains, she slipped quietly off into the forest wilderness, taking with her a box of native pearls which she had carried under De Soto's covetous eyes all this way.

The progress of some one thousand persons through a dense forest is a complex business. One of its disadvantages is that on all sides the game immediately flees. So that, while the Indians lived fat upon venison and turkey and rabbit, the Spanish knights went gaunt in the midst of plenty.

At length the conquistadores came to Guaxule, a large Indian town with a conspicuous mound which has been identified as the famous Nacoochee Indian Mound near present-day Clarksville, Georgia. Here De Soto was hospitably received, and lodged in the town house or council lodge, a characteristic feature of a Cherokee settlement. From Guaxule he proceeded down what is evidently the Chattahoochee made famous by Sidney Lanier's poem. At this moment the hoofs of these Quixotes' horses were tramping over the sixteen million dollars in gold that has since been taken out of the Dahlonega lode. But the wily Cherokee said nothing, and the Spaniard rode on, his eyes on the horizon.

The proud conqueror passes from our scene, to find a grave in the Mississippi. Besides being the explorer of that river, De Soto was, then, the discoverer of the Appalachians as well, though they never mention this in our schoolbooks. He left no memorial or trace, except the name Appalachian itself (from the Appalache tribe of Muskhogeans on the Gulf Coast), misapplied by him to the fair mountains he traversed so long ago. He was the first, and most famous and colorful, of all our explorers here. He was also the worst—the cruelest, most fantastic, the briefest, and the least appreciative. Little that we can recognize as peculiarly Appalachian in its flavor comes out from his chronicles; the mountains to him were a stone in his greedy path, on which he stumbled, and cursed as only a Christian can. It might be true to say they were a windmill at which for a moment he tilted, seeing in it fabulous wealth, and that its great arms flung him off in disdain.

Twenty-six years later, in November, 1566, the Spaniards came once more. They had established themselves on the South Carolina coast, near Parris Island, at a settlement they called Santa Elena, where their commander, Pedro Menéndez de Avilés, established a fort called San Felipe. He seems to have intended the serious conquest of all "Florida," but his means were pathetic. For instance, Captain Juan Pardo had orders to "discover and conquer the interior country from there to Mexico" with thirty men. In attempting this he reached the foot of the Blue Ridge and built there an ultimate outpost, the tiny blockhouse fort of San Juan. The location of Fort San Juan is in doubt. According to D. D. Wallace, the latest historian of South Carolina, it must have been in Pickens or Oconee County, in the extreme northwestern corner of the state. But from Lowery's commentary one might conclude it was near Old Fort, North Carolina, at the foot of the Swannanoa Gap and the Mt. Mitchell country.

The season was late; snow was falling in the high mountains, and after an attempt to cross them, Pardo gave up, and left fifteen soldiers in the foothill fortress. There is some account of the fighting and the dealings of Sergeant Boyano and his fifteen men with the Indians, but it is not very reliable. We know that Pardo returned the following year, in 1567, to lonely Fort San Juan and reinforced it with about twenty-five men. Probably he expected to come back again and raise a chain of forts.

But Pardo disappears, and even more completely does little Fort San Juan. We cannot know for how long the standard of Spain was raised and lowered, morning and evening, to float on the light wind from the hills. Nor for how long the sentries paced and challenged, nor what they thought, remembering far-off Spain, as they stared at the silhouette of the mountains where the sun went down, and at the heavy curtain of leaves that hangs so still on hot days when the pewee calls, and when the whippoorwill, our ceaseless nightingale, lashes the night air with his song. Vaguely the chronicles state that all the forts hereabout went down at last before the red tide; they were like children's sand castles, which crumble in the sun, and are washed by the waves into mounds that are soon obliterated.

Yet in June, 1935, a farmer named W. Bryson Hammett, near Inman, a town in South Carolina on the railroad between Spartanburg and Asheville, turned up in his field a shaped stone which bore such curious markings that the historian Wallace hastened to see it. A picture of the stone shows it is no Indian artifact, since Indians do not carve dates in Roman numerals. And that date is 1567, when Pardo, and only Pardo, was in this upcountry. The stone further exhibits a parallelogram suggesting, perhaps, a fort. An arrow on the stone points toward it. A symbol of the sun indicates, perhaps, a day's march. Not only is the date right for Pardo but so, too, is the location. For an old Cherokee trail is known to have led through this neighborhood from the Savannah River to the Broad, in sight of the mountains. From Windmill Hill, near by, you can descry the mountains—Glassy, and Hogback, and Rocky Spur, and then the Tryon Range. Somewhere, to the east or west, a day's march off, stood Fort San Juan.

There is no further record of the Spanish in our mountains. But in 1690, James Moore, secretary of the colony of South Carolina, began exploring toward the mountains. At one point he was told by the Indians that there were Spaniards still there, not twenty miles away, digging in the earth for metal. Near Lincolnton, and away up on the Toe River, far over the ranges, in the Valley River country, ancient mines have been discovered. They are the work of white men, for they have mine props and crossbeams and drill holes and broken windlasses in them; they are three hundred years old or so, to judge from the great trees growing on the sides of the excavations. Who made them? And did the miners get their gold out? Did they spend it and enjoy it; or did they hoard it for greedy heirs to quarrel over?

The energies of Spain were pouring into tropical America. Interior "Florida" was soon forgotten, as a bad joke. The Southern Appalachians for more than a century disappear from history. The boughs of the balsams on the high tops were weighted with winter snow. The foothills rolled in an opal haze of summer heat. The dogwood blossomed in spring, and in fall the mitten-shaped leaf of the sassafras was bloody orange. And always the rushing streams hurried down, over winking mica and milky quartz, carrying the spinning corollas, the flaming leaves. In peace the red men hunted the deer, and the red women planted the sacred corn.

THE CHEROKEES

Out West, wherever the scenery cries for an Indian to complete its nostalgic grandeur, one promptly appears—and sells you a piece of jewelry. But in the Southern Appalachians where every old field with corn stalks in it, every quartz stone like an arrowhead reject, every western ridge with its crown of trees like men walking, every veil of blue mist like pipe smoke from some fine old calumet speaks of the red man, the scene is empty of its most natural actor.

True, there *are* Indians in these mountains, Cherokees, though one has to make a journey to their distant reservation to see them. But once this great people held all the southern mountains in their sway. Their territory coincided almost exactly with the limits of this book's focus, from the Roanoke Water Gap in the Blue Ridge, to the end of the Appalachian system in northern Georgia, and to the foot of the Unakas in Tennessee. They claimed an even larger territory—almost all of Kentucky and Tennessee. And though the Shawnees and northern Iroquois also laid claim to this region, the Cherokees were one day to sell Kentucky and Tennessee in the no doubt conscientious belief that it was theirs to dispose of.

The Cherokees belong to the Iroquoian linguistic stock, and had originally a strongly Iroquoian organization. According to their own tradition, they were migrants to their present home, and came from the north, having at one time inhabited the Shenandoah. So the Cherokees formed a northern salient into the southern Indian groups, who belonged to very different and hostile stocks—the Muskhogean Creeks, the Algonquian Shawnees, and the Catawbas, who were a feeble eastern branch of the Sioux.

The Cherokees believe that when they came to these mountains they displaced another race, a group of albino pygmies. Whether this is so or not, they certainly built their towns in some cases upon the celebrated mounds of some predecessor people whose culture, in part, they may have taken over. These mounds are not usually found in the mountains themselves, but in the Great Valley of eastern Tennessee, and the valleys of upper Georgia and, in North Carolina, occasionally in the basin of the Hiwassee.

The word Cherokee has no meaning in these Indians' own language. They call themselves Yunwiya, meaning principal people, and Cherokee is literally Choctaw to them. It is a name given them by their neighbors, and seems to mean cave people.

The Cherokees were grouped by early students into Valley Cherokees (living in the foothills of the Blue Ridge, chiefly in South Carolina), Middle Cherokees, living in the interior basins of the mountains, and the rich and powerful Overhill Cherokees, who dwelt behind or beyond the mountains, in the Great Valley of eastern Tennessee. There were the most populous towns, the richest farms, the widest trading paths. And there if anywhere was the Cherokee "capital," the big town of Echota. This was a sacred or peace town. It was considered a sanctuary, and anyone who could reach it was safe from that blight of Indian life, clan revenge. Other towns were sometimes called fighting towns, and were rudely fortified.

Far more than most Indians did the Cherokees live in towns. It is hard to locate some of these, for Indians moved their smaller towns from time to time, as the fields around them "wore out," or the game grew scarce, or fancy dictated. But these people were organized upon a town basis, and the destruction of their towns by their enemies meant almost as serious a disruption as it does to more civilized peoples. Indeed, like several other southern Indian tribes, the Cherokees are commonly spoken of as "civilized" Indians. The word is comparative, but no less appropriate for that. At least they had evolved a strong social organization, sufficient for themselves.

Cherokee towns were organized around the town council, held in a special lodge called the town house. William Bartram and other early travelers have left us descriptions of this. It was capable sometimes of seating five hundred; the seats, or rather the couches where the members half reclined, were placed in concentric rows, the highest of course at the back. In the center, around the sacred fire, sat the chiefs. The only illumination came from the fire, the ventilation from the open door. The heat was quite suffocating to the white visitor, but the Indians did not cry when smoke got in their eyes.

Usually the town house, which was domed over with earth, stood upon a natural eminence in the heart of the town, or else upon one of the great ceremonial mounds. It is said that the squaws sometimes had a town house of their own; there was a chief squaw in such cases, a sort of prophetess, called Beloved Woman. Ordinary dwelling houses were built of upright logs or boards with cane interlaced between them, and grass for thatching. Later in Cherokee history the Indians imitated the log cabin.

The agriculture was limited to only a few crops—corn and native beans, and a little tobacco, as well as pumpkins, gourds, and squash. But the fields, tended by the squaws, were extensive. In many places white settlers found that the land had long been cleared by the Indians. At the head of the New River, and on the fertile plains of Tellico, as well as in the Watauga, Hiwassee, and Little Tennessee basins, settlers encountered these openings. They called them "old fields."

The Cherokee weapons were the ball-headed war club, spears and bows and arrows, and they hunted, too, with darts and blowpipes. Even shields were used. Children, especially, were allowed to use these last, practicing on grasshoppers. The blowpipe is still made on the Qualla Reservation.

The most famous of Cherokee artistic products were their beautiful tobacco pipes, carved with much artistic imagination out of stone. These, and the arrowheads and spearheads made of flint and quartzite, were usually the work of men, and so perhaps were also the fishhooks and awls of bone. Women made the basketry and prepared the skins of the now vanished elk and bison, of bear and beaver, otter, mink, raccoon, skunk, and deer.

For the Indian knew his quadrupeds as neighbors; no behavior of theirs, as we see from his rich legends and animal fables, was not intimately and fondly familiar to him. It is startling to note that the origin of the Uncle Remus story of the rabbit and the tar baby is to be found in these mountains, among the Cherokees. The Cherokee mythology is the most varied and delightful I remember having encountered anywhere among the American Indians. It is extremely rich in humor, almost always at the expense of the animals, whose characteristics are limned unfailingly. The ghost story is developed with eerie effect. And certainly there is great originality in the wonder tales—about the enchanted lake, the underground panthers, the haunted whirlpool, the stone cannibal and the slant-eyed giant.

But in nothing does Cherokee imagination show up so surprisingly as in the stories of the Little People. They are about the size of children, very pretty, with long hair falling almost to their feet. They do the work of good Indians at night, and are fond of Cherokee children, leading them home when lost. They do not like selfish and prying people, however, and you must not follow when you hear one of their tiny drums beating. They are fond of music and dancing, like the Cherokees, who boast of their sacred Green Corn Dance and of their Eagle Dance.

Dr. Robert Redfield in his work on the Yucatan Indians points out that belief in fairies goes with forest life and vanishes with the trees and their mysterious half lights. In the young days of a mythology, belief in fairies belongs in the category of sacred things. But in its old age, fairy tales descend to the nursery and are believed only by children. So the little spirits troop off toward oblivion.

Probably the first Englishmen who ever visited the Cherokees in their own mountain homes were James Needham and Gabriel Arthur. Needham was an explorer, trader, and experienced wood ranger, in the employ of Abraham Wood, a merchant of Charles City, Virginia. His servant or assistant was Gabriel Arthur, an illiterate but clever youth. Wood's trading post, which he called Fort Henry, was then (1646-75) on the Indian frontier, though today the little town of Charles City seems to us practically on the seaboard. To this trading post, the most important in the English colonies for thirty years, came Indians from as far off as Georgia and Tennessee. The astute Wood, finding that other merchants waylaid the Indians with their furs on the trail, decided to send his employees to the source of supply, to bring in the furs direct. So he sent out Needham and Arthur, with eight Indians, on a memorable April 10, 1673, to cross the mountains to the homes of the proud Cherokees.

On June 25, the traders met a party of Cherokees and were conducted by them for nine days in a southwesterly direction, to the last town of the Catawba Indians at the foot of the mountains.

A few pages of description in Arthur's narrative leave us no doubt of the course by which the Cherokees then led their guests. They toiled over the Blue Ridge, crossed the rolling valley of the New River with its high canebrakes and sandy bed; then came a toilsome passage of the Unakas, through rains and mists, and at last the travelers arrived in the long meadows of the Holston Valley, low ridges bounding it far to the west, and high mountains to the east. There was "great store of game all along as turkes, deere, elkes, beare, woolfe and other vermin very tame." So at last they came to the "Cherokee Towne," a very populous place, undoubtedly one of the prosperous, numerous Overhill villages. Here the crowd was so dense and so curious that a friendly chief built a platform for the two white men to stand upon so that they could be looked at without being crushed. The only horse of the pack train to survive the exhausting passage of the mountains and virgin wilderness was regarded as a divine creature, tied to a post in the center of the village, and fed by its red admirers.

Leaving Arthur to learn the language, Needham hurried back to Fort Henry, and set out again with a pack of trading goods; near the foot of the mountains in January, 1674, he was murdered by a treacherous Occoneechee guide, who tore out his heart and held it out threateningly toward the east, where the white men came from. The murderer then instructed some Cherokees to return home and kill Arthur, and never have anything more to do with the white man.

How that lucky lad was saved from the stake at the last minute by the return to camp of a friendly chief, how he was carried, armed with bows and arrows and painted like an Indian, on war parties that took him to Florida, South Carolina, and Ohio, how he was wounded, captured by hostile tribes, escaped, and returned, is not part of our story. Needham and Arthur undoubtedly began the English trade and sowed the first seeds of the English alliance among the Cherokees, bonds which were to have such fateful consequences in American history. But these first adventurers did not, however daring their explorations, open a practicable way to white merchants, for the trail the Cherokees took was suitable only for themselves.

The first white trader to remain among the Overhill Cherokees was one Cornelius Dougherty, who appeared in 1690. This son of Erin passed his life with them, taking Cherokee girls to wife, and occupying among the Indians that unique position accorded the trader, combined of banker, counselor, ambassador, importer and exporter, which, if he was at all astute and trustworthy, made him the leading citizen, friend of the Indian, and host of the visiting white man. Even when the Cherokees were at war with the whites, they did not molest the trader, a very important munitions merchant in time of war, and a valuable adviser at the peace councils. The presence of Dougherty therefore marks an important event in Cherokee history.

He was also the first to introduce white blood among the children of the tribe, a process that has gone on for almost three hundred years, resulting in half-breeds, quarter-breeds, eighth-breeds until, amongst the exiled Cherokees of Oklahoma, the white blood may be said to have swallowed the red with a corresponding total change in culture. With the eastern Cherokees the process has not gone so far; they are still Indians and proud of it, though they are proud, too, that they have been voting citizens of North Carolina for more than a century. The names of those early traders are preserved still, it is said, on the Qualla Reservation in western North Carolina—little Doughertys and Galpins and Adairs from the country of the shamrock, and McIntoshes and Vanns and Rosses from the land of the heather.

There were two original main trading paths to the Cherokees, in existence before the white man came. One led from Virginia west of the mountains, to the Overhill Cherokees by a "warrior's path" that ran from present-day Roanoke, Virginia, and the Shenandoah, to Chattanooga, Tennessee. The other came up from Charleston to the Valley Cherokees in the foothills of South Carolina, and led up into the interior mountain basins to the Middle Cherokees—at the headwaters of the Hiwassee and Little Tennessee, and over the Great Smokies to the Overhill towns. A third, made much later, led from the Hiwassee Valley to Augusta, Georgia. Along these paths came the traders, with their strings of horses, each with its jingling bell and pack. If the trader was going upcountry he had tin and iron implements, and knives, guns, traps, powder, rouge for war paint, cotton and woolen stuffs, mirrors, cheap jewelry and trading beads; the traders even sold blankets, tomahawks, and tobacco to the Indians! On the return to the white settlements, the horses plodded under great mounds of skins and furs. Cherokees, too, took these roads, in full regalia, paying visits of state or commerce or curiosity to the white men's settlements. They passed white settlers coming slowly upcountry, their chattels and children wobbling on the pack horses. It is said that trader Dougherty first introduced horses among the Cherokees. The savages leaped to the backs of these new beasts like centaurs who had been born with only half their bodies, and soon became not only great horse traders but incorrigible horse stealers, for by Indian morals a strayed horse was his finder's property—and how easy to help a horse to stray!

With the introduction of guns and traps, the fur trade flared up into a roaring business. Soon the white man's domestic animals were popular with the Cherokees. They were especially delighted by pork, though they appreciated beef and milk too, and poultry and eggs. Peas and potatoes were added to their agriculture, and honey sweetened life for them. Coffee cheered it. The peach became their favorite fruit, and they planted thousands and thousands of peach seeds, and plum seeds, too. The simple savages still saw little but good in the white man's civilization with its goodies and gadgets.

At this time they probably numbered twelve thousand well-contented, suddenly prosperous souls, whose mortal enemies, the Creeks, Catawbas, and Tuscaroras, were being crushed by the Europeans. They themselves could muster about five thousand warriors. They were a formidable power to their foes, and their friendship was courted by the English in the east and by the French in the west.

That eccentric, wandering, lovable genius, William Bartram, the Quaker botanist, saw these people at the height of their power. Other travelers have left their impressions of the Cherokees, and they do not much resemble Bartram's descriptions of the Indian character and habits. The difference, I think, lies in the mentality and attitudes of the visitors. Bartram came as a friend of the Indians, or at least a respectful and objective observer. He makes things sound idyllic where others refer only to filth and savagery. But Bartram did not expect the Indians to be anything but what they were. And if he found them courteous, hospitable, peaceful and interesting, is it not likely that the ingenuous redskins were reflecting their guest's thoughts and actions? If others found them greedy, devious, and cruel, what then are we to conclude?

In 1738, smallpox was brought to the Carolinas on the slave ships. It traveled up the trading paths, and burst upon the Indians with fearful effect. One half the entire population is said to have been carried off. Rather than await the ravages of this horror, many Indians committed suicide even when in health, and others killed their wives and children while they slept. Once established among them, the disease lurked about, endemic and ready to blaze up again and again. So the Cherokees began to pay the cost of contact with the whites.

That cost now mounted. For the British Crown regarded this mountain tribe as an ideal buffer state between the English colonies on the coast and the power of New France, slowly approaching from the west, up the Tennessee and Cumberland rivers, through the water gaps. The French were penetrating Alabama with forts and alliances, inciting the dangerous Creeks. They were coming east through Tennessee, making the Shawnees their allies. The Cherokees must be won over to an alliance with England, and the English took the surest way to do it; they encouraged traders to permeate the whole fabric of Cherokee life, until indeed the Cherokees admitted "they could not live without the traders." As for Cherokee lands, the Crown may have had designs on the best of them in Kentucky; probably it intended to give them as political plums, or sell them to London land syndicates. But it was distinctly opposed to letting the American colonists take up tomahawk claims on them; that would enrage the Cherokees and ultimately balk the Crown.

George II, in 1750, sent for a delegation of seven Cherokee chiefs, among whom was Oconostota, soon to figure in fateful events. They came to Whitehall and took the king's hand; they were shown his throne and his crown, his palaces and ships, and his great town. And they gained the impression, true enough so far as diplomatic friendships go, that the English were their friends.

The American colonists, even more truly, saw in the Cherokees their inevitable future foes. For westward expansion was not possible to Southerners without crossing the Cherokees' path, and the Indians held a strong position in their mountain passes. Treaties made by the Georges in far-off London, guaranteeing the Cherokees the inviolability of their boundaries, were made over the heads of the pioneers. And they were hollow anyway, for on every occasion the white settlers had already penetrated far beyond the said boundaries, making tomahawk claims, and defending them with blazing rifles. The individual pioneer did not go through the diplomatic hypocrisy of pretending peace, love, friendship, and inviolable agreements with the Indians. Declared or undeclared, the war was on. The forces propelling westward expansion were beyond the pioneers' control, and so far from controlling them, they set their shoulders to the wheels of their wagons and exulted in rolling them up-country.

The Indians soon saw, too late, that their most formidable foes were not Creeks and Tuscaroras and Shawnees, still less the French, but the Americans who had used them as a club to crush all the others. They saw that from the Americans they had everything to fear, and no relenting mercy to hope for. Even when the pioneers and Cherokees were allies in the French and Indian War, they fell out. The whites complained justly that the Indians did not really want to fight the French, and stole the white soldiers' horses. The Indians retorted truthfully that the pioneers saved themselves by expending their red allies in every dangerous corner, and that for a trifling misdemeanor like horse-stealing the Cherokees were tomahawked and had their scalps sold in Charleston for the bounty then placed on Shawnee locks! And while the braves of the sanctuary town of Echota were off helping the whites, some soldiers stationed near it ravished the Indian women.

There were sharp clashes, and the Cherokees tried concessions. They gave up a portion of their ancient holdings, in the supposition that the settlers might be satisfied with that. They submitted to becoming the unquestioning allies of the Crown, in offense and defense. They agreed to the strict regulation of their trade, to the appointment of a white agent for their affairs. They allowed the Americans to build and garrison two forts in their midst—Fort Prince George in Oconee County, South Carolina, on the trading path at the foot of the mountains, and Fort Loudon far beyond, among the Overhill clans of Tennessee, where its guns frowned ostensibly on Shawnees and Frenchmen, but also covered the Indian "capital" of Echota.

But still the settlers were not satisfied. In 1759, Governor Lyttelton of South Carolina precipitated a war, in spite of every effort of the Cherokees to make peace. And though the Cherokees won a great victory near the present town of Franklin, North Carolina, and massacred the garrison of Fort Loudon, they did not succeed in taking Fort Prince George, and the next year Colonel Grant decisively defeated first the Valley and then the Middle Cherokees. He burned their towns and their crops, cut down their orchards, drove off all their horses, pigs, cows, killed without quarter every Indian male, and hunted fugitives into the mountains. So the Overhill Cherokees sued for peace. Once again they gave up territory and were guaranteed the new boundaries. George III issued an order for all squatters to return to the white frontier.

But none answered that call. Every year now thousands of immigrants were pouring down upon the mountains from the north. They were a new people, quite different from the Carolinians and Virginians of the coast. These newcomers hated King George; they hated the Episcopalian aristocrats of the coast; they despised the Negro slaves; they had nothing but death in their hearts for the Indians. And, Bible in one hand, rifle in the other, they sought a new Canaan, confident that God had appointed it for them.

To understand how these people made themselves masters of the complex mountain system, one must now turn and consider the mountains themselves.

GEOGRAPHIC INFLUENCES

Probably no portion of North America has a more intricate physiography than the Southern Appalachians. A first glance at a map of the ranges and valleys of our area fills one with despair; the mountains seem to go every which way, and half of the rivers exactly contrariwise. A heavy rainfall descends upon these highlands. The result is the most abundant and elaborate drainage system on the continent. Every stream has a hundred tributaries, every tributary a hundred forks, every fork a thousand tiny streamlets. And all of them have their gullies, side ravines, little valleys and bigger valleys.

The mountains have been carved with all this water erosion as distinctively as the Alps are ice-carved. At the same time they have had a will of their own; they have buckled and folded, and ancient stream courses grown sluggish were thus rejuvenated. The mountains forced them this way and threw them that way, so that the streams squirm and fight through the seismic chaos. The mountains are not dynamic at the present time, and the streams would have it all their own way except for the forests. For the heavy rainfall produces a dense, tall, three-tiered forest with a mantling carpet of moss and herbs upon the ground. All these plants hold the soil, store or filter the water, or sponge up or delay it on the surface or in the ground. The virgin forest has the run-off of the moving waters in check, just holding it in exquisite balance. So they battle—river and tree and hill.

The people who came to these mountains had to battle all three. That is the story. To follow it we must unravel the geography, find some reason and order in chaos and complexity. Else we will not understand why so many of the mountain valleys were entered from the west instead of the east as one would normally expect. Or why the Indian frontier was not a north-south affair but soon became a circle, with the beleaguered red men fighting for their lives inside it, and the whites galloping round and round it, whooping and shooting. Or how it is that the mountain whites formed a salient of Union sympathy deep in the heart of the Confederacy. Or why they form a salient of eighteenth-century Old-World culture in twentieth-century America. Or how it is that, having so close a cultural and blood relationship, these people until recently scarcely knew each other, much less the outside world.

Indeed, their disunited character is one of the most striking things about the mountain people. Until the advent of the automobile, they betrayed, sometimes, the most astounding ignorance of near neighbors, even when separated only by a moderate mountain range. Many instances of this have been told; I have met some striking ones myself. Probably nothing would be more universally understood, however, than the case, discovered in these mountains by Dr. Asa Gray, the famous botanist, of the valley that forgot God. In a few generations, from isolation and neglect, it had lost contact with religion. Whatever may have motivated the men and women of this valley to their good, it was not knowledge of God; the birth of the child Jesus was not commemorated among the children of that valley on December Twenty-fifth, for the Child was not remembered. The example may be extreme and without parallel elsewhere in these mountains, but the mountains explain this anomaly, just as they explain how the beautiful handicrafts of these people were preserved when more cosmopolitan communities lost their heritage of traditional domestic art.

Let us then have a look at these friends and foes of man, the Southern Appalachians.

One clear topographic feature does emerge at once from the intricacies of our mountain map, and that is the Blue Ridge, the east wall of the Appalachian system that runs from northern Georgia to northern Pennsylvania. It makes some bends and loops, and it is cut repeatedly, from Virginia northward, by a characteristic feature of Appalachian geography, the water gap. Still, it is essentially a straight front wall or escarpment of mountains, and though north of the Roanoke Water Gap the Blue Ridge is indeed nothing but a ridge, easily surmounted even in the absence of gaps and passes, yet in North Carolina the Blue Ridge becomes a formidable obstacle, the surmounting of which was only possible through a few passes.

The passes of the Southern Appalachians have been somewhat neglected in the interest which has centered on those of the Central Appalachian system, like the renowned Cumberland Gap.

True, modern engineering, given time and money enough, will surmount any declivity that the Appalachians can show. But the first settlers here had no state money for the building of roads that simply contradict geography; they had little powder for removing the great mountain rocks and enormous trees. So their penetration of the mountains depended upon passes.

Now, a pass, to have human significance, must be more than a mere gap between peaks. It must be low enough to be serviceable. The land passes of the Unaka chain, almost all five thousand feet high, or higher, were all but useless. Further, a pass to be of importance must lead from one important natural site of settlement to another one, through an otherwise intraversable wall. Many of our passes here merely connect two forks of the same valley system, reducing them to second-rate or third-rate importance. The first-rate passes are none too many, and some, like the Swannanoa Gap, Hickory Nut Gap, Saluda Gap, Rabun Gap, Watauga Gap, and Wayah Gap, have been channels for history, for a pageant of Spaniards, traders, explorers, armies, and settlers.

As the Blue Ridge approaches South Carolina, in the Tryon region, it begins to weaken. From Chimney Rock to Caesars Head its inner rim is only a little higher than the Hendersonville-Asheville plateau behind it. It is therefore not surprising that settlers found here an easy access to the fertile French Broad Valley. Or that early in the nineteenth century the Charlestonians, seeking a cool summer retreat, came up through Saluda Gap to Flat Rock.

From here on, the Blue Ridge appears like a festoon looping between the terminal abutments of the mighty transverse or cross ranges. Here it was that De Soto lost himself, in the Toxaway country, or the Shortia country as botanists call it from a famous rare flower. The transverse ranges are often as lofty and craggy as the Unakas, or more so. They might be compared to the rungs of a ladder of which the Blue Ridge and the Unakas are the poles. The transverse ranges, bearing such picturesque names as the Balsams, the Craggies, the Black Mountains, the Newfound and Snowbird Mountains and the Nantahalas, have kept the Southern Highlanders apart from each other, in their separate interior valleys; they have delayed road building and in many cases deflected railroad construction. They are mightier than the Blue Ridge itself, are pierced by few low gaps, and have added greatly to the complexity of mountain peopling.

In Georgia the whole mountain system begins to break down. The Rabun Gap was destined, when at long last settlement crept to this point, to let in armies and settlers just as once, perhaps, it let De Soto out of the highland wilderness. In Georgia the Appalachians proper end; they are like the stern of a great ship, with a wake of diminishing ridges behind it. Those who do not want to cross the mountains in this neighborhood, have only to go around them, as the Creek Indians did on their trading paths, as the South Carolinians were to do in the eighteenth century, dragging their cannon through the wilderness, to build Fort Loudon behind the mountains, in the valley of the Tennessee.

Now, in addition to the Blue Ridge itself, which may be defined as the watershed between Atlantic-draining and Gulf-bound waters, there will be noticed on the map a remarkable series of discontinuous or even quite isolated mountains that, like flying buttresses, are thrust east-northeast into the piedmont, at an acute angle with the true Blue Ridge. These are miniature Appalachians, sometimes having the form of ridges and hogbacks, sometimes almost butte-like, monadnocks of some pre-Appalachian highland, perhaps. They should have a collective name, and might well be called the Outer Blue Ridge. From north to south they are the Brushy Mountains, the Hickory Nuts, the South Mountains, the Tryon Range, and, in South Carolina, the Saluda Mountains, Table Rock and Pinnacle Mountain, the Oconees, and others.

These deserve more fame than they have received. Many writers do not even mention them because they are not "high,"

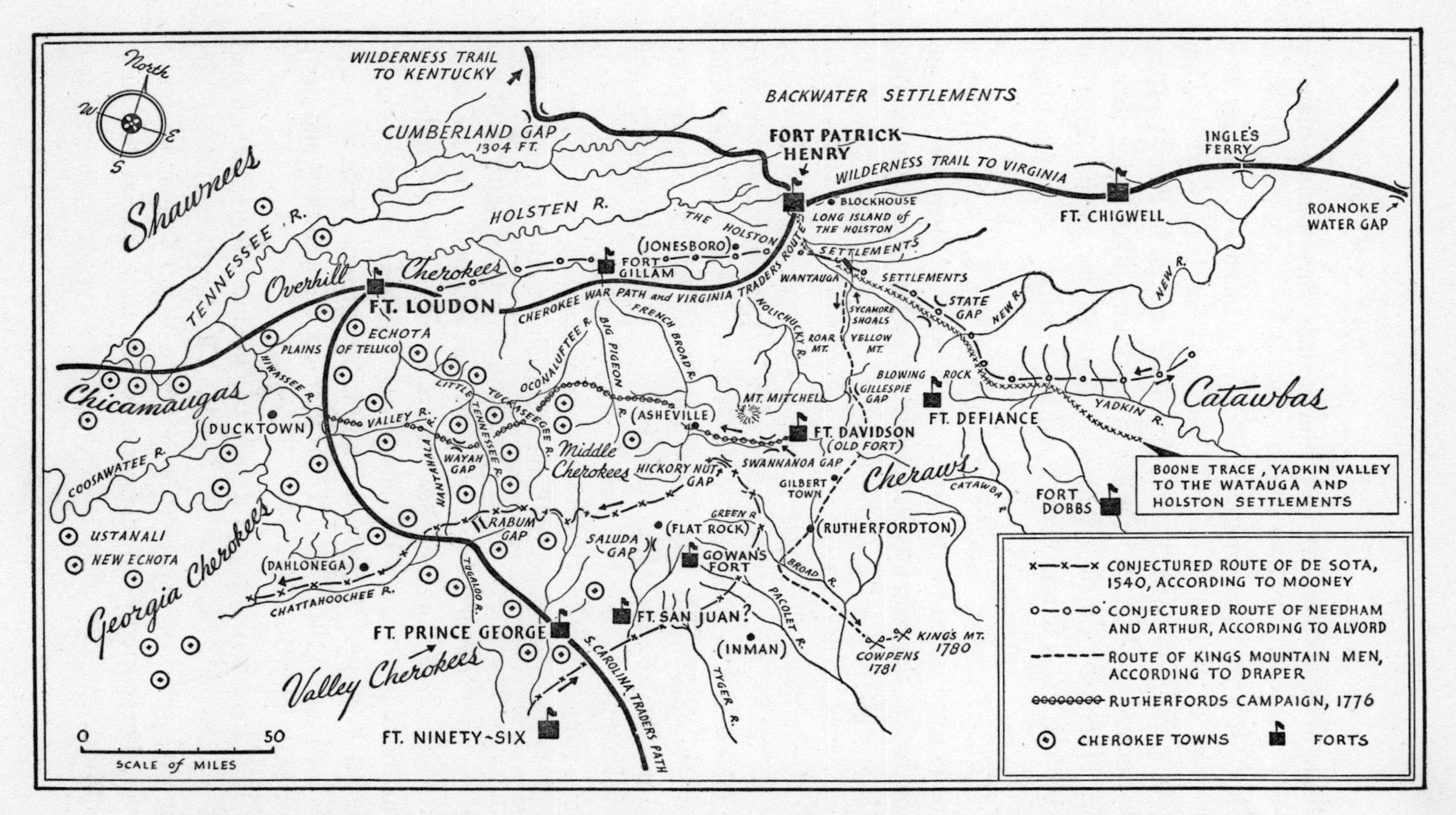

A MAP TO SHOW THE INDIAN TRIBES AND TOWNS, ROUTES OF EXPLORERS, TRADING PATHS, TRAILS, FORTS, BATTLES, AND CAMPAIGNS OF THE INDIAN AND REVOLUTIONARY WARS

although they stand as high above their surrounding plains as many technically higher peaks above their environing plateaus. They are a true part of the Southern Appalachian province. It is in these mountains, above all, that gold has been found. They have a drier, sunnier climate, almost frost-free in certain places. Settlement is older and thicker in the Outer Blue Ridge than in any other part of the highlands. And, so far as the American Revolution was fought in the Southern Appalachians, it was fought here.

This, of course, could be attributed to the fact that settlement had not proceeded much farther at that date. When the Revolution broke, the colonists were still entangled in the Outer Blue Ridge and were settling the beautiful coves between it and the main chain. That settlement had gone little farther is explained by the terrain. The early colonists were not eager to leave the coastal plain, for the advantages of tidewater communication with England and between communities were great. The piedmont, with its unnavigable rivers, was sought out only as coastal plain farm soils deteriorated, as malaria drove settlers up-country, and new immigrants found the low-country claims pre-empted. Slowly the piedmont was to fill with settlers of English, Scotch, German and Huguenot descent. Still the approaches to the mountains presented increasing difficulties. The natural path of settlement was up the river bottoms, on rich soil. But the mountain streams, some of which descend at their headwaters 2,500 feet in five miles, are usually found in deep V-shaped gorges between ridges of an inverted V shape. Rocks and inhospitable streams drive man and his roads up on the ridges. The settlement from the east and south was truly uphill work!

But there was a key to unlock the mountain gates, which had been discovered as early as 1671 by Thomas Batts and his Virginians, who went through the Roanoke Water Gap and found a river, unexpectedly flowing west, which they named the New.

The key they discovered can best be understood by another glance at the map, which will show that by coming up the Shenandoah, or breaking through the Blue Ridge wall by the easy water gaps of the James and Roanoke rivers, access is had to the Great Appalachian Valley.

This is the negative of the Appalachians proper, earth trough to their cresting earth waves. This depression makes itself felt from New York State to Alabama. The Shenandoah flows in it, and was early settled by the Pennsylvania "Dutch" (Germans) and Pennsylvania "Irish" (Ulstermen). Once within this great valley, traders, hunters, explorers, armies, and immigrants found themselves in a natural corridor. No formidable mountains separate the headwaters of the rivers in this valley. With ease one passes from the sources of such Atlantic-draining streams as the Shenandoah, the James, and the Roanoke, to the Ohio-draining New River. Over slight divides one can find the way from the New River to the Holston, the Clinch, and the Nolichucky which run south through Tennessee.

Here, among natural meadows dotted with herds of bison, elk, and deer, where the valuable beaver and otter lived in the streams, the Overhill Cherokees had their towns, their rich farms and happy hunting grounds. Here ran their path for war and trade, their strategic interior lines of communication. Anyone entering the Great Valley would find himself on a deep rich loam above sweet limestone rock, on level land, ever broadening as he moved south. The rivers were navigable and became increasingly so, at least for canoes and pirogues. So, inevitably, the Great Valley was likely to be settled from the north at least as fast as the Blue Ridge could be crossed from the east.

The Blue Ridge is the dividing line between east-flowing and west-flowing rivers. But the master chain of the whole Southern Appalachians is the high, very rugged and densely forested Unaka Mountain system of which the Great Smokies are a central part.

Yet the west-flowing rivers all cut right through this chain. They do this, say geologists, because they are older than the mountains. As the rocks buckled up in the upheaval of the Unakas, the rivers, with equal energy, sawed through the rocks. The Watauga, the Nolichucky, the French Broad, the Big Pigeon, the Little Tennessee, and the Hiwassee all rise on the inner (western) rim of the Blue Ridge, but escape from the mountains by deep water gaps in the Unakas.

Thus it came about that the explorers and settlers of the Great Valley, by turning eastward, could enter the interior mountain valleys by the back door as easily as these could be reached by forcing a way westward over the Blue Ridge. Perhaps the "easiness" of doing this from any direction, in the face of fierce Indian opposition, should not be exaggerated. But the fact is that the New River headwaters and the Watauga Valley were pioneered from Virginia while the slow tide of settlers from Carolina was still hesitating at the foot of the Outer Blue Ridge far to the east.

To think of the Appalachians as do the dwellers in them, one must know the mountain people's terminology. These homely words may not sound as scientific as words of foreign origin like *massif*, *glacis*, *crevasse*, and the like, or as elegant as gorge, pass, peak, range. Yet the natives' language for their scenery could seldom be improved in descriptiveness.

A pass is usually a gap or, rarely, a notch. The word peak is found on our maps and might be understood in this region but it is really not native to it. The equivalent is top, or knob; high top and high knob indicate lofty peaks. Dome may describe a shape, but often indicates a barren rock summit. But a bald is usually a mountaintop with a permanent grass meadow. Botanists speak of heath balds, meaning an area crowned with an intricate shrub tangle of the heath family, but mountain people call these slicks, and distinguish between laurel, rhododendron, and ivy (Kalmia or mountain laurel) slicks. A balsam is a mountain crowned by balsam fir or spruce or both. A hogback vividly if inelegantly describes a type of mountain so characteristic that it might almost be called an appalachian, as one speaks of an alp. Ridge and spur are designations very common, highly descriptive, and characteristic.

A valley usually means a big valley; a small one is a hollow or a cove. Most of the native life of these mountains is lived in the coves. Level alluvial land among the mountains is usually a bottom.

A river denotes a large stream; its prime tributaries are creeks, and pronounced creeks, too, not "cricks" as in the Middle West. The word brook is never heard; run is employed in Virginia but not to the south. Branch and fork are common names for minor tributaries.

Into this densely forested province, with its two great parallel chains of the Blue Ridge and the Unakas, connected by powerful cross ranges, between which flow the twisting rivers of the interior drainage, are to come streams of immigrants with little experience of mountain and forest, and with none of the red man. Let us see who they are, and why they came.

THE PIONEERS

In the year 1607 when Jamestown, Virginia, was founded, James I, for whom it was named, himself instigated quite another sort of colony. For he declared that the lands of the rebellious earls of northern Ireland were forfeit to the Crown, and he opened them for settlement. Then began a great emigration from the overcrowded Lowlands of Scotland, where a breed of warlike, intensely Protestant, land-famished people were ready to jump at the King's invitation to colonize Ulster. Certain tracts were reserved to the Irish but, for the rest, the land was seized by fifty thousand invaders who, as Lord Bryce understates it, "somewhat unceremoniously drove the Irish into the glens of Antrim and the mountains of Mourne."

At first the Ulstermen were well content in northern Ireland. They did a fine business exporting beef, pork, mutton and wool to England. The people were a lusty lot, "Presbyterians and phanatiques," as one old account puts it, "able-bodied, hardy and stout men. . . . They are very numerous and greedy after land." But between 1655 and 1699 Parliament passed a series of acts prohibiting the Ulstermen from exporting their products to England and Scotland, and at the same time it put Presbyterians under severe disabilities, and tithed them for the support of the Church of England.

The act of 1704 imposed final indignities. Presbyterians were forbidden to hold any civil or military office, and their clergymen were forbidden to celebrate marriages. Thus driven by economic necessity, goaded by attempts to cramp their every natural ability, these high-spirited Ulstermen began their exodus to America. Along with them came native Irish too, and some Welsh—a Keltic company altogether.

Usually they disembarked at Philadelphia, at Lewes and at the old Swedish settlement of New Castle in Delaware. It was at this last point that the log cabin (unknown to the early New England, New York, and Virginia colonists) was introduced from the Swedish forests. Here, or more probably somewhere on the frontiers of Pennsylvania, our future mountaineers picked it up—the perfect first shelter for pioneers in a forest country. In its quick construction these immigrants were soon to become past masters, helping each other at log raisings so that a new home could be erected before nightfall, and as soon as logs were chinked with dobbin, the puncheons for the floor were in place, and the stick-and-mud chimney was up, a man and his family had their home ready. No part of the country, today, still clings so fervently to the log cabin as the people of the Southern mountains do. It is their own style of domestic architecture now, the very symbol of their homes, as it has been the symbol of the heroic age of American life for generations.

But I am hastening ahead of these immigrants. In 1729 six thousand arrived in Pennsylvania in one year; soon after that, twelve thousand a year. They were "bold and indigent strangers, saying as their excuse when challenged for titles, that we had solicited for colonists and they had come accordingly."

The price of Pennsylvania land went up, in the presence of the new demand for it, and sterile soils to the west also deflected these "indigent strangers" southward. So for the next fifty years a steady stream of migrants—known more or less incorrectly as the "Pennsylvania Irish"—moved across Maryland and into Virginia. They came up the Shenandoah (that is, southward) and also along the eastern side of the Blue Ridge. These two streams, divided by the Blue Ridge, flowed parallel through Virginia. The western stream diverged into the "Backwater settlements" of southwestern Virginia and so, by the route mentioned in the foregoing section, into what is now northeastern Tennessee, then called the Holston and Watauga settlements. The eastern stream of migrants continued on down the upper piedmont, having much of the time the Blue Ridge in sight on their right. They settled first the valley of the Yadkin, and then of the Catawba, sharing these lands with a simultaneous stream of Germans (Pennsylvania "Dutch"). And, keeping straight on, leaving the German element behind now, they entered the upper valleys of the Broad, the Pacolet, the Saluda, and the Keowee, until they reached Georgia, where, at the stern-end of the Appalachians, they joined forces, after the Revolution, with their Tennessee brethren. Wherever there were land gaps in the Blue Ridge and water gaps in the Unakas, they sought a way—themselves like some permeating flow—to fill every cranny of the mountains.

It would be wrong to think of this stream as swiftly moving; it was merely more sudden than the Anglo-American frontier approaching from the coast. The first of the Scotch-Irish stayed with the Germans in the Shenandoah and on the Virginia piedmont. The next-comers had to go farther to find unclaimed land, and so passed the first-comers' doors, and stopped as soon as they encountered free land to the south. So, by a sort of leapfrog practice, the immigration progressed. The immigrants had wagons if they were well-to-do, but many, like Morgan Bryan, Daniel Boone's future father-in-law, had to dismantle their wagons for lack of a road, and pack the parts on the horses' backs. The typical mountain pioneer had only a pack horse or two, and wife, chattels, and children joggled so into the wilderness. Their progress might be slow, but more than four hundred of these families, with horses, wagons, and cattle, came to North Carolina in a single year (1752-53) and before long these immigrants had doubled the population of that erstwhile slow-growing colony.

By this time it is hardly necessary to state how distinct were these people, in blood, tradition, religion, culture and political sentiment, from the English colonists of Virginia and the Carolinas, who had come earlier and had still barely reached the foot of the mountains by a direct approach. The difference was borne in upon me again only recently, when I stopped in tidewater Virginia and read the list of young men's names posted by the Selective Service Board of Gloucester County. These names might have come from the tombstones at Stoke Poges churchyard where Gray wrote his *Elegy*, so purely English were they. Two days later I was up in the Blue Ridge, and there one saw called to the colors nothing but McAlpins and McCoys and Rosses and Kerrs and other Scotch-Irish names. The Ulstermen, then, in their line of immigration southward, cut at right angles to the slowly approaching English line as it moved westward. Swiftly they filled the gap between the English frontier then on mid-piedmont, and the mountains.

Perhaps someone who knows well the Lowland Scotch and the Orangemen as they were in the eighteenth century could paint the background of our mountain people. One writer has stated that our best clue is to read *Kidnapped* and *David Balfour* to understand the intensity of clan love and interclan hatred and clan revenge, the poverty and squalor mixed with incredible courage and chip-on-shoulder pride, and the strange unwritten laws of these people who, by other standards, seem to hold law in such contempt. Certain it is that the Scotch-Irish brought with them the blood feud and clan revenge, the right of man to brew his own whisky, and an unquenchable land hunger. These people were clannish before they came and had been so for untold generations. The geographic isolation of the coves of the Southern Appalachians fostered that clannishness. And the tradition that the man hunts, fishes, and fights, and the woman is a hewer of wood and a drawer of water and a plower of fields, was not learned from the Cherokees (who held the same views) but was brought over in the very hands that carried the Bible to the hills as militantly as if it were scourge of the heathen and title to Canaan, all in one. The conditions of pioneering in these heavily forested mountains reinforced that primitive division of man's work and woman's: the men were indeed amply busied with fighting off Indians, and hunting game and pelts. Without resentment, the women folk unquestioningly assumed the other duties.

It is true that these conditions have now all tended to disappear. But they persisted a long time. I can remember back to several shooting feuds when I was a child in these mountains, and I have been in several moonshine blockade stills. I am not passing judgment on these matters. The historical reasons for these conditions are all I am attempting to state.

The Scotch-Irish, however, brought finer things with them. They brought the old Scottish ballads about which Mr. Niles writes in this book, and the traditional weaving patterns about which Mr. Erskine tells. They brought a tradition of the highest courage and of political freethinking and independence that saved the American Revolution at a critical moment, and certainly helped to save the Union. They were from the beginning, and they remain today, some of the most gifted and courageous and interesting people that ever came to this country. But from the first they have suffered by characterizations at the hands of outsiders who have made everything of the uncouthness of some of these people, as if that indicated a defect of mentality or character instead of a defect in opportunity, while at the same time their detractors have never taken the time (and it does require time) to make friends with these hardy mountaineers. In particular they were held in contempt and looked on with hatred by the Tories and the Englishmen who came to America as appointed officers or as travelers. One of these early observers has left us his reflections. The back country people are, he said:

"hospitable in their way, live in plenty and dirt, are stout, of great prowess in manly athletics; and, in private conversation, bold, impertinent, and vain. In the art of war (after the Indian manner) they are well-skilled, are enterprising and fruitful of strategies; and, when in action, are as bold and intrepid as the ancient Romans."

Another, quoted by Henderson, describes their appearance at this time:

"Their whole dress is very singular, and not very materially different from that of the Indians; being a hunting shirt, somewhat resembling a waggoner's frock, ornamented with a great many fringes, tied round the middle with a broad belt, much decorated also, in which is fastened a tomahawk, an instrument that serves every purpose of defence and convenience; being a hammer at one side and a sharp hatchet at the other; the shot bag and powderhorn, carved with a variety of whimsical figures and devices, hang from their necks over one shoulder; and on their heads a flapped hat, of a reddish hue, proceeding from the intensely hot beams of the sun.

"Sometimes they wear leather breeches, made of Indian dressed elk, or deer skins, but more frequently thin trowsers.

"On their legs they have Indian boots, or leggings, made of coarse woollen cloth, that either are wrapped round loosely and tied with garters, or laced upon the outside, and always come better than half-way up the thigh.

"On their feet they sometimes wear pumps of their own manufacture, but generally Indian moccossons, of their own construction also, which are made of strong elk's, or buck's skin, dressed soft as for gloves or breeches, drawn together in regular plaits over the toe, and lacing from thence round to the fore part of the middle of the ancle, without a seam in them, yet fitting close to the feet, and are indeed perfectly easy and pliant.

"Their hunting, or rifle shirts, they have also died in a variety of colours, some yellow, others red, some brown, and many wear them quite white. . . .

"The women wore linsey (flax) petticoats, and 'bedgowns' (like a dressing-sack,) and often went without shoes in the summer. Some had bonnets and bedgowns made of calico, but generally of linsey; and some of them wore men's hats. Their hair was commonly clubbed. Once, at a large meeting, I noticed there but two women that had on long gowns. One of these was laced genteelly, and the body of the other was open, and the tail thereof drawn up and tucked in her apron or coat-string."

This gives us a glimpse of the physical appearance of these pioneers; other English observers complained of them that they were defiant, lawless, hard-drinking, licentious, and irreligious, differing from Indians only in line of descent. All of this is true, and not true; that is, it was true of some, and no doubt the farther these folk traveled from the original font of their culture and religion and law, the more they took on the ways of the wilderness. But it must not be forgotten that many of them came of families that possessed distinction in the Old World, and these did not fail to distinguish themselves in the New. Such clans as the Davidsons, the McDowells, the Donelsons, the McClures, the Rutherfords, the Calhouns, the Bairds, the Vances, the Alexanders, and the Robertsons came not only with fine stocks of horses and cattle and sheep, and a rich store of Old World culture, but with the stuff of heroes in their bones, and they were first not only in war and pioneering, but the first to get a church up, or a school, or a courthouse. It should be remembered that the blood of these Scotch and Welsh and Irish Kelts flowed in the veins of Woodrow Wilson, David Crockett and Abraham Lincoln, Patrick Henry and John Calhoun, Andrew Jackson, Samuel Houston, and Daniel Boone. Almost all their ancestors were poor in the things of this world, but the pioneers' poverty was chiefly that of "do-without," which does not necessarily entail poverty of spirit. And the resources of the mountain land to which they were coming were, though so hard to win, at any rate richer than anything the thin woods and sandy soil of the coast could boast.

Looking back on those early times, one cannot but feel that in some ways the pioneers had the best of it. The game, certainly, was plentiful. Tens of thousands of deerskins were exported in some years. The ham of deer could be marketed or smoked for home storage. Deerskin, like bearskin, could be dressed and might even be cut into plow lines, bridles, and traces. The horns and hoofs of deer served for spoons and buttons and the antlers for coat-rack and rifle-rack in every home. Sometimes a ton of bears a day would be brought down by a hunter, who, since he could get only one shot at a time from his rifle, must be an expert marksman. Bear meat and hide, however, were not exportable and could only be used at home. Wild turkey was everywhere, at first, and beavers abounded. A horseload of beaver was worth five times its weight in deerskin.

Those were the days when all the soil was virgin. The woods were full of wild peas on which the hogs fattened. So big were the trees then, so far did the forest stretch, that it was more than a man could do to clear his land with an ax. He had to girdle the trees, and let them die; then he burned them down, with the result that a pioneer cabin was usually surrounded by desolate-looking silvered trees, and the air was often filled with a pall of smoke. Still, all the streams ran clear, and you could drink anywhere. A barrel of fish could be captured overnight in the rushing streams. Beyond the mountain, adventure beckoned always.

I have talked about the peopling of the mountains by the Scotch-Irish and their fellow Kelts, the Irish and Welsh, as if it were something that took place without interruption. That is an over-simplification of a very complex movement. It should be divided into two phases, the pre-Revolutionary and the post-Revolutionary, for in the Revolution the mountain folk had to fight on two fronts—the Indian and the Tory. For the moment, migration was halted.

On the eve of the Revolution one stream of the Keltic immigrants, paralleled by a German (Pennsylvania "Dutch") movement just to the east on the mid-piedmont of North Carolina, had moved south at the base of the Blue Ridge, through the Outer Blue Ridge, filling up in succession the headwater coves of the Atlantic-draining rivers. The most numerous settlements, of course, were to the north. The visitor to the headwaters of the New River is impressed, for instance, by the air of old colonial settlement, by the way that so many of the surrounding hills, especially the Brushy Mountains, are cleared of forests and farmed to the top with fine grain fields and ancient-looking orchards of apple, cherry, peach, and plum. The churches, the houses, the public buildings, the gardens, all look old.

In the next valley to the south, on the Yadkin, a young man named Daniel Boone, in times immediately pre-Revolutionary, had already been farming for years, dutifully trying, though eaten alive with taxes and loaded with debt, to support his annual crop of children with all that the bottoms could yield, and fuming because the last elk had long since been shot out of his woods. Near by might have been found the farm called "Roundabout," belonging to Ben Cleveland, a hunter who had preceded even Boone into Kentucky; as yet he had not attained quite all of his legendary four hundred and fifty pounds, but he was already boiling with a dislike of Tories that was soon to make him the fattest, jolliest, and cruelest patriot of them all.

Where the Catawba headwater tributaries come out of the gorges at the foot of the Mt. Mitchell country, conditions were wilder; still there were stout-hearted men in the sweet Quaker Meadows and at Morganton, ready for savages and king's troops alike. Down on the Pacolet, and on the head streams of the South Carolina rivers, conditions were more primitive still. Yet there were farms, and a line of blockhouses; there were a few roads, here and there a lonely church; there was a spirit brewing that would stand the test in the days ahead. In the mountains above these settlements, the Cherokees still held sway, suspending their threat.

On the other side of the mountains, to the west, the peopling moved forward swiftly at first, down the great Appalachian Valley, a natural corridor. In 1750 the surveyor-explorer-physician, Dr. Thomas Walker, had threaded his way with a party of hunters over the ridges, through the valleys of the Holston, the Clinch, and the Powell, and discovered and named Cumberland Gap, the most historic land pass of the eastern United States. Thus was the way to Kentucky opened, along the route of the future Wilderness Trail.

So this natural corridor became a famous path, of which Daniel Boone was to blaze the section from the Long Island of the Holston to Boonesboro, Kentucky. But at the Long Island those immigrants destined to become Tennesseans of the future kept straight on down the forks of the Holston. Many of them turned to the left (eastward) and followed up into the Unakas through the water gaps, the valleys of the Watauga and the Nolichucky and their tributaries, there to clear and farm the beautiful coves. Thus as early as 1769 William Bean built his cabin on the Watauga, the white man's chimney smoke rising for the first time into the air, the whir of his brave wife's spinning wheel singing merrily above the churning of the river, the laughter of his little boy echoing from the virgin forest that hung all about, cool-breathed, on the steep sides of the mountains. At Bean's cabin door were to stop the great men of the age in these mountains, Daniel Boone from over the mountains, on his way to hunt in forbidden Kentucky; John Sevier, the bold young Huguenot Virginian, young as his young bride; John Findlay who showed Boone the way to Kentucky. There too came James Robertson, the future great Indian fighter, then only a farm boy sent by incredulous neighbors to test the truth of Dan Boone's fairy tales about the smiling land beyond the mountains; and Isaac Shelby, hero of two wars, future first governor of Kentucky. These were but some of the outstanding leaders among the settlers that came pouring in to the Watauga vale, where they formed a fateful and curious association, with a mentality quite its own.

In the first place, most of them thought they were still in Virginia, the survey not having been completed at that time. Indeed, they were Virginians, though only some of them were born in that state. Civilized eastern North Carolina of that day was even farther off than Virginia for practical purposes of travel, trade, and communication. Hence the Watauga settlers felt no allegiance to the Old North State, and in turn it felt no responsibility for protecting these wild Virginian squatters. The Cherokees realized, if the whites did not, that these settlements were inside territory expressly guaranteed by treaty to the red man. This left the Watauga settlements in a dangerous position—not that the fiery pioneers had any intention of backing down from it.

Into the midst of these hardy independent Keltic immigrants came a sudden influx of quite another stock, the refugees from the Battle of Alamance (1771), in which the Regulators of North Carolina were defeated by the party that no doubt considered itself that of law and order. But it was King George's harsh law. And it was order in favor of the oppressive tax collectors, the greedy lawyers whose fees for title were enough to ruin a man before he could occupy his land, who set even the cost of a marriage license so high that indigent young people waived the formalities. The Regulators may have been a rash lot, little more than a mob; but they really fired some of the opening shots in the American Revolution. They were the simple folk of the times, landless or squatters, or what we would now call sharecroppers, the descendants of English yeomanry who had come to America as indentured servants, as political or religious exiles. And they nourished a deep hatred of England, and of the moneyed classes, as well as of tax collectors, lawyers, and ministers of the Established Church.

As many as could migrated to the Watauga settlements. They went west over the Blue Ridge, crossed the upper coves of the New River and then the Unakas, and so came down upon the Watauga from its headwaters. The Virginia settlers already there were glad to receive their additional strength. All were united in their sullenness toward eastern North Carolina, their hatred of royal authority, and their determination to hold their own against the Indians.

The last act in the pre-Revolutionary drama is the great meeting at Sycamore Shoals on the Watauga, when the Overhill Cherokees and the Watauga settlers came to hear Richard Henderson, colonel, judge, and financier, buy most of Kentucky and Tennessee from the Cherokees. It must have been a memorable scene. Handsome Henderson in his scarlet coat spoke for the watchful North Carolina speculators. The Wataugans looked on—wild tough boys who were to become deathless heroes in a few years, stouthearted Isaac Shelby, and those two fast friends, the darlings of the pioneers, James Robertson and John Sevier. Daniel Boone, and his brother Squire, Benjamin Cutbirth and old Mike Stoner were waiting, twenty miles away, at the Long Island of the Holston to begin cutting the next section of the Wilderness Road to Kentucky.

On their side, fifteen hundred Indians had come to see the barter goods for which they were bargaining away Kentucky. The shrewdest of all their diplomatists was Attacullaculla (Leaning Wood), an English-speaking Cherokee. White men called him "The Little Carpenter" because he could join the pieces of a treaty to the nicest advantage. Hanging Maw was present, a suave brute who would one day kidnap Daniel Boone's daughter. Aged Oconostota, who had been to London, looked on under fine eyelids, and spoke in bitterness of the Americans, while Dragging Canoe warned his people of dire things to follow this bargain. But the glister of ten thousand pounds' worth of barter swayed the Indians. The bargain was struck on March 17, 1775, and Henderson followed Boone north on the Wilderness Road. The Wataugans remained to complete their own purchases from the Cherokees, making safe their homes. Two months later the embattled farmers of Concord, Massachusetts, would fire upon the British regulars and rout them.

REDSKINS AND REDCOATS

When the American Revolution opened, the Cherokees made a fatal decision to side with the British, for the British government made a show of protecting and favoring the Cherokees. But plainly the Indians saw that their ultimate foes were the relentless American pioneers, who pressed on with ax and gun, wife and child, ever further into Indian territory. These were foes who did not really wish for peace, who did not disguise their ultimate aim of driving the Indians from their lands or exterminating them. The longer the clash between Cherokees and pioneers was delayed, the stronger the white men would grow. So, in the summer of 1776, seven hundred warriors of the Overhill towns started up the rivers of eastern Tennessee, to wipe out the settlers.

But warning was given the whites in time by a secret message carried by the traders from Nancy Ward, the "Beloved Woman" or high priestess and seer of the peace town of Echota. "Queenly and commanding"—so whites who saw her described her. Her uncle was Attacullaculla, a chief always reasonably friendly to the whites. Her father is said to have been a South Carolinian officer named Ward, probably one of those at old Fort Loudon, in the days when every soldier in the garrison had a Cherokee "sweetheart" and the Overhill lodges were filled with their half-breed offspring.

Warned by this woman, in whose veins flowed the blood of the two races, the settlers on the Holston were ready for the enemy, and on August 20, 1776, they met the Indians at the Long Island and completely defeated them.

Next the Indians swept up the Watauga Valley, driving the settlers before them in terror, till they came to the closed gates of the little blockhouse. Perhaps it was on that day that John Sevier met his second wife, mother-to-be of eight of his eighteen children. Tradition states that Catherine Sherrill was milking her cows when she saw the redskins coming across the meadow. She dropped her pails and ran, the enemy close behind her till she came to the fort. The gate was locked, but Sevier saw her as she leaped frantically at the palings, and drew her up by the hands, and into his mighty arms. Captain James Robertson, lifelong Oliver to Sevier's Roland, was in command of the fort that day, and so stoutly did he defend it that the Indians retired, completely discomfited.

Their only real triumph was the capture of Mrs. Bean, wife of the first settler in the Watauga coves, who had many a time been host to Oconostota, Attacullaculla, and Dragging Canoe. A boy who was taken with her was burned at the stake. Then she herself was led to the pyre, and bound to it. Though even Oconostota pleaded for her life, her captor, the vicious Dragging Canoe, would not listen to pleas. Then, suddenly, Nancy Ward appeared. Sacred in her person, she had the unquestioned prerogative of life and death for prisoners. By her hand the white woman was untied; she was returned to her family at the subsequent treaty of peace signed at the Long Island.

But the whole Cherokee nation was on the warpath. On the eastern flanks of the mountains, too, the Middle Cherokees raided and killed. While Tories were harrying the foothills of South Carolina, the Indians in the mountains co-operated with them. Together they surprised the little fort at Gowansville, at the foot of Hogback Mountain. Colonel Joseph McDowell, with five hundred American militiamen stationed at Earle's Fort, in present-day Polk County, North Carolina, felt so weak in comparison to the horde moving upon him that he withdrew to Gilbert Town up in the Hickory Nut Mountains. The settlers on the headwaters of the Pacolet were in a desperate plight when a young chief, Skuyuka, who had once been befriended by Captain Thomas Howard, came to his house in Dark Corners, that flowery cove at the foot of Rocky Spur, and informed him that the Indians were dancing their victory dance over their prisoners in a gap in the Tryon Range. Howard mustered out every man with a gun, stole behind Round Mountain, and caught the unwary red celebrants in the rear, signally defeating them in what has, ever since, been called Howard's Gap.*

The rage in the Southern colonies was white-hot when it was learned that, with the British thundering at Charleston and Savannah, the Cherokees had stabbed the patriot cause in the back. Virginia, Georgia, and the Carolinas had but one thought, to punish the Cherokees instantly and break their power before the final test should come between the colonists and the British armies.

So each colony launched a thunderbolt of vengeance. Colonel McBury with 400 Georgians, 1,860 South Carolinians under Colonel Andrew Williamson, 2,400 men of North Carolina under

* I am indebted for these details to Mr. Carroll Rogers, the historian of Polk County.

General Griffith Rutherford and, under Colonel William Christian, 2,000 Virginians from the Backwater settlements, would converge upon the Cherokees. The total number of whites engaged was thus near to 7,000 troops, many of them veteran Indian fighters, Scotch-Irish immigrants, Moravian Germans, and stout yeomanry from the piedmont, of English descent.

The Cherokees had no such force to muster. With a few exceptions they dared not risk a pitched battle, but preferred to fight from tree to tree and day to day, in typical Indian fashion. But their foes could fight that way too; they could pursue the Indians into every little cove, to the tops of the ridges, and into caves. The answer to the Indians' partisan warfare was an individualized policy of man-by-man extermination, where marksmanship counted, and the white man was the better shot.

The Georgians met with no opposition, and destroyed the Indian towns and carried off prisoners. The South Carolinians defeated at Oconoree a large force of Cherokees, led by the British agent Cameron himself. They burned every town; they burned the standing corn, they cut down every peach tree, and dug every store of grain out of the villages and destroyed it. No quarter was granted to any adult, and the children were left to starve in the woods. Twenty years later, children of the refugees from the Valley towns, then living in the Georgia hills, ran screaming from the face of the white man. Marching up through Rabun Gap, Williamson reached the villages of the Overhill tribes from the south.

Meantime the largest of the armies, under the daring Ulsterman, Rutherford, accomplished a feat that the white man had never before attempted. The North Carolinians had mustered at Fort Davidson (now Old Fort, where the railroad from Salisbury to Asheville strikes the mountains). They drove up the Swannanoa Gap, descended on the wide valley of the French Broad, forged over the high mountains to the valley of the Big Pigeon (the most inaccessible of all the big interior basins, never before entered by white men), and passing by what is now Waynesville they crossed the Balsams—a terrible scramble—and descended on the valley of the Tuckasegee. Thus they proved that determined men could force their way anywhere in the mountains; even the wildest parts would hold no terrors after Rutherford's campaign. Indeed, the fine soils, the delightful climate, the beauty and fertility of the mountain valleys were revealed to soldiers who, as soon as the Revolution was over, came surging through all the gaps to stake their claims. Nothing so hastened the mountain peopling as the Cherokee War, which dispelled the mystery of the mountains.

On the Tuckasegee the work of the North Carolinians began. For here they encountered Indian towns. At Wayah Gap they fought a sharp encounter, but the Cherokees were defeated. Flying detachments from the main force turned up every side stream. Even the wild valley of the Oconaluftee, one of the most inaccessible fastnesses of Indian resistance, was combed clean of redskins. All of the Middle Cherokee towns and crops were destroyed everywhere; every male, and every woman who resisted, was slain. The Rutherford expedition specialized in young prisoners; although the officers objected, the men insisted they would kill the captives if they were not immediately auctioned off. An untold number of these savage children were accordingly sold amid the smoking ruins of their homes and, their families' scalps swinging in their conquerors' belts, were led away into slavery.

Rutherford completed the ruin of the Middle Cherokees, and then (September 26) in the valley of the Hiwassee joined forces with Williamson's South Carolinians. Both then prepared to attack the Overhill towns from the south and converge with Christian's Virginians. Colonel Christian had been slow in getting started. But his Backwater men completed their muster at the Long Island of the Holston, and swept down the Appalachian Valley, burning the Overhill towns and taking prisoners without opposition, for apparently most of the Cherokees' forces were fighting Rutherford. To the disgust of the Carolinians, Christian spared the ancient capital of the red men, the sanctuary town of Echota.

The Indians now sued for peace, making treaties with each state. Old Attacullaculla even offered to lead five hundred young warriors against the British and Shawnees. But many of the Cherokees did not attend the peace conference. These remained to the end irreconcilable enemies of the Americans. Dragging Canoe, disgusted at the submission of his tribe, drew off the die-hard refractories down to the present site of Chattanooga, where, joining with Creeks, Chickasaws, and "bad Indians" generally, he organized a terroristic band, the Chickamaugas, that kept up the war relentlessly. Old Oconostota, who had once shaken the hand of George II, still regarded himself as an unconquered king. Through the jungles of the Great Smokies he journeyed, a prophet of hatred, keeping alive the spirit of opposition among the refugees.

The Revolutionary War itself did not reach the neighborhood of the mountains until 1780, five years after the opening shot at Concord Bridge. That was the dark year in the South, when Charleston and Savannah were captured, and Cornwallis had everything his own way, with Tarleton and Ferguson raiding for him far up-country, rousing the Tories everywhere. The hatred of the backwoodsmen for Tories and Indians was intense. From the battles of regular troops—Redcoats against Continentals—going on down on the seaboard, they felt remote; their job was to hold off the powerful Indians, from Kentucky to Georgia.

But when Colonel Patrick Ferguson's redcoats had swept Colonel Charles McDowell's patriot militia from the fords of the Pacolet and the Broad, and, advancing to Gilbert Town at the foot of the mountains, sent by a paroled prisoner a message to Sevier and his Wataugans to submit to George III or he would come and hang them, the answer was a spontaneous rising of the clans. Without the full knowledge of American army headquarters, without a single officer amongst them experienced in fighting well-drilled regular troops, the men of the vales of Watauga and the long meadows of the Holston resolved to cross the mountains and teach Ferguson a lesson. Could George Washington have seen these gaunt determined men as they mustered out at Sycamore Shoals, he might not have written, as he did at this time, "I have almost ceased to hope."

There was a sharpening of long knives, a cleaning of old Detchard muskets, while the womenfolk ran the bullets of lead taken from Sevier's own farm. Money for the expedition came from a curious source. John Adair, the entry-taker from North Carolina, a man hitherto not too popular, who had compelled the settlers to pay North Carolina for the lands they had bought from the Cherokees and won with their blood, simply turned over the funds to the patriots. Records show that they eventually repaid him. Themselves unpaid, the mountain volunteers furnished their own horses and guns. Without tents, commissary, or supplies, they made ready to seek out Ferguson's redcoats. Theodore Roosevelt has described the appearance of the "King's Mountain Boys":

"They were led by leaders they trusted, they were wonted to Indian warfare, they were skilled as horsemen and marksmen, they knew how to face every kind of danger, hardship, and privation. Their fringed and tasseled hunting shirts were girded by bead-worked belts, and the trappings of their horses were stained red and yellow. On their heads they wore caps of coon skin or mink skin, with the tails hanging down, or else felt hats, in each of which was thrust a buck tail or a sprig of evergreen. Every man carried a small-bore rifle, a tomahawk, and a scalping knife. A very few of the officers had swords, and there was not a bayonet nor a tent in the army." *

The autumn woods rang with shouts, as redheaded Colonel William Campbell led his "fighting Presbyterians" into camp

* From *The Winning of the West*, by Theodore Roosevelt, published by G. P. Putnam's Sons.

from the Backwater settlements of western Virginia. Sevier's young sons were there, his younger brothers. Pioneer Bean's boy, James Robertson's son—they were almost all boys, with the grimness of frontier boyhood, the thin, tight, straight mouths, the narrow eyes, the high cheekbones. So they start, four hundred under Campbell, two hundred and forty under the dashing Shelby, a like number under Sevier, their parched flour under their saddlebags, their tough horses between their knees, their rifles on their backs.

They rode up out of the hollows of the Doe River, right over the Unakas, through Elk Hollow between bald old Roan and lofty Yellow Mountain, where already the snow was shoe-mouth deep. Down into the coves of the Toe they swung, the crooked vale twisting between the wildest of our mountains. But here, too, were pioneers. At the sight of the passing cavalcade, men left their plows or their dinners, snatched a rifle and forked a stallion, to ride after the band that was sweeping, quiet and swift and dark as a raven's shadow, over the ridges and hollows. Down through Gillespie Gap they file, and, after only three days from Sycamore Shoals, out on the Quaker Meadows, where McDowell joins them with one hundred and sixty veterans, all that is left of his old guerrillas. And up canters enormous Ben Cleveland, roaring at his three hundred and fifty rough-riders from the bottoms of the Yadkin—Dan Boone's old neighbors, and James Robertson's.

Warned by spies, Ferguson had pulled swiftly out of Gilbert Town. The mountain men, like hounds, tracked his hoofprints and his campfires through the gap in the South Mountains, to the fords of the Broad. There torrential rains had washed away his trail, but the men of what is now Rutherford County were mustering out to join the avenging host. Its campfires glowed on the Green River. In less than a week it had crossed the mountains and gathered itself into a force that was driving the enemy before it. And now at Cowpens (Spartanburg County, South Carolina, where four months later General Daniel Morgan will defeat the dashing

Colonel Banastré Tarleton and his cruel redcoats) up rides Colonel Williams with four hundred South Carolinians, who have been hanging on Ferguson's flanks, skirmishing, to tell the rest that Ferguson has not gone down to Fort Ninety-Six, but has hurried off to the east, trying to get in touch with his master, Cornwallis, at Charlotte. That junction he must not be allowed to make. The hounding backwoodsmen go belling after him; they ride all day, and they ride all night. At a Tory household one girl is patriotic; she tells the Americans that their quarry has drawn up on Kings Mountain.

It is a long ridge, the very last monadnock of the Outer Blue Ridge. But worn down though it is, it is still a comparative mountain, and the tactics of the battle that took place there on October 7, 1780, are typical mountain fighting, by the Over-Mountain men. On its summit the ridge is bald, so that anyone on the top is silhouetted against the sky. But the slopes are densely wooded, so that anyone coming up the mountain is concealed. Thus Ferguson's artillery is little use to him, and though he has the repeating rifle of his own invention, the mountain men with their clumsy old Detchards are the better marksmen, as they steal from tree to tree. First they surround the mountain and, like all backwoods fighters, dismount, keeping their horses in the rear and preferring to fight on foot from ambush. The words of Cleveland to his men are typical American talk; they might almost have been addressed to the jungle fighters of New Guinea in our day:

> "When you are engaged, you are not to wait for any word of command from me. I will show you, by example, how to fight; I can undertake no more. Every man must consider himself an officer and act from his own judgment."

In an hour and a half the battle was over. Ferguson lay dead, his silver whistle at his lips, and the entire British Army of 1,125 was either killed, wounded or captured. Not a man escaped. The mountain men had won with only 900 of their force in the field; they had outshot an enemy who held the ridge above them. On the battlefield a few swords of British officers were passed out among the victors. Probably most of them, even the colonels like Sevier and Shelby, had never had a sword at their sides before. It is doubtful if they were even distinguishable in costume from the others, in an army where "every man is his own officer."

At Bickerstaff plantation (near modern Rutherfordton) the worst of the Tories captured at Kings Mountain were summarily hanged, the lesser flogged. Stomach for this brutal work was supplied by the jolly Little John, old "Roundabout" Cleveland. Sevier did not attend these ceremonies. He was riding with all speed back over the mountains. For there James Robertson's tiny rear guard was hard pressed; the Cherokees were on the warpath once more. Without stopping, without warning, Sevier struck the Cherokees like a hawk from a cliff. On December 16, 1780 he defeated them at Boyd's Creek (near modern Sevierville, Tennessee) and then swept down upon the Overhill towns. This time Echota was not spared; the ancient sanctuary and peace capital was destroyed, its historic town house laid in ashes, its sacred council fires extinguished. Joined by Campbell and his Backwater Virginians, Sevier swept south, refusing peace talks with Nancy Ward, until the Hiwassee towns too were ruined. Then, in March of 1781, the Middle Cherokee still being defiant, Sevier crossed the wildest parts of the Great Smokies and descended on the Tuckasegee Valley. Warriors and boys he slew; women and children he carried off prisoner, to be held as hostages, or sold in slavery. Where he passed, nothing lived. Then, before a force could be collected to meet him, he vanished back over the snows of Clingmans Dome and Thunderhead, as swiftly and mysteriously as he had come.

Indian fighting to this young man had already become a vocation, perhaps his most successful in a highly varied and adventurous life. To him, as to his followers, it was practically a sport, at the same time that it shone in the light of a high-minded crusade.

Originally his family name had been Xavier; his father's family were of French Huguenot extraction. Jack himself, though, was a Virginian, born in 1745 in the Shenandoah while it was still an Indian battleground. And he grew up with the Appalachian pioneer's itch to know what lies beyond the ridges. As a boy he went to school in Fredericksburg, and was thus far better educated than his friend Robertson who did not learn to read until his wife taught him. At the age of sixteen, Jack took to wife Sarah Hawkins, a girl of his own years, and carried her dauntlessly off to the frontier; the boy set his plow among the flowers of the Long Meadows, sowed his wheat and his five first sons and five daughters. Farmer, hunter, trapper, trader, storekeeper, he had his first brush with the Indians when he defended his trading post from Shawnees who wanted to take back the skins they had sold him. In 1771 he first visited the upper Holston settlements. Attracted by the fertility of the soil, by the bounding game and the type of men and women, he moved there the next year with his wife and children, his mother and father, his brothers and their families, and became the hope of the Tennesseans, the scourge of the Cherokees.

John Sevier, in his log castle on the Nolichucky (near present-day Jonesboro, Tennessee), "Chucky Jack," as his foes and admirers the Indians called him, was the Appalachian pioneers' *beau idéal*. He thought as they thought, but more astutely than most; he lived as they lived, but in rather grander style; he fought as they fought, but he was their natural leader, to be Governor one day of their strange, shadowy, rebellious coonskin republic of "Franklin," the lost state that grew out of the Watauga Association, and would become the nucleus of Tennessee. Arrested by Tipton of North Carolina, he would be carried over the mountains to Morganton to stand trial for high treason, and would escape from the courtroom by the window and mount the horse his sons were holding, to flee over the mountains and strike the Indians again. Yet he was to live to recoup his fortunes and become first Governor of Tennessee.

But now he is smiting the Cherokees, thigh and hip. When Sevier finished his campaign there was no fight left in them, except for the cruel, depraved Chickamauga band of mongrels and outlaws down on the Tennessee. In 1782 Sevier, with two hundred mounted men, again made one of his lightning strokes, utterly surprising this ogre gang in their natural rock castles. All who did not save themselves by flight were slain, to the last brave.

The English defeated, the independence of the American colonies won, there was now no road for the Cherokees but the stony one of submission and remorse. All that would be necessary in the future would be to summon them to a fresh treaty-making and then dictate to them what further territory they must cede.

Those thirty treaties were never understood alike by the high contracting parties. The establishment of an Indian boundary meant, to the white settlers, that the Indians renounced everything outside them, and agreed to remain peacefully within them. Not for one moment did they construe a boundary to mean that a white settler could not cross it and take anything he wanted, from a deer to a tract of rich bottom. The simple savage supposed, each time, that the whites had made their last territorial demand and agreed not to pass the boundary they themselves set up. So, no sooner had the abject treaties been signed after the Revolution and the old capital of Echota raised again and its sacred council fires lighted, than the Indians had reason to complain that every year the white settlers penetrated deeper among the Overhill towns, taking the finest lands as their own, and demanding of their governments that their acts be legalized by fresh treaties with the Indians.

So Echota was abandoned in despair. Old Oconostota, who had once led his tribe to victory, resigned in favor of his son, Terrapin.

Legend has it that he passed the last years of his life a beggar on the contemptuous bounty of his foes. The whites had won their mountain homes, never to be displaced from them. But the feet of the Cherokees were set upon the road to sorrow.

THE TRAIL OF TEARS

In 1800 the Cherokee nation in the Southern Appalachians had so far recovered that it is stated to have numbered 20,000 souls. The capital had been removed to the town of Ustanali, and a little later to New Echota, both in Georgia, where the Indians sought again to revive the grandeurs of the old Echota, now trampled by profane feet. In the Georgia mountains, indeed, there was a distinct revival of Cherokee life, with prosperous towns and new town houses dotting the coves. Farming had now gone far with these people, enabling them to survive the loss of the big game, and they had borrowed good ways from the whites. The lowing of the Indian's cattle could be heard, and the murmur of his bees, the purr of his cat, the whir of the spinning wheel, the sound of the churn. Horses were so plentiful that even squaws rode. In the bottoms Negro slaves tended little cotton fields! For the Cherokees had long had slaves; first they did a business in capturing runaway Negroes, and selling them to the whites again; presently they kept the runaways and exploited them, though in many cases the blacks seem to have secured their freedom, and to have lived as members of the tribe.

Christianity had made some progress by this time. The Moravian Brothers in 1799 had established missions and by 1820 had four among the Cherokees, while the Baptists had one. These were the sources of the civilizing influences among the Cherokees, where they were educated, taught the secrets of the white man's civilization and given a sense of equality and citizenship which so annoyed the Cherokees' white neighbors.

A powerful reaction against the white influence in the tribe took place during the 1812 war between England and the United States. Tecumseh, the great Shawnee chief, seized the moment to try to weld all American Indians into a league to resist the further aggressions of the white man. Soldier, diplomatist, and statesman, he labored in every field to bring into being his great confederacy. His brother, called The Prophet, took charge of the mystic and emotional side of the movement. Like some Old Testament character, he went amongst the Indians recalling them to their ancient faiths, seeing visions, and rousing forgotten passions. Under his influence the Indians were whipped up to hysterical fanaticism. Very soon he came among the Cherokees, and preached to them at Ustanali. The Cherokees, he cried, had strayed from the path beaten by their ancestors' feet. They had put on the white man's clothing and trinkets, they sat on chairs and ate at tables and lived in log cabins, and drank coffee and whisky. Some even had cats and books and such effete and heathen things. Let them kill their cats, and their bees, and throw away their books; let them strip naked again and paint themselves red, as in the days of their health and strength! For their gods were angry, and terrible events were now at hand.

Emotion like that at a revival meeting shook his listeners. They would put away profane things. Many cut down their orchards, slew their cattle, abandoned their horses, and withdrew into the Great Smokies to live again upon roots and wild beasts, while they awaited the storm which The Prophet had promised to rouse, which should destroy the apostate world. When the storm did not come, when the whites were not destroyed, when Tecumseh was slain in battle, these red Fundamentalists sadly returned to their dead orchards and their weed-high fields. It was too late to turn back, the Cherokees saw.

So they assisted the United States in its great war with the powerful Creeks. At the Horseshoe Bend, they turned the tide of the battle (March 27, 1814) which General Andrew Jackson won. On their return they found their towns burning and their women ravished by bands of white soldiers, and heard of fresh demands for their territory. "If I had known that Jackson would drive us from our homes," Chief Junaluska was to cry, "I would have killed him that day at the Horseshoe."

There was a constant pressure being exerted to oust the Cherokees. They were told that they could remove across the Mississippi, though the Government did not explain how they were to take the land of the Osages and Quapaws from them. In 1817, however, some 3,000 of the Cherokees, foreseeing the inevitable, agreed to make the removal, and after incredible difficulties accomplished the change. But all offers and temptations and threats to get the rest of the tribe to depart were scornfully rejected.

Probably no Indian people ever gave greater promise of bridging the gulf that divides not only the two races but technical civilization from a New Stone Age culture than the Cherokees in the period from 1820 to 1830. For it was then that they adopted a tribal constitution which put them on a footing with the best in white politics. The law of revenge was written off the Cherokee moral code forever. Schools were established, supported by taxes; officers were elected by democratic vote, and laws were passed by a freely elected legislature. The traffic in liquor and the treatment of slaves were strictly regulated. And whites were not allowed to vote or hold office, or buy Indian lands except by permission of the nation. In 1820 their agent, Return Meigs, considered the Cherokees so advanced that further paternalism by the United States government was unnecessary, and President Monroe recommended that the Indians be given full citizenship rights. This, however, the states of Tennessee, North Carolina, and Georgia resisted bitterly. Already they were breaking their own treaties, and plotting the day when no Cherokee should be allowed to stand on his own land and live.

At the same time occurred the great literary movement among

Is this the origin of the expression "To get the Gist of" something?

the Cherokees. This was due to the invention by Sequoyah, or George Gist as the whites called him, of an alphabet, or rather a syllabary of seventy-seven characters which, unlike English letters, really express Cherokee sounds. These were so easily learned that in a few lessons old men and children alike were able to read their language with ease. Copies of the syllabaries went to the remotest Indian cabins; there were no chosen teachers; anyone who could read instructed the rest. The Cherokee syllabary, indeed, carried to the western bands by Sequoyah, has proved adaptable to Indian languages all over the country, and has caused a literary awakening in tribe after tribe.

The giant among his tribe, Sequoyah, for whom the redwoods of California are so appropriately named, had an uncertain parentage. He was born about 1760 near old Echota, and his father may well have been one of the South Carolina soldiers stationed at Fort Loudon. Sequoyah when young came under the influence of the Moravian missions, and though he never became a Christian, he did seize upon the elements of white culture. In a few years after he introduced his syllabary it is probable that the literacy among the Cherokees far exceeded the average among their white neighbors.

The first book in Cherokee characters was a translation of the Bible. Arithmetics, spelling books, histories, geographies, were written in the language, each copy at first laboriously prepared by hand. Later a printing press, with Cherokee characters cast in Boston, was shipped by water, dragged up to New Echota with almost as much trouble as the guns of Fort Loudon had once been wormed over the ridges, and a Cherokee newspaper, the *Phoenix*, was printed, the first number appearing February 21, 1828. But many of their white neighbors, particularly the Georgians, looked on with contempt, suspicion, and hatred. The last thing such men wanted was to have the Indians educated, Christianized, organized, sobered and intelligent. They blamed the missionaries and nursed their race hatreds.

One day in 1815 a Cherokee boy in the Dahlonega region was playing beside the Chestatee River in upper Georgia when he found a shining yellow pebble. He brought it to his mother, who sold it to a white man. In 1827 his paleface brothers finally found where that stone had come from. The cry of gold rocked Georgia with excitement, and the Cherokee civilization, just beginning to flower after the terrrible winter of the past hundred years, was blighted even as it opened.

Georgia instantly declared all Indian lands forfeit. No Indian might dig for gold on his own lands. No Indian might testify against a white man (which opened the way to murder), nor assemble in council, nor resist the seizure of his lands, house, stock, or other property on penalty of death. In the United States House of Representatives, Edward Everett pleaded in the Indians' favor, and David Crockett, Henry Clay, and Daniel Webster also raised shocked voices in protest. Alas for the Cherokees! Andrew Jackson, an inveterate Indian-hater, was soon elected President. When he heard that the Supreme Court had rendered a small decision in favor of Indians, he snorted, "John Marshall has made his decision. Now let him enforce it."

And, indeed, a Georgia judge, ignoring a United States decision, caused to be hanged, before his eyes, a Cherokee whose crime was to testify against a white man. Now began a systematic destruction of all opposition. The Cherokee newspaper was suppressed. The white missionaries were arrested and held in defiance of their constitutional rights, without charges against them. That noble fellow, John Ross, chief of the Cherokees, was arrested. At the time, the poet John Howard Payne was visiting him, studying Cherokee literature. So the authorities clapped Payne in jail too, for good measure. Thus did the author of "Home, Sweet Home" become the guest of the sovereign state of Georgia and a witness of the way the Cherokees came to lose their homes in the sweetest mountains in the world.

Listen to the testimony of James Mooney, a Cherokee writer:

"Even the Georgia laws, which deny us our oaths, are thrown aside, and notwithstanding the cries of our people, and protestations of our innocence and peace, the lowest classes of white people are flogging the Cherokees with cowhides, hickories, and clubs. We are not safe in our houses—our people are assailed by day and night by the rabble. Even justices of the peace and constables are concerned in this business. This barbarous treatment is not confined to men, but the women are stripped also and whipped without law or mercy. . . ."

But no pleas availed. Employing tactics never used by Sherman and equaled only by De Soto, who had the same yellow gleam in his eye, the Georgians proceeded enthusiastically to sell off "gold lots," and sent soldiers to protect the white marauders.

For his part, Jackson was determined to get the entire Cherokee nation, whether in Georgia or its neighbors, out of the country forever. For pretext, the President produced a "Treaty" signed by fifteen Cherokees, out of a nation of 20,000, who had never been delegated to speak for the tribe. After they had signed, Jackson rewrote parts of the Treaty making it infinitely harsher. True, the Indians were to receive money—a paltry sum—for their lands, and the cost of their removal and subsistence was to be borne by the government. By this means, the grab of the Cherokee lands was charged not to the grabbers but to the whole country!

But General Wool, who was sent with troops to disarm the Indians in 1836, had nothing but pity for them, and nothing but condemnation of the Georgians. The kindest thing he could do for the Indians, he wrote, was to remove them beyond the reach of such vultures. General Dunlap, in command of the Tennessee troops sent into the mountains to prevent an alleged uprising of the Cherokees, called his men together and delivered an address indignant at the injustice. He called on his troops to give the Indians every protection. The whites, he stated, needed and deserved none.

Finally, with the Cherokees still peaceably protesting and refusing to leave their homes, General Winfield Scott was called in with 7,000 soldiers to drag the disarmed Indians to exile. They were hunted out of the remotest fastnesses of the Great Smokies. One Georgian who was present, afterward a colonel in the Confederate Army, confesses: "I fought through the Civil War and have seen men shot to pieces and slaughtered by thousands, but the Cherokee removal is the cruelest work I ever knew." The Cherokees were herded into "forts" which were really pens or concentration camps, and then marched as fast as possible to their desolate home upon the treeless flat prairies of Oklahoma. Four thousand, out of the 17,000 rounded up, died on the way; the wife of John Ross breathed her last in his arms. No words can express the brutality, injustice, illegality, and destructiveness of this march. But the Cherokees have a word for it.

They call it the Trail of Tears.

At last the exiles came to a halt on the dusty, wind-torn, treeless flat plains of Oklahoma and Texas. From their homes in the mountains covered with noble forests, laced with pure, tinkling streams, they had come to this, leaving the blood of their feet on a trail a thousand miles long. Here, among other defeated, dispossessed Indian tribes, they would live and die in a prison without walls.

BURIED HATCHETS

From some one thousand or more fugitives who fled to hidden recesses of the Great Smokies is descended the present "eastern band" of the Cherokees. For many decades they lived in the winter snows, the cheerless caves, the gloomy balsam tops and in the sunless tangles of the laurel slicks. Fortunately, their friend

W. H. Thomas, a wealthy merchant, legislator, and later a colonel in the Confederate Army, never lost touch with the hiding bands. And when the California gold fields had reduced the Dahlonega boom to an insignificant pop, and the greed and hatred of the Georgians had died down, Thomas was able to bring about a gradual adjustment of relations between the eastern Cherokees and the state of North Carolina and the United States Government. He bought lands for them in the wildest parts of southwestern North Carolina; he helped them rebuild their towns and revive their tribal and cultural life; he gave them a constitution to live by.

With the passing of the years, the eastern Cherokees have recovered from their poverty, sorrow, and degradation. True, their way has still been hard. In contrast with their brothers who suffered exile more than a hundred years ago, the eastern Cherokees have not found themselves on the richest oil deposits in the world. Some of the Oklahoma Cherokees ride in Cadillacs, attend directors' meetings, and can dispose of great fortunes. Those people have lost almost every vestige of their original cultural heritage. The manly sport of the Cherokee ball play is as forgotten among them as if it had never been; they are fast losing the memory of the great national mythology. Their way is the white man's way. The eastern Cherokee, on the Qualla Reservation at the foot of the Great Smokies, have rebuilt their old national life, and have built it in the hard way of patience and economy. Today they are on the warpath again, but this time against Germany and Japan. Between white Americans and red Americans there is peace in the coves and on the ridges, a peace that, this time, the white man will honor.

CHAPTER TWO

THE MOUNTAIN PEOPLE

by Alberta Pierson Hannum

Probably no other group of people in the world have been so much caricatured, with so little actually known about them, as our southern mountain people. But there was a man in Altamount, North Carolina, named Jacob Carpenter, who knew them from the inside, for he was one of them. And he kept a diary.

It is more tanagra than diary, for when someone in the community died, Uncle Jake made note of it in an old red-backed account ledger by setting down his private opinion of the deceased's way of living.

One of Uncle Jake's neighbors told me that "Jake warn't no scribe, and he warn't no hand at figgurs, nuther." That is quite true. The diary is all but illegible. Yet it is important. Its dates, for one thing, beginning with the death of a Revolutionary War soldier and ending with World War I, cover the whole span of our southern mountain people's existence as a separate people. For another, although in itself it is the record of only one small community, it is typical of mountain communities all up and down the range.

And when Jacob Carpenter's own name was added, that red-backed ledger closed on a rare record of the prolific vigor, the courage, the patience, as well as the love of liberty which have been in America since its beginning and which Uncle Jake's people helped to bring in. He left a culmination of old English and early American traditions we are coming now to value. He left a guide to an earthy humor, and a mental calmness, that can help steady a nation's thought.

Jacob Carpenter's people have played a great part in all our wars, and they will take their part in peace.

THAT FIGHTING THING CALLED FREEDOM

Wm Davis age 100.8 dide oc 5 1841 war old soldier in rev war and got his thie brok in last fite at kings monton he war farmer and made brandy and never had drunker in famly

William Davis was a Pennsylvanian. During the Revolution he happened to be with that part of Washington's troops who got into North Carolina. One day when the camp ran out of food, he was sent out with a foraging party for game. When he got up into the mountains, he thought it was the prettiest country he had ever seen.

I happened to hear this about William Davis at the top of Linville Mountain, with the Linville River too directly below to see and too far down to hear. But the opposite side of the gorge does not drop sheer there. It lies back, full and lush with all the greens there are—wide and spreading with unplungeable depths of woods. And away and beyond reach miles and miles of sun and shadow, with the shadow at some indefinable place becoming blue mountain; blue mountain and blue mountain and gray mountain until it is hard to say which is gray cloud and which gray mountain. There is no one thing the eye can get hold of. But all the senses grow lulled as you look, and at the same time heightened. I could understand how William Davis had thought it was pretty country.

"Of course," explained the old timer who was telling me the story, "hit war the b'ar and the deer made hit so purty to him."

At any rate, whether from the aesthete's or the hunter's view, he liked it, and he swore right then and there if he lived through the war he was going back to Pennsylvania and get him a woman and come there and live. And he did.

In some such way, almost all mountain family histories go back at least as far as the Revolution.

"The first of my folks to come," a North Carolinian—a woman—told me, "come over to fight for the King." She was a woman with an evident amount of spunk about her. She was sitting on a low-legged hickory chair on her porch, her feet planted substantially wide so her aproned knees could clamp a big wooden bowl of red apples she was peeling for apple butter. Occasionally she'd lift the end of the apple knife and scratch her nose.

"But when he got hyur," she said, "he saw the Colonists were bein' imposed upon, so he swapped sides and started fightin' for America. And," she finished dryly, "that contrary streak still kindly runs through all our family."

Most highlanders can trace their beginnings back even further. One old man in Tennessee obligingly took his ancestry clear back to Christopher Columbus for me. He 'lowed that *his* folks had come over with Christopher Columbus, on an old sail ship. "But when they got hyur they got kindly wild, and tuk to follerin' the game, a-wanderin' to and fro, till the generations they all evaporated, and the only ones of 'em that war left war them with strength enough to climb up into the hills."

Despite the Christopher Columbus part of it, the rhythmic recital has an element of soundness in it. No doubt many of them did come over on an "old sail ship." There is a record of the "Eagle Wing" setting sail from Ireland as early as 1636 filled with the Scotch-Irish Presbyterians who were destined to become his forebears.

The story of our southern mountain people never has been set down fully in history. You can piece it together only from incidental bits in the copious records of the early New England and seacoast colonies, and from old church records, family histories, and biographies. However, in the main, the story of their being is very much like that of America itself—the story of a people daring to leave the known and fare forth into the unknown in search of religious and political freedom.

In the beginning, in 1607, James I transplanted Scotch and English Presbyterians to the northern counties of Ireland, and called them Scotch-Irish, although they never got along with the Irish. A quick-tempered, visionary, highly independent people, they also quarreled violently with the British crown. It has been said of them that their fear of God was so great it left no fear in them of mortal man.

Early in the eighteenth century they left the old country entirely, and came in large numbers to America. But upon arrival at the new shores, they found the seacoast crowded and many of the same conditions there that they had left at home. Impatiently they pushed on westward, to the frontier borders of Pennsylvania, beyond the Palatine Germans and the English already settled there. A great many went into the Valley of Virginia. But there especially the Church of England was firmly established, and again they found themselves forced to worship in a way to which they were unsympathetic. Furthermore, they were heavily taxed, and received little in return.

Again they moved on—southward along the Cumberland Valley, westward into the Shenandoah: the intensely independent and determined Scotch-Irish, picking up a strong lot of the Palatine Germans, intermarrying with the English, being joined by a few French Huguenots and Swiss—their numbers mounting, their power snowballing. They were becoming an element to be taken into consideration in the new country. The consideration was that the King's law spared no pains to bring them to heel. But it was not in their history to back off weakly before authority. So once more they pushed on, in further search of that elusive thing called freedom.

After the acquisition of territory west of the Alleghanies from the French in 1763, England, to prevent her colonial population from scattering, put out a proclamation forbidding emigration beyond the mountains. To this proclamation the Scotch-Irish and their friends and relations paid not the slightest attention. Consequently, by the time of the actual outbreak of the Revolution, that "western" territory had been well explored, hunted, and settlements were begun.

But still they found themselves coming short of their ideal of religious and political freedom. With their numbers scattering to remote hollows in the mountain wilderness, church services naturally grew infrequent, and the churches and schoolhouses which they used to put up side by side wherever they settled were now few. However, the long arm of the King's law still reached in to them. They were still being governed according to colonial precedent in the lowlands which—according to a positive old man who remembered an opinionated grandfather who was in the Revolution—"didn't have a continental to do with the way things was up in the mountains!" Heavy taxes for a government in which they had no part were still being imposed. That they felt this was unfair is shown by a few old records of formal resolutions of rebellion against "paying any officer any more fees than the law allows, unless we are obliged to do it; and then to show our dislike and bear open testimony against it."

The resolutions were followed by actual resistance in the form of an organization of North Carolina piedmont men known historically as the Regulators, who met the King's army in the Battle of Alamance in 1771. News of that open rebellion spread, and sympathy with the cause of freedom was aroused in other colonies.

In 1772, in the beautiful valley of the Watauga in what is now Tennessee, a group of these rebels formed the first self-governing community in America—the community of Franklin. In his *Winning of the West,* Theodore Roosevelt writes of this Watauga Association:

"It is this fact of the early independence and self government of the settlers along the headwaters of Tennessee, that gives their history its peculiar importance. They were the first men of American birth to establish a free and independent community on the continent."

Occasionally among mountain people you will find someone who claims proudly that his or her ancestor signed the "Declaration of Independence." This was indeed the first declaration of independence to be drawn up in America. But it was not that of Thomas Jefferson. It was written by indignant citizens of Mecklenburg County in 1775—and its spirit was very much like that later one which was hailed by the whole country.

By the time Washington was appointed commander in chief of the army, the Revolution was already under way in the mountains. The mountain frontiersmen had been guarding the back door of the American colonies, holding the fort against the Indians who were fighting as emissaries of the British as well as defending their own hunting ground. Such bloody border warfare as the Battle of Point Pleasant in Virginia and the battle at Boonesboro, Kentucky, mark this earlier period of the Revolution. An American historian, in speaking of the unyielding determination of the Boonesboro men to stand their ground says: "The feeble little handful of 'rebels' at Boonesboro were true to the last to the principles of the Revolution, and battled as valiantly and suffered as nobly for their freedom and for country as did the men of Bunker Hill or the shivering heroes of Valley Forge!"

As the scene shifted to the south, the mountain people had a very definite part in bringing the war to a close.

Cornwallis, on his march to Virginia, sent the men of the mountains a message that if they did not desist from their opposition to

British arms he would march his army over the mountains, hang their leaders, and lay the country waste with fire and sword. Whereupon the mountain men promptly took up fire and sword of their own—in the form of scalping knives and tomahawks and hunting rifles—and delivered their answer personally. They met the Cornwallis army at Kings Mountain. George Washington, in his report of this battle, framed it in noble words—he called it "proof of the spiritual resources of the country."

In the mountains you will find it remembered in smaller ways. I've seen in a Kentucky shack a little cedar cask which carried water in that battle. From Kentucky comes also the story of the women of a family staying up all night to make gunpowder out of cave saltpeter, redbud ashes, and brimstone, with their vengeance-browed men riding out of the yard with it yelling, "The Sword of the Lord and of Gideon!" A Tennessee family's hero at the battle dodged into the hollow side of a sycamore and shot through a knothole with a gun named "Sweet Lips," for his sweetheart on Back Waters.

In North Carolina there was a man who remembered hearing a joke on De Peyster, the second in command to Ferguson. As the wild-looking army—in homespun and leather hunting shirts, a balsam sprig or a buck tail stuck jauntily in their coonskin caps, and their long hair flying in the wind—charged the hill, he heard them give a cheer for liberty. He had heard it before, at Musgrove's Mill, and groaned, "This is that damned yelling set again!" But after the battle was over, and the "yelling set" ordered him to dismount while they gave *three* cheers for liberty, De Peyster thought all hell had broken loose.

A South Forks family has an ancestor who was so seriously wounded in that battle that, after the valiant Ferguson fell, he could not get up to see the corpse, and had to be carried. By the time he saw it, Ferguson, to his disappointment, had been stripped. It was not a courteous battle.

From Uncle Jake's own neighborhood comes the story of Benny Wise's wife, who couldn't rest easy in her mind at home and had followed the army to Kings Mountain. She waited just outside Charlotte, in a farmhouse. The day went by, and every time one of the great big old guns yonder on Kings Mountain went BOOM! she would cringe, and say, "Oh God! Did that one git Benny?" The last fighting was the worst. Then the mountain men began thundering down off the hill, shouting and putting forth some of the best cussing it's ever been permitted a woman to hear. But Benny Wise's wife wasn't interested, because Benny wasn't one of those who came thundering down off the hill in the flare of Ferguson's burning wagons.

"Hasn't anybody," she kept asking frantically, and then finally in dreary breath, "seen Benny Wise?"

At last a smoke-grimed somebody from home came past. "Yes, I seen him."

"Is he—?" Now that there was someone to tell her she could not ask. But the man from home said kindly:

"He's hit, a little, but he's all right."

"Oh, thank God!"

"And ain't you heard? We won!"

And Benny Wise's wife could listen then and hear it—hear the pound of freedom in the hoofs of the victors' horses still thundering past. She did not know it was news that would thrill the whole country, shock it out of the darkest period of discouragement it had yet known, and give it heart again. All she knew was that the mountain men had won!

A SEPARATE PEOPLE

Franky Davis his wife age 87 dide Sep 10 1842 she had nerve fite wolves all nite at shogar camp to save her caff throde fire chunks to save caff the camp war haf mile from home now she must have nerve to fite wolf all nite

"It took a brave woman to leave England behind," said a mountain man once, thoughtfully, "a still braver one after the boat had landed to follow the rivers on inland, and when the rivers stopped, it took the bravest ones yet to come on up into the hills."

When you walk in the hills, even the mildest of them, it is an ever-recurrent surprise to find that within half an hour from the main highway, you can be out of sight and sound of anything civilized. Following a little creek your whole preoccupation becomes a wonder at the variation of tone in the crystal clear stream; at the high dry sound of fall in the trees overhead if it's coming on toward that time of year; or the separate sharpness of the first snow to hit. And every now and then you think of that woods when it was really wilderness.

The quiet then was an awesome silence, broken not by small reliefs from mechanization, but by the scream of the panther—that long piercing, quivering, half-human wail which people who have heard it say seems to come from nowhere and yet be everywhere. Such a sound must have frozen the pioneer woman in her tracks with horror, and sent her faint for an instant with dread of the wilderness still ahead of her. Even more than the sounds of the wilderness they say they dreaded those opposite times when there was a suspicious lack of sound. That was the sign that Indians were about. Those were the times when their men told them to keep their eyes and ears open and their mouths shut. Those were the times when their men left them, to go ahead, telling them if they heard a shot to get behind a tree and wait.

A salty West Virginian who is a "dear Lover of antiquity" and takes great pains to dig up everything he can concerning his forerunners, told me with a chuckle that one of the womenfolks in his history once got behind the wrong tree. An Indian grabbed her. But she was husky—she had some fight in her, and got away. She was the only one of the family who did. But he said she was a woman with life, and at their last family reunion there were enough of her descendants to cover an acre standing solid.

The woman of the wilderness, though wolf packs howled and wild cats screamed and every tree shadow held the lurking fear of Indians, did not turn back. She went on, because her man was being driven by some spirit of search, and she was staying by him.

The daring of those early days of search is still there. It is in that unwieldy long barreled rifle hanging honoredly over the fire place, with the old shot pouch and powder horn beside it. That rifle brought the first woman of the household safely through the wilderness, to the particular high piece of globe her man had decided he wanted to be his.

The homing note of those days is still there. It is in the clumsy old looms that sometimes still are found taking up too much of the small house far back off the road, although more likely they will be found moved down into the community weaving room set up by the local school to keep the time-old arts alive.

The daring and the homing—it is still there. It is in the well-set head and steadfast eyes of the best of the mountain women. That young girl to come into the mountains—strong, lithe, vivacious, daring anything at the side of the man of her choosing, a man of unbreakable will and cautious determination, a border chieftain—still lives in the free, sure swing of the mountain girl's walk.

It is in the faces of the old mountain women. There is something magnificent about the old mountain woman—in the patience and endurance in the thin set of her mouth, in the friendly interest in all pleasant things at the wrinkled corners of her eyes. There is a slow wisdom there, steeped in elemental things. It is a saneness amounting to serenity, letting her wait the end of age calm in the knowing that though her kind may not have found all they set out to find, they have found a place in which to search for it.

They had set out to find freedom. And that first pioneer man and woman, climbing up into a high place where the very air was that freedom they were seeking, where the mighty loops of the hills made a hallelujah garland around the sky, could not know that the clock of time would stop for them there.

They did not foresee that that hallelujah garland would become a wall—a potent barrier shutting off their descendants from the rest of the world; shaping their political and economical and social lives along entirely different patterns than those of their outland compatriots.

There were no maps to show them they had chosen a place without waterways which make the natural routes of communication. They knew the roads they had followed, or made themselves, into the mountains had been bad. But at the time of those early migrations all roads were bad, and mountain passes not much worse than others.

They could not know that for the next hundred and fifty years their roads, and their pioneer way of life, would change as little, that they would become a separate people, set apart from all others by virtue of custom, character, dialect, by certain physical and mental traits they had brought into the wilderness with them, which their long isolation there would accentuate.

SINS OF THE FLESH

Charley Kiney age 72 ma 10 1852 war farmer liv in N. C. on blue rige at Kiney Gap he had 4 womin cors marid to won rest live on farm all went to feld work to mak gran all went to crib for the bred all went to smoke house for ther mete he cild bout 75 to 80 hogs ever yere and womin never had words bout his haven so many womin (if it) wod be this time thar wod be hare puld the raz 42 children belong to him all wen to prechin together nothin sed they des everibodi go long smoth with won nother he made brandy all of his lif never had any foes got long smoth with everibodi i nod him Jacob Carpenter

Every man—at the head of his own house, the law in his own hollow—lived his own life. But when a man carried that independent way of life to the lengths which Charley Kiney did, that made him a character. However, although the wild lavishness of that particular patriarchy was unusual, every mountain state has had in it some man of like stature whose progeny spread out over several counties and came to be counted on to carry the vote for that section. But the others maintained several separate establishments. Charley Kiney is the only such potentate within my knowledge who so blandly attempted—and evidently succeeded—in carrying it off all under one roof.

Irregular unions, on a much lesser scale, were not uncommon all through the mountains, and might occur anywhere along the social ladder. There was the youngish woman who did the local wash in one mountain community, and took things comfortably as they came. She had a likable, bony face with a healthy curve to it. All her children were healthy, too. There were three of them. She kept the two oldest dressed in their respective fathers' old clothes, cut down, and they bore their respective fathers' names. But she was uncertain about what to name the new one, and sincerely troubled.

"I prayed all night the night hit come," she said earnestly, "tryin' to think who hit's pappy is—because if thar's one thing I'm particular about, hit's my honor!"

Going on up the scale, the attitude tightens. The better people do not condone such laxness by any manner of means. Still, should the misfortune occur, they feel the condemnation should fall on the parents, and not on the child. That the child have a fair chance, therefore, it takes a place without stigma in the household, along with the children born into the family rightfully.

In the days of the mountain life when creek beds were the only roads there were, which was not so long ago, sometimes it might be months, or even years, before the preacher got into remote districts, and marital strictures necessarily grew lax. A state of marriage was often declared by the enamored young couple merely moving into a house of their own further up the creek.

But the general lack of social shock accompanying illegitimacy goes back further than that. It was not unknown among their forebears. Irregular unions, in fact, were so common in the old country they were recognized by law. An old English map shows widely spreading properties as belonging—quite simply, in unashamed type at the top—to "William, Bastard Duke of Normandy." Even the Irish St. Brigit herself was born out of wedlock. And certainly the sins of the flesh were regarded as amiable frailties of mankind in Shakespearean times—and our southern mountains have been called "Shakespeare's America."

Time, however, has caught up with the southern mountains in the last quarter of a century, and that moral viewpoint, along with other carried-over ideas and customs, has been supplanted.

THE DEVIL'S WIFE

Franky Carpenter age 56 dide oc 25 1862 hard workin womin on farm made corn oates

What it was about that broad place in the mountain road that made it immediately so exciting, I don't know. But there was excitement even in the way the store light fell out the open door and lit in the mud puddle. It was Saturday night, and the store was keeping open for the movie crowd. The movie was being held in a barn just back of the store, and in that strange clarity which mountain air has you could hear faintly for a long distance the wail of the orchestra as it whanged away at "Barbara Allen" while Tom Mix galloped across the screen. The orchestra was a fiddle and a banjo and a comb, and played for the price of admission. Up the hill from the movie house was a café (CAF'E it said in the window), where you could get ice cream on these Saturday nights. There was also a white church and a white school and a gasoline station, and all around lay the slaty suggestion of mountains.

The high winding road had rounded a curve in the clear dark

of great trees, and then there ahead lay the town, in moonlight and mist on a Saturday night, and it was mine.

As an excuse to stay, I taught in the school. Since then the school has greatly improved and is more particular about pedagogic qualifications. But it was a high-hearted experience for everyone concerned, and early in it I became aware that the people living in our southern hills have a unique contribution to make to our national literature, in the form of a mythology. It takes time and loneliness to make mythology, and nights when even so sure a thing as a mountain wall is no more than a mark in a dream; it takes hunger. And historic imagination.

Not many places in America are so equipped. Those mountains happen to have been. Their people, coming to America years before the Revolution, brought the beginnings in with them, in the lore of eighteenth-century Britain and western Europe. They stopped long enough in the settlements already made along the coast to give the old lore a colonial turn, and then they pushed on "west"—to the mountains. There, by geography and circumstance, not only were they sidetracked from the strong surge of empire building which had brought them to the new land, but their very existence was forgotten by the rest of the world for a hundred years or so.

In that strange historical pause they had the time—and the need—to create a mythology. Begun in the long-gone past, raised up in the raw ways of the young country, they have struck out something new—different from anything else in America, and yet peculiarly American.

My first experience with it came one morning when I found myself confronted with such mathematical paralyzers as "If an ice factory makes ice in half-ton cakes how fast does the ice melt in thirty minutes"—or problems equally unfathomable. I was writing a wild undercover note to the seventh-grade teacher for help again, when Ingaby came up to the desk.

Ingaby had bright blue eyes and fair hair, skinned back tight from an alert little face. She had a quick mind and usually a merry one. But this morning she was solemn, with her solemnity carrying an extra load of importance.

"My Aunt May died."

Not knowing her Aunt May, still I looked up, of course, and made the perfunctory expression of sympathy. "Oh, that's too bad. What was the matter?"

"She got spelled and turned fitified," said the child simply.

I looked at her blankly. She nodded.

"The old witch on yon side of the mountain done hit."

"Did it," I corrected automatically, hitting on the one thing I could be sure of at the moment.

"Did it," said Ingaby dutifully. Then she added, "She's the very one all right!" She grew sad. "And Aunt May used to be the prettiest woman to look at in the face!"

"Really?" By this time I was even more mystified by Aunt May than by the ice factory, and much more interested.

So Ingaby told me, her bright eyes on fire, a little girl in a very clean calico dress repeating some tale from home. As she told it her childish voice took on a lilting sweetness, minored with plaintiveness. That strangely fascinating quality of voice also was something she had come into from hearing a long time back.

"The old witch was jealous. She wanted Aunt May's man for her own daughter. And one night when Aunt May's man was out coon huntin', the old witch come over and into the house. And she made Aunt May eat nine witch balls, made out of nine needles all wrapped around with fine little hair. Then she turned Aunt May into a horse, and rid her up and down the valley. Every night and every night, my mother said, she done hit—did it—till the once beautiful woman got poorly, and ugly, and turned fitified."

"Well—" I said, inadequately. It was the first witch story I ever had heard; a few days after I went home with Ingaby to call.

If she had not showed me, I could not have found my way there alone. We went up the hill from the schoolhouse and dropped down the other side to a hollow that fingered out deviously. She knew which way to choose and we followed that creek clear to its head. Sometimes we were in the creek bed, but oftener on a narrow path beside it. It was the kind of path where rhododendron and scrub oak and blackberries close in quickly, letting you see only a little at a time ahead or behind you; even the creek beside you is known only by the sound of it on the rocks, like feelings too clear to be thought, and shortly all sense of familiar things is left behind you and lost, so that you marvel again—even on a narrow path with no vista—"Wild, wild country still!" The witch story did not seem so incongruous here.

Ingaby had said her Aunt May once had been a beautiful woman. So had her mother, hauntingly so. Plenty of meat and potatoes, for it was a good farm, but still the woman was hungry. She kept looking at me—not at me, but at the unknown life which lay beyond the narrow work-worn boundaries of her own. Dreams that had gone empty looked with tired blue eyes from under the brim of the man's hat she wore. I turned from her to the man, wondering what he was thinking about as he sat with his chair tilted back against the house wall staring at the opposite bank of the creek, and decided not much.

I had brought a present for the "least one," a little boy about four. He and Ingaby were the last children left at home, and Ingaby, with the older one's invariable pleasure in the younger, had told me about him. It was not a particularly appropriate present, but the best my belongings offered, a paperweight in the form of a wild young glass horse.

The little boy, who had drawn back shyly close to his mother's drab skirts, took the package silently, not knowing what to do with it.

"Look what for a present the teacher fotched you," encouraged his mother, pleased herself.

He opened the first layers of white tissue strangely, and did not seem surprised when nothing showed up. I had to urge him to keep on unwrapping. When the little glass horse finally revealed itself, he looked at it, and handed it back. When I assured him it was his, he ran a grubby finger over it awkwardly, giving the promise of knowing it more intimately with time—like a small bud that would open slowly and with a wonder it would never lose. Then all at once he let loose. He flew around gathering up chairs from all over the house, although each of us already had one. He came out carrying one on his head. He was like a quick tickled little animal.

His mother watched the antics that showed his delight, smiling a little, but with a heavy kind of wistfulness attending the smile. She sat holding the little crystalline horse for him carefully and quite as though it were his and none of hers. She held it as though it were too late. Once, as we sat on the long porch talking, when Ingaby was telling something about the school which held the excitement of wide horizons, the woman lifted her hand and pushed back her hair restlessly, and then seemed to grow tired, all the way through, as though exhausted by a hint of great things she would never know.

The world of fact and science and philosophy and art was unfolding to Ingaby, as the tissue wrappings had opened up before the younger child. But, for their mother, up in that wild shut-in, there was no such promise. She was a "hard-working woman on the farm," and the only way she knew to break the monotony of that, the hard sameness it had fallen into, was the way her people before her had done—imbuing with drama from the days of the Witch of Endor such present squalid circumstances as a woman dying with fits.

The people of our southern mountains have stepped aside to let two centuries go by. But sitting on the porch of that old house, which itself had been there "right at a hundred years," I had a strange sense of time kaleidoscoping—the mother standing back still, but watching her children stepping out into line again, to take their place in the procession of the world.

They enter it with much to contribute from their long seclusion, and if the old lore is one of the minor contributions, it is a flavorsome one.

What other part of the country except the thin air of the mountains—sometimes smelling so sharply of nothing, sometimes "stinking so spicy"—could have nourished such an extravaganza as Skilly Pendergast originated in the outhouse? Her man was away to the widow Lance's, looking at the widow's brindle cow again, and Skilly was starting to cook supper, when she heard the fiddle music in the outhouse, and lots of people dancing.

She didn't have much wood in the house, but she put it all on the fire to have light, and who should she see coming in but the Devil, and four little devils and nine of the prettiest-dressed women she had ever seen, and a whole pack of hellcats. The Devil's wife put apple dumplings on the table.

"Lord, I didn't know where they'd got those dumplings," Skilly would say afterward. "They were big as my fist!" The Devil asked her to eat with them, but she wouldn't.

After the Devil had finished eating and was feeling good, he laid the fiddle across his knee and sawed on it. The Devil's wife opened up the waists of the nine pretty women and made a cross on each of their breasts. Then they all danced. The little devils were playing around the hearthrocks, so close to the fire that Skilly said, "You little devils, you'll git burnt up!"

They didn't answer her. Skilly liked to have an answer when she spoke to people. It made her mad when they didn't pay any attention to her. So she took off her shoe and flung it at them. They all turned on her and made the awfullest faces ever she saw.

"Some people," she reported afterward, "say thar hain't no children in hell. But thar shore war four little devils in my house that night!"

A trout pool on Hogback Mountain

Nahantahala Gorge

Looking Glass Falls, Pisgah National Park

Then the hellcats began snooping around till she didn't feel to stand for that either. So she threw a kettleful of boiling water at them. But they bowed up their backs and the water rolled off steam. The house got so steamed up she couldn't see her hand before her face, and the air so flavored with brimstone she couldn't fetch breath.

When it cleared, the Devil and the Devil's wife and the little devils and the nine pretty-dressed women had all disappeared. But Skilly knew she had got a vision of some sort. She studied on it, and when her man came on in home, she told him about it. He was just about the uneasiest man she had ever seen.

"Skilly, you just drempt hit," he sputtered.

"How could I a-drempt hit," she retorted, "when I used up ary stick of light wood to see 'em by?" Then, she said, careless like, "Well, did you git the widow's cow bought?"

"No I didn't—" fumbled Harry. "Because hit was a-comin' on toward dark by the time I got over thar. I figgered, maybe, I'd just step over and give her another look tomorrow—"

"Who?" asked Skilly sweetly. "The widow's brindle or the widow?" Then she lit into him. "I can fair see you out in that pasture, a-lookin' at the widow's brindle, and then a-lookin' at the widow."

"Now, Skilly—" protested Harry. But she cut him short.

"I'm a-leavin', that's what," she told him. "Hit's been give to me in a vision that I've been livin' with a man a-goin' on in sin."

"Skilly, hold on—"

But Skilly wouldn't hold on. She went to a neighbor's house and told her tale. "The Devils have routed me," she told them.

The need for something new to talk about acted like tow, and sympathy for Skilly like spark, and they burned together. And Skilly, quick anyhow, took advantage of the flare to strike a pose. She began to claim to see things other people could not. She did seem to have a knack for bringing out the half-thoughts in the lurking places of everybody's mind, and it was a talent which grew with her use of it. She lived with first one neighbor and then another, and they were glad to have her. Long evenings picked up when Skilly Pendergast was there to tell her tales.

In course of time, Harry tried to get Skilly to come back to him. (He had married the widow, but she had died. At the funeral, somebody ventured with awe, "I'll 'low Skilly Pendergast put hit into the Lord's head to do that—just out of punishment to Harry." The man to whom it was said was disgusted. He said back sarcastically, "I don't reckon the Lord's takin' orders from Skilly Pendergast. Not yet awhile, nohow." But the other was not convinced. "Um mebbe not. But I wouldn't put hit past her to use her influence.")

When Harry asked her to come back, Skilly studied him, like she was pondering it. He wasn't a bad-looking man, although he could have shaved up and looked better. But finally she told him she guessed she wouldn't. She was making her own way now, and getting along good. When she'd lived with him there was nothing about her more than another. But, now she had prestige. It was a prestige which she kept clear to the end.

She was staying at Jake Taylor's place, at the time, and was out at the side of the house washing clothes. Suddenly, Jake's wife heard a queer sound, and looked out, and there was Skilly, standing on her head in the washtub!

They got her out and stretched her on the ground and crushed on her ribs. But she hadn't drowned. When the doctor got there he said she'd had a stroke. The Taylors figured she must have felt it coming on and knew she was heading for the tub, and bewitched herself so she wouldn't drown. Because when they took the snuff stick out of her mouth it was dry!

It is an elemental mythology which our southern mountains have created for us, of the soil, sometimes romantic, sometimes brutal, often humorous; always restless—a substitution for the life-want set deep in everybody from the beginning, which those of the world can lull with worldly things, but which those out of reach of the world have to go down into themselves to satisfy.

Martha Thomas was one of those women made for a strong man. And from the name her husband left behind him, Arzy Thomas was dangerous enough. But his danger lay in the devastation that can be wrought by a little mind. Any capabilities Martha may have had for being a great woman got sapped out of her in little ways. And something of all that had been wanting in her living with Arzy Thomas, she put contemptuously into the telling of his dying. Her voice was deliberate, with that ominous quiet that holds back power.

"I knowed he war a-goin', because all the dogs from fur and nigh come around and howled. The cows come down out of the woods to the barn lot and lowed and lowed. I went to the door and looked out. White chickens war a-scratchin' on the doorstone, and la, we didn't have a white chicken on the place!

"Hit war a dark night. But plain as day, comin' down yon side the mountain, through bresh so thickety a butcher knife couldn't cut hit, I seed the Devil a-comin'. He war ridin' a coal-black cart, drivin' a coal-black oxen. The cart come down to the door and stopped. When hit come—"

—The voice releasing its power now, the tones going straight down the scale to cold depths and scraping on the bitter bottom—

"—hit come empty. But when hit went away hit had a big black ball in hit that war Arzy's soul."

Naturally some of these experiences with the supernatural are vouched for by people who would let anything else that came along do for thinking. It was a nervously wrinkled little woman who introduced me to the idea that if anyone ever tried to borrow anything, you had to be careful, because the borrower might do you harm. She told me that one day a neighbor woman came to the house to borrow a blow of soda, but she made an excuse not to lend it. The neighbor came back three times, and finally just grabbed up the soda and ran.

"And what happened?" I asked.

She got a dimly harassed look. "That's what I ain't never been sartin about."

She was not certain about anything, including herself. Even when she sat down, she would sit not quite in the middle of the chair seat, and then look dimly troubled, as though wondering why the seat didn't feel right. It was easy to imagine that she'd been a little off center, always, about everything—a little off center and wondering why life didn't feel quite sure.

Then there was a lurid account in a rapid undertone in which the teller went to extraordinary lengths to be ordinary, about a great big old fleshy girl—"La, her big dinners!"—who got bewitched and her stomach just swelled and swelled. The particular details of her bewitchment I've forgotten except for the wild eyes in the old woman who told it, and the snuff that dripped down from each corner of her loose mouth.

It was, however, in the living room of an attractive modern bungalow in a rapidly-changing mountain community—which the up-and-coming members of that house were helping to change—that I learned the proper way to do away with a witch. You draw the witch's picture on the gatepost and then shoot the picture through the heart with a silver bullet. The young woman who told me this is thoroughly intelligent, with a quick sense of humor, and an enviable verve of expression. She told me the old stories because she knew I was interested—casting off any belief in them herself, and yet somehow their substance was still in them.

"Sometimes when we were little," she said, "people would sit around at night and tell those tales. Mother'd never let us listen. But we'd peek down and hear."

That any of the old lore at all has survived the sweeping changes which the last quarter of a century has made in the mountains, is due to the mountain people's natural ability at story-telling. They tell the old stories easily, unself-consciously, and with an instinctive eye for the dramatic. And they delight in an audience—if the audience is sympathetic and responsive. On the other hand, one of the best raconteurs I know, a veritable "tale-tellin' devil charmer," stopped short at an exchange of amused glances between two of his listeners. He shut up like a burr, and thereafter did not bother to put himself out about them.

They were guests at the summer resort where he was "helping," and had asked him to tell the story. He had been quite willing to do so, if it would please them and make their visit more enjoyable. Mountain people are interested in outsiders, feel a natural friendliness toward them, and are famously hospitable—until they feel they are being imposed upon, or made sport of. Then they draw back into a reserve. If the outsider mistakes it for backwardness he is indeed making a foolish mistake. The highlander withdraws into a sense of his own dignity as instinctive as his sense of the dramatic, and regards the less well-bred outsider now with a complete disinterest.

The story which the summer people interrupted was an old murder tale of the district, which the teller had heard from his father. It concerned a man named Asa Meters who claimed that one day while he and his brother were out shearing sheep, his brother fell off the sled and the upturned shears went through his heart.

Nobody believed him. People did not "confidence" Asa Meters. Mountain people are used to earnestness of purpose being masked under a leisurely detachment. Asa was a small-eyed driver. And his driving determination to get ahead bothered them. When his brother was killed, everybody thought Asa had done it so he would get his brother's share of the property. They thought that showed in his face. They would look at his hands as though they were full of blood.

But nobody could prove his guilt, and the brother was buried up in a field back of the house. There was not even the dark dignity of a cedar planted, to mark the place. In course of time Asa decided to turn that field for rye, and make some money out of it. He got Henry Holt to come plow for him.

The dead man had been buried in a shallow grave, and when Henry with his bull-tongued plow came upon it, he pondered the matter, and then he decided what to do.

A proved way to find a murderer is to place the murdered person's skull above the suspect's head, high up and out of reach of water. Then, when the question is put, there is no power in the suspect to lie out of it. On some pretext, Henry got the skull up into Asa's loft, near the fireplace. Then he watched, and when Asa went under it to fix the fire, he accused him.

Asa neither denied nor affirmed the accusation. But he began to shake. It seemed he would shake himself to death. After that he never could eat, because every time he'd try, the vapor of his brother would grab the food away. He couldn't lie down to sleep, because his brother's ghost would throw itself down on top of him and smother him. He could only sit by the fire, and try to beat his brother's ghost with a stick. A gray something hovered over him all the time, all the time.

Nobody called the law. Nobody felt there was any need. Nature was administering due justice.

That story came out of a group of people who had brought into the mountain wilderness with them, along with other strong colonial traits, dislike of the British courts. Through their taxation experience with them, they had come to mistrust all authority except that of natural justice. And often a touch of the supernatural, as in the case of Asa Meters, helped that course along.

Needless to say, even in the early times, there were many people who would scorn interest in any such supernatural nonsense. Saying that mountain people natively are superstitious is like saying hemlocks are native to the mountains. They are. Yet there are many places where there are no hemlocks. Sometimes you can go for a long way through an oak woods where each tree stands in its own dignity, with no underbrush except rhododendron—the rhododendron, too, growing singly there and immaculate. Then there are the chestnut knolls where the bears come to feed. Or there are fields with white rock like sheep in them. There are no hemlocks in these places. Yet hemlocks grow in the mountains, and so have the superstitions of early America and time before that rooted and grown up there.

Much of the southern mountain legend can be traced very directly back to that of England and Scotland and Ireland. In comparing mythologies, you will find a legendary dog of West England called the Spectre Hound. It was a fearful thing to see, evidently. Sir Walter Scott has it as a paralyzing spectacle: "For he was speechless, ghastly wan: Who spoke the Spectre Hound of Man."

The English dog was shaggy and black, with long black tail and ears. The American variety is yellow and spotted, and not so terrorizing. At least one man who was telling me about it said his father had seen it many a time when he was riding back from Morgantown after salt, and it was company along the lonesome road.

He said the yellow dog would appear out of nowhere, and for a while follow along like any ordinary little old dog. Then slowly it would rise, and run along in the air. For a time it would run along beside him, then gradually it would skim forward to a place beside the horse's head.

The old-time terror of a baby dying if it is not baptized was not only a doctrinal part of the Presbyterianism of many of the mountain peoples' forebears, but also wound back to Irish and German folklore. The old Gaelic belief was that unbaptized infants wandered the air till Judgment Day, wailing in distress. The German idea incorporated a mysterious lady known as Frau Bertha, attended by those troops of unbaptized children who formed "the wild huntsmen of the sky." Sometimes an old crone, on stormy days in the mountains, can hear their wail and peer out to see them sweeping homelessly across the dreary sky on the cold wintry winds.

The fires of a real mountain house never are allowed to go out. The fact that had they been allowed to go out in the old days, someone in the household would probably have had to walk miles to borrow fire to light them again, is no doubt a very sound functional basis for the habit. However, the highland fires of Scotland and Ireland were not allowed to go out either. The hearth traditionally is a sacred place—a place of warmth and security; the center of the home.

In that regard there is another ghost story about a household which was roused every morning by a scraping sound across the hearthstone. The mother seemed to have an exceptionally nice pair of eyes while she told about it. She said it was the ghost of her man, come back to scrape away the night ashes and freshen the fire for his homefolks. He always had been good to them, and every morning he still came back to fix the fire.

The story of the ghost of the sawmill I heard at the store one morning while I was waiting for the mail. The general store of any mountain town—and often the store is about all the town there is—is a good place to find a guide for hunting, or to get information about fishing or homespun. But most of all it is a place to sit and rest yourself.

Mountain people never at any time appear to feel pressed by the necessity of making a living, but at mail time they drift in to the store to wait as though they could wait all day, and all night, and tomorrow morning, and have a very pleasant time doing it. To someone from the strained world outside which is always in a hurry this leisurely social hour in the middle of the morning may be a matter of amazement, scorn, envy, or habit—depending on how long you can stay.

This particular June morning the sky overhead was fire blue, and the mud out front was cracking open and loving it. Everybody was loafing around in the sunshine as though it were, as one ruddy blond in overalls, leaning in the doorway, expressed it, "just come day, go day, without a thing on earth to study about." A little boy named Jerkwater got a man with handlebar mustaches and a couple of mild black devils for eyes, who was taking his ease on a bench against the store wall, started on the mill story.

Jerkwater's freckles were so thick his cheeks were mustard brown, and what brought on the story was that Jerkwater had divulged to his chums out front that he had a penny to spend. They all came trooping up the store steps to help him spend it.

"Git horehound, Jerkwater," one of the little boys was urging in strident whispers, although there was little else he could have gotten, the store being "fresh out" of almost everything—a regretful piece of information which the storekeeper gave out philosophically, without excuse or offer of substitution.

"A stick of horehound," teased one of the men on the store porch, "will last you a week, Jerkwater, and you suck light on hit."

At that Jerkwater, in an agony of grinning embarrassment, let the penny slip through his fingers. It rolled gaily off the porch and all the little boys scurried to go find it.

"You shoulda spent that penny, son, afore hit got away from you."

"Why, certainly, he should have."

For a few minutes lazy wit was free and everyone enjoyed himself immensely at the mild expense of Jerkwater. Then the mustaches leaned down over the edge of the porch and got themselves a piece of hay from a clump growing wild there, and nibbled at it, and the man behind them said that reminded him of the time Dave Kinder let a fortune get away from *him.*

It seemed that Dave Kinder himself never had seen the ghost at the sawmill which was a couple of miles up the road. Neither had anyone else. But a few people had said they heard it. Riding by, they claimed they could hear it shivering in the night. It was the ghost of a man who had been drowned in the cold millstream. The stream is held back by a dam at the side of the mill, so that the water there lies still and dark, deep and sufficient—until those moonless nights when the invisible ghost rises up out of it to shake terribly.

The mill got itself haunted years ago by a man traveling north on foot. Nobody knew who he was nor a thing about him. But he had a little sack of something so heavy he could hardly carry it. There was some talk of its being gold. He spent the night in the mill, and it was bruited around afterwards he had been killed there, for nobody ever saw him again. But people going past the mill on dark nights began to hear that blood-churning sound of shivering.

One night Dave Kinder took him a good slug of corn and said he wasn't afeared. He was going to go in that mill, just to see what the hell a ghost was like. He took a lantern with him, and some sulphur matches, but he didn't figure on fetching light till he heard something to make it worth while. That shivering noise took up. Though he was waiting for it, when it came, his hair rose straight up on his head, and his chin whiskers like to pulled spang out. Dave said it was the awfullest sound ever he heard! He said he couldn't understand why he'd ever wanted to come in there in the first place—and then by golly there came another sound! A kind of little rattling, all around his feet! He got that placed, though, directly. That was the sulphur matches dropping one by one from his shaking hands. He made out to get the lantern lit—and then liked to died.

That shivering had ceased. But someone was coming. He could hear the slow footsteps, coming nearer, and nearer; nearer still. When they stopped, whatever it was was right alongside him. Well, Dave finally got up strength enough to raise his eyes to look; there stood the dripping *re*-mains. The eyes were great sunken stares, and the flesh was all rotting away. The mouth was open, and Dave got a good view of the teeth and the blue purplish gums. The teeth looked about to fall out. Dave said the whole thing just looked like a corpse that had laid in the river and then got up and was walking around.

"In the name of the Father and Son and the Holy Ghost, who are you?" quavered Dave—using the ancient idea of referring to the Deity when talking to a ghost.

The ghost didn't answer flat out, but led the way through the mill and up back of it into the brush, and pointed to a spot on the ground. Dave marked the spot with a honeysuckle stick, and then got himself out of the place as fast as his tottering legs would take him.

"I'm drunk," he said hopefully to his wife. "I couldn't hold my pint and I've the ague and I'm a-goin' to go lay down." Then he told her all that happened.

"You're not drunk!" His wife was plumb delighted. "You've just found yoreself a fortune! I'll lay to hit that whoever killed that traveler got scared out and buried the money, and run. That ghost was tryin' to tell you whar that money is buried at! You go get in the bed and take a good sleep, and in the mornin' I'll help you dig."

The next morning they went back to the spot, and sure enough, there the honeysuckle stick was, still stuck in the ground. Dave figured he hadn't been drunk after all, and maybe his wife was right for once, and they started in to dig, he and his wife both. But the earth took to trembling so, they got scared and ran away. Every time he'd ride by the mill after that, something seemed to try to pull Dave off his horse, and up toward the spot. But he'd cut his horse a lick and ride clear of the place.

Dave said he'd like to have the money, but not that bad. He never did get it.

By the time the story was over, one of the little boys had found the lost penny in some weeds.

"Hyere's yore penny," they called. "Come rake it out, Jerkwater."

Jerkwater came to with a start. He had moved unconsciously closer and closer to the teller of the ghost story, his eyes in his freckled face "biggin" and "biggin," and watching Jerkwater had been almost as good as listening to the story.

Jerkwater would remember that story. And some day he would tell it to somebody, who would remember it, too.

LURE OF THE HUNT

Soonzy Ollis age 84 dide June 10 1871 grates bar honter & turkies bee trees by honders and ratel snak by 100 cild deer by thosand I no him well

There is a current weekly newspaper in West Virginia, *The Pocahontas Times*, which is running ads for bearskins as usual. Its editorials lean to hunting. Not that such a matter as a war throwing six continents into travail is ignored. Not at all. In its last issue the two columns at the left of the front page are devoted entirely to news of "Our Army and Navy Boys"—scattered all over creation and thinking about Pocahontas County and wanting to get back home to it. That they might get back there honorably and safely, the Pocahontas Board of Trade had a big box ad about buying War Bonds. The Minnehaha Farm Women's Club had met to learn to fix rib-sticking lunches for their men out doing war work, and the women along Beaver Creek had got together for a Red Cross meeting. That covered the war news.

There were no last-minute flashes from far fronts. There were no headline accounts about Big Men meeting to decide Big Things. There were no spreads about national labor arguments—although there was a long piece about a Pocahontas housewife who had gone to work in an airplane factory and had received a merit award for an efficiency which had such grace and ease she seemed to be playing. The friendly, meandering hill paper goes on the evident theory that Pocahontas County does what it can in its own way and need not keep itself harassed by conditions beyond its power to control.

It is the local Rod and Gun Club therefore that gets the steady front-page space, and in the issue at hand the editorial starts out to be on Victory Gardens but shortly veers off into fishing. "The next time you are in a trout stream," begins the third paragraph enthusiastically, "and hit a piece of luck with trout all of a sudden beginning to jump crazy for a fly—" *The Pocahontas Times* with its news of hunting and fishing is famous for its effect of a little bit of quiet in a noisy world.

Ever since Daniel Boone got Kentucky settled with his fabulous tales of the game there, and led the way to it by joining buffalo trails into a road, the southern mountains have been happy hunting grounds. And surprisingly, the diversion of the hunt there is not much different today than it was in the early days of our country when those first bold spirits broke the bondage of routine, oppression, banalities, or things they would like to forget—to set forth for the free life of the wilds.

There is an old account of one Sam Pringle's adventure with a bear near Tygart's River in what was then the Virginia of 1846, which could nearly double for a similar one in North Carolina two years ago.

"Sam Pringle," so goes the account, "was no coward, but the huge size of the beast loomed so formidably that even the intrepid hunter felt a sensibility akin to fear come over him. He realized that he was alone in that boundless wilderness, within twenty paces of a beast of crushing strength. Should his shot fail to reach a vital spot, he well knew the infuriated monster might charge—that it would be a hand to hand fight, with knife and tomahawk pitted against gnashing fangs and ripping claws—"

It goes on tensely to tell about a mighty avalanche of claws, tusks and iron muscle, with bloody froth dripping in ropy strings from spiked jaws.

In the more recent encounter, if the bear were not exactly a monster, it was, according to admiring observers, "too big to stand under." The present day "intrepid hunter" is a mountain man by choice, having arrived at that by way of what Robert Louis Stevenson termed for himself "The 'Circle' "—that "advancement from complexity to simplicity." The excitement about his brush with a bear had been spread by the observers, the hunter himself not being inclined to dramatize, although the whole drama of these present-day stories lies in that very ease, with away back in it quietly, humor. But sitting around a picnic fire one night, the picnickers finally prevailed upon him to tell about it.

The stars were very near that night, and red sparks flew to heaven from the whole balsam tree somebody had chopped down and kept feeding to the fire. The fire was in a kind of balsam valley almost at the top of a mountain, between two peaks that were blacker than the sky. One rose as though the flat of a hand had made a gesture upward with one superb movement. The other peak was cragged and cut. All down around and below us the wind in the hemlocks was a wild, mad thing—it sounded like a million maniacs ripping up cellophane. But it was very quiet where we were. Even so, we had to listen to hear, the story was told so incidentally.

"One particularly mean bear had been getting the dogs, so we set off after her. I saw her once up the branch, but my gun hung up and wouldn't fire. It had done that once before, and I'd knocked it against a stump. So I tried it again. But this time I broke it. So I left it at the stump and ran on.

"I met the bear at a sharp turn, and we stood there looking at each other. She looked like she couldn't make up her mind what to do, but mine was already made up. I turned around and ran. I looked for a club to hit her with, but by the time I'd found one, she'd loped off in the other direction.

"The next time I caught up with her, I was up on a bluff and she was down a ways, leaping on a favorite dog of mine. She had it in her paws, and would hold it and fall on it. That made me mad. I got excited and started down toward her, rocking her as I ran. I hit her, but I didn't do any good. Then I remembered a knife I had in my pocket, and I jumped on her and started to hack. I could feel the knife cut, but I didn't seem to hurt her. Then I realized I was cutting on her ribs and moved over.

"The bear was mad, too, and we rolled downhill together. I had her about cleaned by the time we hit bottom, but still she wouldn't die. Doggonedest bear to die I ever saw. I looked up and saw Bert Aldridge aiming at it—or me, one or the other, I couldn't be sure—he was so excited. But I was glad to see him. I yelled, 'Bert, shoot this bear—only come down here and do it.' "

Once caught by the fascination of bear hunting, everything else is put second. Whenever the right kind of day comes along to carry scent, any other occupation or interest is dropped promptly to train the bear dogs. Whole intent days are spent dragging a piece of bear-hide tied to the rear bumper of the car, over the country with the dog pack in tow, teaching them the scent.

Even politics are forgotten. They tell the story in eastern Tennessee about the time the Governor got up that way. The local politicians, by way of cottoning up to the mighty man, produced their best for him—a bear hunt. But they grew so interested in listening to their own particular dogs giving tongue out over the hills and valleys, that they forgot about its being the Governor's party. Suddenly one of them took a whiff of the midnight supper they had intended. Then he drawled, "How do you like yore meat, Gov'nor?"

"A little burned," sniffed the Governor obligingly.

"Wal, she's a-burnin'," sang back the hunter cheerfully.

Almost anywhere in the mountains you can hear bear stories. In Avery County in North Carolina, they talk about Spenser Shooks' traps. He contrived very ingenious ones. He contrived one so ingenious he got caught in it himself. Fortunately he happened to have a hand hatchet with him, and hacked himself out. It took him three days.

Uncle War Clark told me, comfortably from his old age on the front porch, about the time when he was young—to use his own words, it was the time in his life when he was "mostly muscle and the rest fool."

"B'ars go to bed about Christmas," he said, "and get up about the middle of April. They make a bed of ivy and twigs in a rock cave. They don't eat endurin' that time, just lay thar suckin' their front paw, so that when they're killed in the spring their guts is just as clean as the inside of yore hand.

"One time a feller I was huntin' with offered to give me the whole hide and half the meat, both, if I'd crawl in a cave whar we figgered a b'ar was, and smoke him out. B'ar meat's good. Hit tastes just like beef, and hit's sweetened. So I said I'd do it.

"I raked some leaves and twigs together and started a fire just inside the cave. And the b'ar was in thar all right. Only hit didn't seem like thar was room enough for us both, hardly, so the b'ar got out. On hits way hit cuffed the gun out of my hands, and knocked me flat, and then clumb out over me. I still got the claw marks. The other feller shot him, and give me what he said he would. I was risky in them days."

The deer and the elk that used to be killed in the mountains by the "100" are not nearly so common now, although almost any roadside restaurant or mountain hotel has a pair of glassy-eyed heads mounted on the wall. That they once abounded, however, shows in the frequent place names referring to them, such as Elk Horn City, Banner Elk, Bull Scrape, Buck Creek. Deer Lick is so named because the deer used to come there for salt. Head and Shoulders Mountain is named after a deer that was head and shoulders bigger than any deer ever seen before. It was so big, that when it fell, all the streams for miles around grew oily.

There is plentiful lesser game still, including birds. That first tang of fall in the air, that first woodbine to turn scarlet, is the signal for many a man to get out his high lace boots, call his setter, check his tobacco supply, and take to the hills with his gun—his pulse quickening in anticipation of that first whir of grouse wings.

Or it may be the pheasant, scurrying ahead of his spaniel, and then leaving the ground to go hurtling through the branches, that has summoned him to the hill woods.

If it is the soft winnowing of woodcock wings that has called, then no other game bird holds interest. Shakespeare gave the name of that odd drab little bird to the foolish, but it is a quarry that holds a peculiar fascination for the hunter. It is said that once a hunter hears the peculiar musical whistle of the woodcock's wings—once that strange little brown creature has scuttled between him and the sun, once on a cold day when the hills are gun metal, the snow being that dark on the northern slopes, he comes upon the whiter chalk marks of the woodcock—he is lost.

The practical hunter, however, goes out for wild turkey. You get more meat per bullet, and better. From an epicurean's standpoint, turkey is the finest game in the world. Also, in its way, it is as sporting a game as there is. That purely North American bird is wary. It is hard to find, and even after a flock has been flushed and scattered and called back, even then the great bronze bird can slip away so silently you feel, rather than hear, its departure.

Down around the Smoke Hole district in West Virginia, a man recently had the misfortune to go to sleep while he was boiling down his sorghum. The huge pot of it represented his whole crop, and when it caught on fire, it made quite a blaze. The neighbors were very anxious—but not about his sorghum burning up. "I hope Dave didn't skeer all the turkeys out of the country with that fire."

Rattlesnake hunting, in some sections, has a charm. One veteran of Snake Den named Oaty told me what to do if I ever came upon a rattlesnake. Of course, Oaty was a liar. It was said of him that he would rather climb a tree and tell a lie, than stand on the ground and tell the truth. However, his wife stood up for him indulgently.

"He only lies enough to enjoy hisself," she told me that October afternoon.

We had gone hoping to find a Faith-and-Fortune quilt I was

hunting, having heard that Mrs. Oaty had some of rare old pattern. We followed a lane with some chinquapin trees along it. The sweet little brown nuts are a lot of trouble, but they are good. The house, when we got to it, was up the hill a ways, beside an oak tree. There is nothing like a mountain oak in October. Its leaves were sparse enough for each leaf in that first moment we looked up to be one thing against the clear blue sky before the wind hit.

The house itself was the kind that is held up in front by a couple of bean poles, and then leans back against the mountain, so that you cross the porch at a decided pitch. But it was a "very" kind of day—very bright, very windy, very carefree, and although I did not find a Faith-and-Fortune quilt, I found out what to do in case I ever came upon a rattlesnake "quirled" up in the road. Oaty told me. First of all, you want to take yourself some tobacco.

"Just take yoreself a good chaw of fresh, homemade tobacco," recommended Oaty. What made him think of it was a neat brown arc he had just sent out himself into the October sunshine. He paused to watch the fluid accuracy of its fall and then went on enthusiastically. "And whilst yo're a-workin' out on hit, step over in the bresh and git yoreself a good stout forked stick. Then step back in the road and ram the fork down over the snake's neck—and stomp on hits tail right quick, so hits tail won't smack! Then ease down, and ease down, until you git right close to the snake's mouth—and hit'll be open—and let fly that wad of fresh, homemade tobacco, and old mister snake'll roll over on hits back, and roll back on hits belly, and die dead."

A good many hunting stories that you hear are inclined, like Oaty's, to handle the truth a little carelessly. Percy Mackaye celebrates a Kentucky Baron Munchausen in his *Tall Tales of the Kentucky Hills*. West Virginia has such a one, too, renowned for his yarns that he builds as he goes, and which his captivated hearers add to as they pass on. Thus the story of the time Grandpappy Sparks went coon hunting has taken on proportions.

"Now Grandpappy Sparks," so the story goes, "was just about the dearest lover of coon huntin' in the world. Thar wasn't nothin' he liked better than to roam the hills with his dogs and his guns, unless hit was to set around and yarn about hit afterward.

"But Grandpappy hadn't been out coon huntin' for oh, two, three years. He'd just buttocked down in his wheel chair—just set by hisself by the fire, the sorriest old man in the world. He'd been settin' like that ever since the night the ha'nt got in.

"That was the night Grandpappy woke up along about midnight feelin' quare. By the light of the moon shinin' down through a peephole in the roof Grandpappy seed down at the foot of his bed, somethin' white and quare, goin' back and forth, back and forth. Grandpappy riz up and drew his gun to him and says:

" 'Speak if yo're human.'

"Nothin' heerd.

"Agin Grandpappy says:

" 'Speak if yo're human.'

"Nothin' come.

"So Grandpappy tuk aim and fired. Shot off all five of his toes.

"Wal, this kindly crippled him some, and jest tuk the heart plumb out of him. So he'd been glummin' thar by the fire, woeful worn and weary like.

"But t'other night he seed his grandsons Hounddog and Squinteye gittin' ready to go coon huntin'. He wheeled hisself over to the door and set thar watchin' 'em a spell, and he couldn't stand hit.

" 'Boys,' he says, 'take me with you! I hain't long for to live, and I want to hear them hounds a-givin' tongue jest once agin afore I die.'

" 'Oh, la, no, Grandpappy,' says Hounddog. 'We're goin' way up yonder on top of Hickory Mountain.'

"And Squinteye says, 'Leastwise, Grandpappy, I don't reckon you'd enjoy yoreself, much. The last time me and Hounddog went we only got us one coon, and hit was so pore we sot hit on a limb and let hit went.'

"But Grandpappy, he begged and pleaded so powerful pitiful that finally Hounddog looked at Squinteye, and Squinteye looked at Hounddog, and they said:

" 'Wal, might as wal.'

"So Hounddog, he hitched the dogs to his belt, and Squinteye he hitched the lantern and the gun to his'n and betwixt 'em they made a kind of cheer and h'isted the old man up into hit. But, la, long before them boys had got to the top of Hickory Mountain they war puffin' and pantin' and thar tongues war hangin' out.

"But Grandpappy, he war feelin' pearter. He sot thar a-laughin' and a-talkin' and a-chucklin' to hisself and havin' a good old time. When hit looked like the boys war layin' out to set him down he says:

" 'Oh boys, don't set me down hyar. Listen to them hounds a-givin' tongue up thar all in one place! Hit's that old holler oak! They've treed! Take me up thar, boys—hit hain't more'n a mile and a half around the shoulder of the mountain—'

"Wal, the boys war too weary to protest. They struggled on—bammin' into rocks, and batterin' through laurel hells, till by the time they got up to that old holler oak they jest had strength enough to set Grandpappy down on a log and then fall down theirselves on their faces.

"But Grandpappy, he set thar a-peekin' and a-peerin', and directly he says:

" 'Squinteye, shine that old bull's-eye lantern up thar on that first branch, son. 'Pears to me like thar's two big old eyes a-shinin' down.'

"Squinteye got up strength enough to rise a little and shine the lantern—and shore enough, thar *war* two big old eyes a-shinin' down!

"Grandpappy war plumb delighted. 'Shine her up thar on that

second branch, son. 'Pears to me like thar's two more big old eyes a-shinin' down!'

"Squinteye shined the lantern on the second branch and shore enough—thar *war* two more big old eyes a-shinin' down. Grandpappy war plumb excited.

" 'Hounddog, take that gun stick, boy, and rub a sulphur match on yore hindsights and yore foresights, and see can you git that top feller, and maybe hit'll knock down the bottom one, and we'll have us two old streaked and striped raccoons with one shot!'

"Wal, Hounddog fired her a crack, keerless like, and la, thar come down out of that tree jest about four hundred pounds of the maddest West Virginia b'ar you ever seed.

"Thar war considerable confusion.

"Somebody kicked the lantern halfway down the mountain, so they didn't have no light to see by. Hounddog had the gun, but the fightin' war so close he couldn't shoot to do no good. So he tuk hit in both hands and used hit like a battlin' stick, only he hit Squinteye right acrost the back of the neck with hit and purt nigh knocked his head off.

"Hit warn't three minutes—oh la, hit warn't but two minutes and a half—till them boys could hear the dogs war a-gittin' the worst of hit.

"Hounddog kicked one of the b'ars to turn hits tusks loose from his dog's skull, and with that the rumpus turned into a clawin' match betwixt 'em. The b'ar riz up and give Hounddog a cuff that sent him britch sprawlin'. The dogs tuk to kiyi-in' and yippin' and stickin' their tails betwixt their legs and lightin' out for home. Hounddog jumped up and lit runnin' hisself.

" 'Run, Squinteye, run,' he said. 'And if you can't run, get out of the way of a man what can!'

" 'We can't go without the gun, Hounddog—'

" 'Yonder hit lays,' yelled back Hounddog—'and you about to tromple hit—'

"Squinteye got the gun, and skun down after Hounddog, and neither of 'em never stopped till they got to their own gate. Then they stopped whar they war. Hounddog looked at Squinteye, and Squinteye looked at Hounddog.

" 'Hounddog,' says Squinteye, 'do you know what we've done? We've done left Grandpappy to be et by the b'ars.'

"Hounddog never said a word. He just spit regular for a while. Then he says, 'Squinteye, I hate mighty bad to see what we're goin' to see. But the only thing for us to do is go to the house and git us a basket, and go up after the *re*mains.'

"So they went on to the house, their heads a-hangin' down, to git 'em a basket and go back for Grandpappy. They opened the door, and the dogs war a-layin' in front of the fire, a-cryin' and lickin' their wounds, the way hounddogs do. And over in his chair set Grandpappy.

" 'Great balls of fire, Grandpappy, how'd *you* git down hyere?'

" 'Boys,' said Grandpappy, 'I come in ahead of the dogs!' "

HERBS AND BITTERS

Alek Wiseman age 80 dide marc 20 1877 war farmer & stilde never had Dronk boy never had Dock in hos for sick he ras 12 in family war good hand to mak brandy

Springtime in the mountains used to mean a good big dose of cherry bark bitters and whisky for everybody in the family, from the granny woman on down to the least one. It was tasty, toned you up, and was good for the system in general. Yellowroot was another tonic guaranteed to pick anybody up who "wasn't much." Yellowroot, however, was bitter. "Hit was *good* and bitter."

All the old-time southern mountain women have a traditional knowledge of herb doctoring. No doubt originally it was a knowledge of necessity, since the trained skill of doctors and nurses, and news of the new ways of doing, has come to them only in the last few years.

They listen with interest to minute dramas over the radio which urge them to hurry down to the nearest drugstore and buy a box of kidney pills—remembering the times they have hurried to the nearest she-balsam, cut off a hunk of bark and brewed it into a kidney tea. Some people preferred ivy tea. Sage was the thing for common colds in those days. If the cold went beyond the simple reach of sage, and developed into "the pneumonia fever," then pennyroyal was called into use. Pennyroyal also was recommended to anyone bad off with neuralgia.

Many a mountain woman has lain in a darkened cabin room with a nervous headache, treating it with cold-packs—of catnip and dock leaves. A poultice of dock leaves could draw the soreness out of boils.

André Michaux made his famous tour of the southern mountains in 1802, incidentally introducing the idea that the ginseng so common in those hills was a highly marketable drug. The mountain women have also been gathering the roots and herbs whose medicinal qualities had been making fireside conversation for generations, and selling them in large quantities to the outside drug markets. And with present-day imports cut off, scientists are putting the time-old herbs of our own hills to surprisingly wide uses.

The mountain women of Kentucky claim that the Indians first gave them their knowledge of the medicinal value the woods around them hold. It was the mountain men, however, who decided that "yarbs hain't nary bit of use without jest a lease grain of whisky."

In some cases it took more than a least grain. "Milk sick," a dreaded illness from milk poisoned by cows grazing in too shady places, was treated first by an emetic, followed by huge doses of apple brandy.

Puffballs, it was held by some, were the proper things to bind on an open wound. If puffballs were out of season, cobweb was substituted, or even soot. The more expert, however, were inclined to scout this whole school of thought. "You don't want to go devilin' around in a wound at all! Blood's the best dressin' a wound can have!"

The garden also was made to yield itself to the sick room. Fried onions with goat "taller" poured over them made a salve which could be rubbed on the throat of a child with croup. Flaxseed and honey were used for whooping cough. A little poke of asafetida tied around a child's neck kept away disease in general—working on the principle, no doubt, that the smell of it would keep anyone diseased at a distance—as well as check the approach of everybody else.

Asafetida and whisky also made a tea used in the cure of hives. If that didn't work, you *could* use the white powdery substance off the top of hen manure.

Shingles were cured by bathing the irritated portions of the skin with the fresh warm blood of a black chicken. For diphtheria a common toad was sometimes split open and bound to the throat—quickly, again while the blood was still warm.

There is an element of sense in all these homemade remedies. A few, however, were sheer superstition. If someone were to be taken with fits, for instance, just bore a hole in a tree, shave the hair from the armpits of the afflicted person, put the hair in the hole, then plug it up.

The superstitious cures for warts are many and well known, being spread over wider areas than the mountain confines: gather as many pebbles as you have warts, make a bundle of them and drop them in the road—whoever picks up the bundle will get your warts; steal somebody's dishrag and rub over your warts; plant as many beans in a circle as you number warts—when the beans grow your warts will go.

Hemorrhage was taken care of by driving a double-bitted ax into the floor under the bed of the person who was bleeding. Thus many a woman in childbirth has died.

And many a woman in childbirth has died because ignorance and the lack of care accompanying even the sounder home remedies have had to substitute for skilled medical aid. Each midwife, of course, had her own authoritative variations of the nothing she could do. Some claimed that if the woman lay on her side and "hollered," it helped the child to come. Others used very strong doses of hot pepper tea to "fetch on the child-thing." Still others made the mother sit bolt upright during the whole of labor. Uremic infection was avoided (it was hoped) by having the mother lie for three hours in the afterbirth before the bedding was changed. In the meantime, the baby which had just been "cotched" was held upside down and shaken by its heels—so its liver wouldn't grow to its sides. After the abrupt introduction into the topsy-turvy world in which it had miraculously managed to arrive, it was righted dazedly and soothed by a little catnip tea. If the digestive system seemed for some reason a little awry after all that and it developed a rash (called the "thrash": two varieties—red and brown) that was taken care of by calling in a man who had never seen his own father to come blow his breath down the tender young throat.

But whatever the hazards of "childing"—as Shakespeare and the mountain people put it—the new baby itself is the most welcomed thing on earth.

"A baby's always somethin' new in the house," one young mother told me gently. "The children love so good to play with hit." She was still lying weakly in bed. She almost had died during this last childbirth—a matter which she dismissed as of no importance now. "That kind of pain is easiest forgot in the world." At that moment she was looking on happily as her husband bent to take up the child from the cradling crook of her arm, with the warm sweet feel of it in his own arms betraying itself on his lean face.

Mountain men as a class are devoted family men. They would do anything for their "babbies"—it has been merely a question of knowing the right thing to do.

Too often, the few native doctors there in earlier times were as uninformed about their practice as their patients, according to the stories of their "cures" which survive them. Occasionally however you find a remnant of that rapidly disappearing hill version of the old-fashioned country doctor—with a little professional education, and a great deal of good sense. One of these told me there were two things important to being a doctor: the first was to diagnose; the second was to use horse sense.

He still is practicing, and people for three West Virginia counties depend upon him in faith—with their faith founded on fifty years of his whittling out this one's appendix, and rolling up his pants to wade the creek when the ice was floating to go bring on that one's baby. His records show he has brought over a thousand babies into the world, with the help of a registered nurse only eight of those times. He depended on whatever help was at hand, I gathered from one of his graphic accounts. It concerned a stubborn maternity case in which, as a last resort, he was preparing to take the child. He commandeered the services of a neighbor, an Aunt Deedy who tipped the scale at around two hundred. The big old woman was bending over the bed to give the anesthetic for him, holding the chloroform rag under the patient's nose, when "b'God," swore the Doctor, at the crucial moment "over Deedy went!"

"I looked up, and thar Deedy lay, stretched out cold on the floor. Nobody else was thar, except the husband, and he was wanderin' in and out of the house, lettin' in drafts, half out of his head with worry. But just then I heard the mailman drive up. I stuck my head out the door and hollered, 'Homer, yo're just the feller I need. Nobody in here's worth a damn.' I got the chloroform rag, and knocked the patient out myself this time, and when Homer come in I said, 'Grab aholt of that leg thar.' 'Oh my soul alive,' gasped Homer, 'I never seen the like!' 'You ain't supposed to see! You're just supposed to keep aholt!' "

The baby arrived safely and the mother did nicely.

Mountain people are usually as heroic in bearing their own pain as they are seemingly indifferent to that of other people. That stoicism is a part of the fatalism which seems to find a natural home in the mountains. It has let them sit helplessly by the bedside, accepting death before it came—"what is to be, will be."

It let an old uncle, who lived over the hill from the school where I was teaching, come in the store at mailtime one morning, get his Sears and Roebuck catalogue, and stand around letting a good little bit of the day go by, before he gave out the news of his wife's illness. Then he mentioned, "Poppy's ailin'."

The next morning he reported, "Poppy's gittin' worse."

The third morning he said it wouldn't surprise him much if she was "tuk." The next morning, as he had expected, she was dead. He shook his head about it. He said he didn't seem to have real good luck with his women, although he had begun at a right young age, too. This was his third.

In spite of this attitude of fatalism, in spite of the dependency on home remedies, in spite of the often tragic results of ignorance and superstition, despite the sometimes appallingly unhygienic living conditions, despite a diet made up mainly of "hog and hominy," with corn bread the staff of life, the coffee strong and black, and even the green relief of the occasional "mess of garden sass" disdained—our southern mountain people as a class have persisted in remaining a sturdy lot.

"We didn't used to know nothin' up hyere in the mountains," one old man admitted to me cheerfully, "except that we war a-livin'."

That they lived at all, and especially to the ripe old age that many of them did, can largely be accounted for by a love of mountain people for pure air and pure water amounting to an obsession. The door was not left standing open summer and winter because somebody forgot to shut it, but because the people within-doors wanted breath to breathe. And they take the pride of a connoisseur in their water, and are as demanding about its quality. A spring must come up in that silent clarity which only springs do whose source lies deep. If it is branch water they drink, it must come from some

Rot! It was because the door-way was the chief source of light in the room!

stream running in laurel and rock, or filtered by the hemlocks dipping in their shadows, so that the water comes sparkling to the sun, achingly cold in its purity.

Pure air and pure water and the cures of nature—the heart stimulant digitalis from the purple foxglove, creosote from the wood tar of the pine or the beech for bronchitis and coughs, belladonna from the deadly nightshade plant for pain of inflammation and constipation, arnica from the dried flower of the leopard's-bane for bruises and cuts, pokeroot for eczema, oil of thyme for diphtheria and typhoid, hemlock to relieve the pain of cancer, jimson root for ulcers and to help palsy, wolfsbane root for fevers, sassafras and boneset and snakeroot for tonics, tannic acid from the prickly ash and the white oak and the blackberry root, clover for salves and astringents, bloodroot for corns—they went to the woods for them. We buy them over the counter.

THE WORLD IS NEW

Jacob Carpenter start colrado Jul3 1888 com home Jan 1889

Even though you are a mountaineer only by adoption, if ever you have once loved the ugliness of a small mountain village knocked up carelessly around a broad place in a bad road, you go back and back to it. And if ever you've gone on an overnight camping party in weather that would give you pneumonia if you had to be out in it in the city, you literally almost break your neck to go do the same fool thing again.

Weather somehow never seems to be a matter of slightest consideration in these camping parties. Somebody gets the idea for one —and the affair goes off with all the good and bad points of lack of planning. Everybody collects whatever blankets they think they can get away with without too much argument. Somebody brings a skillet, and somebody else an ax. The mood stays spontaneously high, but the food is apt to be uncertain. Larders are raided for whatever cakes and bread happen to be on hand, and chickens are sacrificed. If it's that time of year, there are roasting ears and tomatoes. If it's later there are peaches and apples.

The crowd collects at the store, and a harum-scarum check-up is made for whatever else might be needed. Then the party is off—in vehicles as haphazardly assembled as the other necessities. All mountain drivers drive with a reckless skill which swings you out to the edges and squeals you around curves, all on the bland theory that there is no other car in the country. Any tired idea you may have had that about as much life was left in you as in a woody turnip, and that nothing exciting would ever happen to you again departs speedily with the first half-mile.

You drive as far up the chosen mountain as you can, and farther than any outsider from the world of wide highways thinks possible. Finally, even the mountain driver agrees that he's gone as far as his springs will take him, and everybody piles out, to park the car in oaks and boulders. Before you quite leave civilization altogether, some stalwart picks up a rail from the last outpost of farm fence, to start the fire in case the tree that will be cut down for the fire turns out to be too wet to kindle quickly. He shoulders the fence rail, and leads the way up.

Wind and mist and darkness, and mountains of white rock rising up out of the darkness. You go on climbing; clambering over an unannounced boulder in the path; by some miracle not slipping on pine needles off the narrow path down into a few thousand feet of fog before you'd hit the first treetop; coming finally to solid footing—a great rock not quite to the top. A stocky balsam, a windrunted laurel, some huckleberries stand their ground in a crevice of the rock and the sound they make is single, lonely. But below, millions of trees are making the soft rainy noises that wind does in them when it blows the fog off leaves.

The mountain fog is not a dank fog that hangs heavy. It is swiftly moving, constantly changing—now revealing enough strange light to promise everything—the next instant wiping it out.

The fog in your face, not too cold. The smoke from the fire built in the shelter of a rock sweet in your nostrils. The night sky is stormy—but not so black, not so everlasting, not so almighty as the black peak.

Everything familiar and trite and tired is rolled up behind you some place. The world is new and raw and beautiful and there isn't a mistake in it. You have come eagerly, needing this. You thought you had remembered. But you find you had forgotten. You had forgotten the power, the power and the peace; the uselessness of petty things. The freedom!

There are not always fogs in the heights. Sometimes the stars are near.

Nor do you have to climb to great heights. You can ascend the steeps of the mildest hill in sight—maybe the rise back of the village church, or by your lodge, which amounts only to a few steps. But, as the mountain woman said once when she had occasion to try to figure out all the sorry sense of the world, "A little height makes a sight of difference in the way a body sees things." When you can get above confusion and look to the quiet strength and calm beauty of the hills, with each going on into the next, and the next, and the next till they take on sureness and sweep—you grow somehow not afraid. It is as though you have ascended to some altitude of yourself, to some inner reserve of endurance you had forgotten about, or perhaps never knew was there.

And you can walk down a mountain road when the sky is a glittering blue and the air is fresh, and you can hear laughter ahead at the store; or you can take a side road that leads by a creek with forget-me-nots along its banks—and you need not climb at all.

We know a man who, after looking the rest of the world over to the extent of two continents, came to the conclusion that the small part of the globe he would choose as his was back in the Blue Ridge in a place tourists don't know they've gone through until the sign at the edge of the "town" tells them so. He has a farm he enjoys, but it doesn't pay. He says he's tried everything except hard work, and he's thinking something of trying that next. One afternoon, when it suddenly struck him as a good afternoon to go fishing, he went fishing. But he went to fish down in a wild part of the gorge, and when three days had gone by and he had not returned, his friends became alarmed. They were about to go see what the matter was, when he came wandering back. They asked him if he'd been lost.

"No," he said. "I wasn't lost. It was just such a lot of trouble to climb out."

Sometimes you mourn the loss of people like that to the world of affairs. Then again, in those drained, weary moments when you stop long enough to wonder ironically just what it is you're struggling toward—you think those others are the only sane people you know.

Perhaps it is a yearning of the mind and body for a temporary suspension of all thought and feeling that takes you back to the mountains. Over after-dinner coffee recently a man much involved and harassed with international affairs, said that when the war was over there was just one thing he wanted to do. He wanted to sit and spit. Everyone in the room laughed, with a mixture of understanding and wistfulness.

Mountains are one of the better places to sit—and spit if you wish; but at any rate to sit and stare off over a valley and not think of anything much, and have a very good time at it.

If you need people, there are people—friendly people, glad to welcome you into the participation of whatever they're doing, and hospitably willing to put themselves out for your entertainment—such as the camping parties. If you like your outdoors hitched to a sport, they will show you which place in the rocky river that goes shouting and bawling and singing between the mountain cliffs is the best to send a fly flashing and pull in a big rainbow trout, or which are the best feeding grounds that year for bear, or in which fall woods is the grouse most likely to be flushed.

As for the participation in everyday community activities, there is the choir practice. The volunteer mountain choir is apt to be the kind which by a slip of punctuation was announced in a Sunday bulletin as "Oh Lord Have Mercy the Choir!" But noise you make yourself somehow always sounds all right, so both in self-defense and for the mild fun of it, if you intend to be there for the Sunday services, by all means get in on choir practice.

The last one I went to started off horribly. Everybody was feeling their way along, and the soprano section was trying notes too high for it. The pianist, a local woman who lived in a slab house which sat eagerly close to the road in front so it wouldn't miss anything and was held up in back by stilts, turned on the piano stool and peered at us over her glasses.

"It don't seem to gee right," she criticized.

So we went over the first part again. It still was not all it should be.

"There's something the matter with my ears, our singing, or the man who made this thing up!" decided the minister's wife, a young woman with bright merry eyes and healthy cheeks.

"Let's sing that line again, 'Let His mercies extend,' " suggested one of the teachers who was singing alto, "and see what it is that makes that funny gap that always comes in there."

"That's middle G," explained the pianist. "It don't work. Now go through the whole thing, and see if you can't stop churnin' on that 'Sabbath day ne'er spent in vain.' "

We went through the whole thing again, and toward the end began to nudge each other in triumph, and everybody gave all they had to the last three notes.

"Well," the pianist was pleased. "Our end is *one* thing they won't be able to criticize."

"For once," said the doctor, a quiet tower of a man, who sang bass and kept the choir going, "I believe we almost got together."

A cabin in the Great Smokies

The mountain folk have fine faces

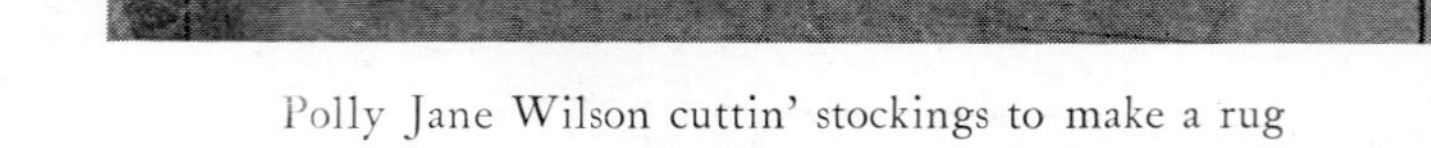

Polly Jane Wilson cuttin' stockings to make a rug

Everybody was proud, everybody wanted to do the ending again. There was a strange satisfaction in the mild humor and wholesome effort of that midweek choir practice for the Sunday services in a little country church.

And you have not laughed for a long time, really, until you have gotten red in the face from the effort of trying the light-toed, loose-kneed shuffling grace of the "play party" dances to the sawing of a fiddle—too busy to notice that you've lost your dignity, and too exhausted afterward from breathlessness and laughing to care.

Many a solid citizen has suffered in an Arthur Murray dancing class—hauled there, needless to say, by his wife, who for the past few years has found him not so light on her feet. Sometimes the solid citizen can stand just so much of it.

That solid citizen, however, finds nothing of the piffling or effete to irk him as the caller of the mountain square dance bawls out, "Big Ring!" Awkward bodies which have grown stiff with the slow labor of highland farms slip into easy repose. Limbs bend freely, and presently, as the fiddler, who has been staring off into space with absolutely no expression whatsoever on his face, gets down to the serious business of whanging the life out of his instrument—the solid citizen finds himself lightfooting it with the other gents "to the center and right straight back." He finds he is a good dancer—there is force to his short, swift steps; a nonchalance to his light smooth spring from step to step. Or so he imagines. At any rate, he swings his lady home like hell a-hootin' for sideways, and whistles the tune all the way back to the inn.

The next morning he may wake up with muscles aching that he never knew he had before. And when he goes to join the rest of the foursome who very sensibly refrained from the whole idea of the country dances, he may find when he bends over to tee up his ball that he can't straighten up again without breaking something. The morning after, he may hate the mountains. But he won't hate them till the morning after. At the moment he whistles of the spirited past, dear and not as dead as he had supposed.

If it's the small aesthetics that need revival, for color, there's the squander of it from May through frost. And even in white winter twilights, there are the rose and purple peaks.

For smell, if you've ever known the spicy aromatic smell of the cool mountain woods—laurel and galax and teaberry and pine, and old logs with their sweetness still in them—then you can understand the utterance that came from the heart of a returned mountain man, who fervently declared, "I'd ruther be a knot on a log up hyur, than the mayor of the city down yonder."

Mountain people come back. They get homesick for friendly faces. "I was just a lonely boy in the streets," said another, who tried it. "Lots of faces, but none I knew. Everybody busy with themselves."

They get homesick for the sight of their mountains. There is a poem by Lillian Mayfield Wright that tells about that. It begins:

> "I think that something in a hill child dies
> When he is taken to the level lands—"

If they can, they come back. Especially if they have gone to the lowlands to work. It is one thing to obligingly go help somebody out—but it is quite another to work steadily for someone who gives them orders. They have never taken orders from anybody in their history, except in time of war. Ordinary servility is intolerable to them.

Moreover the idea of plugging along steadily at a job for the sole reason of getting enough money ahead to be able to quit some day, does not strike their sense of reason. It seems to them much more sensible to work, when there's work to be done. But when a pretty day comes along, stop and enjoy it. Why strive frantically toward something ahead, when you can have it as you go along?

They come back for earnest reasons. Many of those who have

gone away to school, come back to give the people at home who have not been so fortunate the advantages of what they have learned. Thus an increasing number of the teachers, doctors, nurses, dentists and preachers who are responsible for the raising of the intellectual and physical and moral standards of the mountains are of the mountains themselves. They have gone out, and come back.

They come back from wars—from all that war is, to the peace of the mountains.

They come back—those with their roots deep in mountain rock and earth; and those who happened once upon the mountains at some magic time or place that took quick hold upon their thoughts and upon their life.

WOMEN'S LITTLE WAYS

Elizabeth Carpenter age 72 dide auges 29 1889 work hard for her livin

It is the common supposition that our southern mountain women as a class are downtrodden, downcast, spiritlessly submissive. And it is true that from time beyond question, it has been "manners" for the mountain woman to obey, just as it is a deep-seated matter of fact that the mountain man is lord and master.

A woman's finer sensibilities, if they happen to come within the man's notice at all, are more apt to annoy him than anything else. He is impatient with a woman he has to "gentle and hand feed." As one practical West Virginia male put it comfortably, "Thar's only two places for a woman: one's in the kitchen, and t'other's in the feather bed."

He forgot their outdoor chores. All mountain women take pleasure in their flowers and their gardens. But when gathering fodder, helping plow, splitting kindling, taking her end of the crosscut saw, and dynamiting stumps, are added to her natural pleasure in planting and watching things grow, it is apt to get "a least mite wearisome."

After she has come in from the fields and prepared the food, then she stands by and serves while the man reaches out and takes his needs. He has been traditionally indifferent to the fact that she is supposedly the weaker vessel. Her services are taken for granted.

Once I was watching one of these sturdy old lords, who had outlived four women, splicing a piece of deerhide into shoestrings. As he made the leisurely, expert splices he told me about the household of his childhood. There were twelve boys in the family, and in the course of the years his father adopted fourteen more. His mother and his two sisters constituted the feminine element.

"My gracious!" I exclaimed. "Wasn't that a lot of work for just those three women, taking care of all those men?"

He looked at me in honest surprise. "Why la no," he decided, when he had considered it. "Hit warn't no work, much. Oh, they aimed to weave us a pair of pants apiece a year, and a couple of shirts. And if they got *bad* tore, they sewed 'em up ag'in. But they didn't have no bother about their own clothes. They warn't goin' no place.

"And they didn't have to fuss much about the house. They didn't have no curtains.

"The cookin' was easy. Oh, they'd keep a mess of corn bread baked up, for anybody who felt the urge for bread. And occasionally they'd cook us a mess of garden sass. But we didn't keer for that much. Mostly we'd just go out to the smoke-house and cut us off a hunk of meat, and we et as we walked.

"And they didn't have no washin'," he finished simply, "because we didn't wear no socks."

It seldom occurs to the mountain man to do or say the little things that pleasure a woman. And occasionally she gets beaten. Even though they are fond of their families, men have considered this a part of their duty as head of the house. One woman told me earnestly, of a particularly stern father and husband: "He was a *good* man. If me or the children ever done anything wrong, he'd whip us." When she looked at him, her eyes had respect. Indeed, a mountain woman would have little regard for a man who did not lord it over her.

Yet, despite their submission, mountain women, like women the world over, have their little ways.

Sometimes it takes them to eternity, and the next generation, to see them work—as in the case of the worn-down woman who departed her life as meekly as she had endured it, reduced to making no protest about anything. Her husband did not bother to commemorate the departure with funeral services. Then he, the meek one's husband, died. Always a demanding sort, for him the best of graveyard meetings was promptly planned. The thirteen-year-old boy of the house was hustled to ask the preacher to come "improve the funeral occasion." His mother had died the year before, just when there was something about her beaten look which was beginning to make him love her fiercely. He had stood in the room stupidly, and watched her go, completely frightened, and afterward had used all his strength to keep from sobbing there with the others who did not know what misery was.

"We'd take hit kindly," he recited to the preacher, when he was sent about his father, "if you'd come give the oration." He'd been warned to be mannerly. The preacher said he would be proud to come. The deceased had been a prominent man.

"And while yo're a-funeralizin' pa," said the boy, come early into that carelessness of his kind which masks iron, "say a few words about ma, too, will you? And say ma's first."

There are, of course, exceptions. When I first knew Uncle Nick, he and Aunt Charity were growing old together and they seemed to find it not a bad experience at all. They had that quiet about them which lets two people who have found satisfaction in each other view the rest of the world with tolerance. They had had their ups and downs in their time, according to their accounts, but when it had been a crest, they had ridden it. When it wasn't, they had roughed it. Either way they evidently had had a pretty good time together. Aunt Charity always had thought, and still did, that the best thing she ever had done was marry Nick. And Nick's chiefest pleasure still was Charity.

Many a time, the neighbors growing up around the old couple would smile a little, in that way you do at a small thing that is thoroughly nice. They would smile to see Uncle Nick climbing slowly up a slope toward the flame of a wild azalea. A "flower pot" he called it, for Charity. Charity was a dear lover of flowers.

But there still is the North Carolina woman who "got so plumb beat out with the no-account ways of her fam-il-ee, that she just tuk to the bed and stayed thar, year in and year out—just gittin' up every now and then to give 'em all a good beatin'!"

OF PURPLE AND SCARLET

Franky Berlison age 86 July 3 dide 1896 she spon & wove cloth by 5000

"And all the women that were wise hearted did spin with their hands, and brought that which they had spun, both of blue, and of purple, and of scarlet, and of fine linen."

The women of Exodus were spinners, and so are the mountain women of today. It is a heritage that goes back hundreds of generations.

The whole process has a timeless measure to it. Standing barefoot in the branch washing the wool, then spreading it in the sun to dry, were tasks that had the width and ease of the whole outdoors in them. And when the big old loom wheel was brought outdoors so the spinner could stand in the sunshine while she spun, the natural pull and flow there is to the movement of spinning became a part of a bigger pull and flow.

A woman could take her satisfaction in color at such work, dipping the skeins she had spun in dye of her own concocting; tomato green, hickory brown, indigo blue, madder pink. And later at the loom she could combine them as she had a mind to, shuttling the wool colors through the white cotton warp into a design.

The thud and clack of the loom marked off something more than an art impulse. It gave a woman's hands something to do while she thought. Or if she had thought too much—about the uncertainties, and had seen so much she had planned go awry—then there was something wonderful in seeing a thing take shape under her hands and stay that way. And in weaving, if she made a mistake in the pattern, she could undo it.

The old coverlet patterns had life running through them; Log Cabin, Castle City, Blooming Leaf, Martha Washington, Lee's Surrender, Pine Bloom, Spider Web, Jesse Wilson, Young Man's Fancy, and Rose in the Wilderness.

It might be the more utilitarian stuff for shirts and britches she was weaving. There was another satisfaction to that. The men thought a good deal of that homespun flax. "Those britches war rough on a feller's hide, but they war *stout*. They'd last a man. They warn't like these boughten pants made so thin you got to be careful how you walk—"

They knitted socks from the wool they spun. Just not so long ago I watched a woman spinning thread for knitting. She was a young woman and made a very pleasant picture whose main sense was poise, as she stood by the wheel in the fall of the lamplight. She was spinning wool thread for her husband's hunting socks. He proudly displayed the pair he had on, which she also had made, but she thought the new ones would be better—the thread wouldn't be so bumpy. She was just learning to spin.

PREACHIN' MEN

Steven buckanen age 70 June 5 1898 he war precher babtis

It had rained in the night, and although it was afternoon now and there was sun, there still was that lush givableness to the earth.

The smell of green things growing and the rank health of roots faintly mingled with the smell of muddy boots and the dim sweetness of snuff, and of people. It had turned out to be a fine day and the mountain church was crowded.

It was small and simple, of raw new plank. It belonged to the congregation in that way anything does which you labor with personally. Someone had given the land, others had given their time to clear it—although laurel and oak and pine still were familiarly close. Some of the men apt with carpentry tools had tithed their labor and built the building, and made the plank pews which lined up on either side of the center aisle. Out by the front steps there was a pile of poplar bark which had been cut into shingles and weighed down with rocks to shape and season. It would be some months before those finishing shingles would be ready to put on, and there was no glass in the windows as yet. "Window lights" cost cash money, and that was slow to accumulate. So the windows were just openings. The fresh smell of the woods was full in the little room, and there was a blackberry twig leaning in from the outside over the front window hole. Every time Uncle Joe, who was preaching, got particularly "tempestuous" and paced the raw plank platform the while he "delivered himself with great liberty," that blackberry twig would wag impudently.

But if the blackberry twig was impudent, it was the only thing in that little mountain church that was. Even the babes in arms were hushed as their mothers swayed back and forth to the ominous rhythm of Uncle Joe's eloquence.

Uncle Joe was just a little man, in little gold-rimmed spectacles. But he was mighty. He had an oratorical gift which any public speaker could well envy. He had begun his sermon with a commanding hush of expectation, which gradually swept up to thunder—only to stop, abruptly, leaving us hanging. Then he picked us up and started over.

Uncle Joe was of that vanishing order of "homegrown" mountain preachers, and one of the few requisites of that regime was that the man of God have "good wind." Uncle Joe did pretty well. That Sunday he had begun with Genesis and he went right straight through to Revelations, with never a pause except for dramatic effect. To be exact about that span, however, it must be said he hit only the violent high spots. The slender thread of goodness which runs with surprising strength, considering its slimness, through that account, he ignored. But he dwelt masterfully on those sections dealing with the everlasting fires. For three solid hours I sat, fascinated, on the brittle edge of damnation, that Sunday evening.

It really was in the middle of the afternoon. But for the southern mountain people "evening" begins at twelve o'clock noon. For them the morning and the evening are the day, as it is recounted in Genesis of a world still in the making.

As the sermon went on, I began to feel a little surer of Uncle Joe's wind than I did of his scripture. He had a way of throwing in his wife Martha's remarks along with the prophets. But it was interesting. At the end I especially remember the way his wife Martha and Ezekiel got together on perdition for the young and frivolous.

"As my wife Marthy says," threatened Uncle Joe—beginning softly on the "wife," then using all his breath on "Marthy" so that the "says" was somewhat like exhaustion, although after all the whole phrase got saved by a last-instant staccato catch upward which gave him a fresh start again—"you young folks are a-goin' to be roasted, ah. Yo're a-goin' to be laid out on the coolin' board only to burn ag'in, ah—as Ezekiel says, ah, yo're a-goin' to *all* be cast down into Hell, ah—" (The aspirate "ah" gives the holy tone.)

Suddenly, moved himself by the completeness of the prospect he was presenting, he stepped to the very edge of the platform, leaned down toward the front row of us staring up at him, and shook a grubby forefinger so close under our noses he almost scratched them, while he gave out his final word on doom.

"A double L," he sang out in solemn pronouncement, "spells ALL, ends ALL, and kivers ALL!"

Then he straightened from that last downward swoop and grimly lined out a hymn. Everybody got silently to their feet and sang. The men carried the bass, and the women swung in and out on it in nasal wails. At the song's end everybody turned subduedly, and started to file out meekly. But the stern little theologian stepped down off the pulpit, and held up a detaining hand.

"Wait a minute. Young Jim Archer up the branch has fell out of a wagon bed and sprung his back. He can't neither walk nor set. Hit's a-comin' on another windin', rainin' spell, and Joe ain't got his 'taters in yet. Now how many of you folks are a-goin' to meet up at Joe's place tomorrow to help git his 'taters in fer him?"

Uncle Joe is a fair example of the old type of mountain preacher who preached a harsh and narrow doctrine which often was quite at variance with his real humanity. In their capacity of spiritual leadership, the better of them came not only into a firm hold on the deeper things of life, but into a sympathy and understanding with their fellows as well. They were peculiarly equipped for that understanding of the particular problems of their charge, for six days a week they lived through the same trials and experiences. For six days a week the "homegrown" preacher tilled his rocky fields just as his neighbor did; or he made wagons, or bottomed chairs, or cobbled shoes, or shoed horses, or made teeth.

This latter means of the cloth making a living came to me a startled first time in an overheard bit of a conversation. In a small Kentucky hill town, two sunbonneted women had stopped to pass the time of day. One was sitting on the seat of a jolt wagon, and the other had a big hickory basket of eggs she'd brought to town to sell. She also had some new teeth, it seemed, from the other's interested observation and admiration.

"I declare, that's the purtiest set of teeth I ever seen in anybody's head! La, don't they shine in the sun!"

"Preacher Goudy made 'em for me," said their owner modestly.

Occasionally, in the mountains as anywhere else, there was to be found a minister whose business sense was perhaps a little clearer than his concept of his divine calling. A preacher who played one of the side roles in the famous Hatfield-McCoy feud, for instance, sold the liquor which was often the cause of renewed trouble, sold the arms which made it active, used the shipping crates the guns had come in to make the necessary coffins, and then collected a fee for the funerals he preached.

For the most part, however, these self-made ministers were earnest in the giving of themselves—poring over the Scripture by the light of a smoky lamp after their weekday's work was done, and then waiting in faith for the "speerit" to give them utterance on the day of the seventh.

The prevailing religion of the southern mountains is Protestant, naturally, since the beginning of colonization there had its source in the second great Protestant migration of English-speaking people to the New World. The first such migration had occurred about a hundred years before, when the Pilgrims landed at Plymouth Rock. Up to a certain point the two histories are very similar—that of a group of people with an inspired, resolute urge which turned them independently from old oppression to a new and larger land where they could build an empire with divine purpose. The parallel stops with the entrance of the second group to that new land.

From odd bits of written sources you can string together the rest of the story. And occasionally you can find someone among the mountain people themselves to tell it. This summer I heard a colloquial but very sound expression of it in a country valley in West Virginia. Like so many such hill communities, it still is back in time although it is only a little way from the main highway.

I sat on the porch of a log cabin in which that part of West Virginia had first cast its vote for the black abolitionist, Lincoln. My host was a shrewd, keen back-country doctor, and the cabin has been his office for a long time. He is quite a student, and has a good deal of scorn for what he has found out.

"Why," he told me in disgust, "our country was first settled by people comin' over here to escape religious persecution, but they hadn't any more than got their pants warmed till they were meetin' the newcomers with the very same kind of persecution!"

He was referring particularly to that group of Scotch-Irish and English immigrants from the Covenanting Wars, who landed on American shores only to find here, too, religious and political persecution—this time in the form of Parliament levying what they considered undue taxes, and insisting upon a state church. But the stubborn Scotch-Irish Presbyterians persisted in building their own meetinghouses. They grew into a force to be considered, and by 1700 their ministers were being granted the right to preach. But still they were harassed by the Established Church, and kept pushing on westward, toward some place of their own, which came to be, finally, the magnificent wildernesses of the mountains.

But once entered, that wilderness closed behind them, and they were cut off from the rest of the world. With that separation went gradually one of the chief characteristics of that great stream of early Protestant migration. High intellectual standards were essential to the right survival of that strong independent force which had turned them from old European oppression to new times. And old records do show that in their first settlements in this country, beside every church, a school was built. But as they went on into the wilderness, pioneer conditions discouraged the continuance of those standards.

Men with learning who might have taught their children, needed all their time to clear the land and make a shelter, break ground for their fields, hunt down meat, and protect the new-made home from the attacks of the Indians. The women, too, had more to occupy them than sitting down with books. They had brought with them into the wilderness a colonial civilization. But the colonial civilization did not include the common school.

Thus the mountain preachers, as the generations went away backward into their strange and unforeseen isolation, came to have little or no education. Sometimes this lack carried all the laughableness, and the danger, of utter ignorance—as in the mountain preacher who declared with pious pride, "I'm jest a pore ignorant man, ah, and I pray God, ah, that He'll make me ten times more ignoranter, ah—" which was a good deal to ask. As often, however, the "homegrown" mountain preacher kept a native sageness which, if it did not compensate for the lack of learning, at least tided it over.

Across a wild part of the Tennessee border from Uncle Joe's church, there was another little one, manned by a mountain preacher. He was a bachelor—a raw-cut man with a big nose that twitched when he laughed, with his thin upper lip marking the strength of his mouth and the full lower one giving it humanness—and a practical sort. And somehow you went out from his church, with its lamplit shadows of people, feeling that the whole earth was quiet and at rest.

It was his unique closing service which gave that feeling. It was homely, direct, and friendly in a way one of the congregation members himself put it, sincerely and with that naturalness which lets mountain people voice unself-consciously whatever good they feel: "It's Godamighty in the hearts of folks that makes friendship."

After "all minds had been discharged and the benediction craved" the congregation stayed on a few moments, while the minister called the Lord's attention to the individual needs and personal reasons for thanksgiving of each and every member. If "Sister Campbell was tired of burning her brains out bending over a stove that het too hot," then the Lord was asked to see what could be done about persuading her husband—who had made some money in his time and still had all of it—to buy her a new one. If some brethern not so regular in church attendance as might be, had got down sick and was up again, then psychological thanks was given that he had been spared to come back to meeting.

When the preacher found that a young widow of the congregation was out of firewood, he prayed that the Almighty would put it into the minds of her neighbors to get together and give her a wood-chopping. The neighbors responded so well that it was the best wood-chopping the country had ever seen. They chopped the young widow enough wood to last a whole year. And when the preacher married her the next day, what was there to do, after thinking it over, but admire him?

That he was sincerely benign, as well as a good planner, was evidenced in the way he included perfect strangers in his influence. One night, after he had made the rounds of his little flock, he opened his eyes and peered carefully around to make sure none had been overlooked. His survey came to a pause with the back seat. A vacationer from the north who had come to play golf at Linville was with us that night. He was a stranger to the preacher, with his particular wants, hopes and fortunes unknown. But after a contemplative moment, the preacher again lowered his great head, closed his eyes, and did what he could in the way of presentation.

"Lord," he said simply, "bless the stranger in our midst. I can't rightly call You his name, but by the cut of his pants he's an outlander."

Since one of the strong traits of highlanders is individualism, it is but natural that religion too, should get its personal interpretation. There is an occasional preacher (he preaches around when they're short on preachers) in the foothills of West Virginia who gives so very free a translation of the Scriptures that I could not help telling him so. His keen gray eyes merely looked at me and through me and into a dispassionate past, and he said calmly:

"It's been translated several times before. I feel free to give it another. Look at King James' men—they sat around and voted on what was to come in and what to go out, just like a political convention."

According to his particular version, "The Lord started out to be a God of Love. But pretty soon His creatures got so derned ornery on His hands, He had to swipe 'em all out and start over again with Noah, who followed the trade of the sea. But it wasn't any time at all before things were gittin' bad again. So He sent Moses up on a mountain to open up a stone quarry and write down a whole new set of laws. But my soul alive, Moses didn't even any more'n get down off that mountain with his new stoneware under his arms, till the people were breaking those laws!"

All in all, his narrow-eyed, unillusioned look-back over the generations that have made not too much progress in the way of human behavior, seems to offer little hope for the future. But when he was quizzed on this point he grew quite earnest. He ran his fingers through his thinning white hair musingly, and granted, "It's a mystery, the perversity of the human family is. But," he insisted—"the Lord started out to be a God of Love—and blamed if I don't believe He's goin' to go ahead and see that idea through, just to prove it! Love," treating it thoughtfully, searchingly, "that's the touchstone. That's the magnet. 'Love the Lord thy God with all thy heart'; 'Love thy neighbor as thyself' and—" he finished practically, "keep your chin up even though your spirits are low."

If scriptural interpretations have been free in the mountains, the lines of the half-dozen sects which rooted and built up there have been definite and narrow, and theological controversy rife. The loss of broad views in the scrutiny of petty points which he had heard argued all his life, swung one man skeptically away from the idea of denominationalism altogether.

"I've tried all the churches there are," he says now, from his seasoned sixties, "and I don't belong to any of 'em. I've done a good deal of studyin' about the whole thing, though. And I've read some in the Book of Nature, too. It's one of the greatest of them all, and the simplest: love and hate—all mixed up in the same breath, and all addin' up to a process of growth. Where the first germ come from, I don't know. And I don't know nothin' about the hereafter. But I do know that if you transgress one of nature's laws, even though you repent and say you won't do it again, you're a-bound to pay for it. Punishment follows as sure as the fall of rain."

Religion always has been a favorite topic of discussion with the mountain people, and evidently a matter of much musing thought —within the limitations of thought without learning.

But perhaps the very mountain boundaries that stranded those first searchers of stubborn courage—that cut off the intellectual arteries that might have flowed in to them and let the inspired resolute urge which brought them there grow to be the power it might have been—in the strange ways of compensation, those boundaries may have been the very thing to keep that urge alive. Differently, but offering something that was not there before.

If they had been stranded or squandered in the middle of ugliness, the spirit might well have dwindled and dwarfed with the going of knowledge. But when the spirit is world-heavy, weighed down with all the mistakes and confusions and sorrows and humiliations that can come in the frail time of humans, it is like promise to stand in a morning when the near hills are dark with the feel of rain, but away off the far ones are in a lighted mist. It is beautiful and good over there, and clean and simple. It is more positive than solace. The very promise that the heart can be light again, lets you turn, and go onward toward that fulfillment.

If the mountain people can produce preachers with intellectual leadership of stature to rise to the natural heights around them, then the first religious surge which brought them to America will know a revival, strengthened and enriched by an American experience.

A FRENCH CREEK HORSE TRADE

An Diling age 86 dide jun 2 1899 ware grate trader

Southern mountain people are born traders, and often they give the knack a little extra fillip. A famous horse trader in the French Creek district in West Virginia had the fashion of justifying all his particular deals with a quotation from Scripture.

Once he found himself stuck with a horse with the heaves. All the neighbors knew the animal's condition and refused even to dicker. On court day, he took it into the county seat, and although it changed hands seven times in the course of the day, he came home that night with the selfsame nag on his hands. He was sitting on the fence looking at it the next morning, feeling low in his mind, when a stranger came by. They got to talking, and in the course of the conversation it developed the man was an itinerant preacher. He was making his rounds on foot, and a long road lay ahead of him.

The horse trader brightened.

His wife, coming to the door a little later to call him in to dinner, found him standing with his hands in his pockets, whistling a little, contentedly, through his teeth. He was looking down the road where a horse and rider seemed to be just making it around the hemlocks of the next bend. His wife shaded her eyes with her hand, to be sure.

"That ain't that ridin' critter of yo'rn with the heaves a-goin' yonder, is hit?"

He admitted modestly that it was.

"You didn't git anything for hit, did you?"

On the contrary, he had made a right good deal.

"Good la," she exclaimed, "who on earth would give you anythin' for that old nag?"

"Some preacher."

His wife stared at him. "A preacher! Why, however in the world could you do a thing like that?"

She was so honestly indignant, that he studied a little bit. Then he said, "He was a stranger, and I tuk him in."

LOGS BY 100

Joef Pyatt 75 jan 15 dide 1864 he war farmer made logs by 100

Likely he needed to "make logs by 100." There was, first of all, shelter to consider. Those logs were hacked out with patient sure blows of the ax and then scribed at the corners so they would fit neatly when the neighbors came to help raise the sides of the new house and were paid in roast venison and a jollification afterward.

There were the great puncheons to be hewn for the floor boards—leaving a few of them loose, so the wife-woman could store her preserves and pickles and jars of wild huckleberries and gooseberries underneath.

There were boards to be split for shingles, split with a frow from straight-grained oak. You still can find some of these first ones occasionally—twice the size and length of our shingles now and grown gray with the years in moss between them. A man had to be careful to lay these shingles in the increase of the moon, or they would cup. Sometimes a low shingle was left loose, to have handy to reach up and get if a "youngin' was just a-hurtin' for a lickin'."

Next there was the mantelpiece—the fireboard; often half a sourwood log, the deeply serrated bark setting off the stone fireplace well.

The solid oak door had to be made, so it could be left open for air unless a man wanted to bar it against someone he didn't want to see. A mountain man likes air. Most of these old houses, they will tell you, had cracks you could put the cat through. Even standing in the middle of the room you had to hang on to your hat, it was so drafty. And when a real "windin'" spell struck, you had to put rocks on the bedcovers to keep them from sailing out the cracks and into the next county. Rain came in one side of the house and went out the other. And many a morning you would wake up with your breath frozen on the coverlid.

Even a present-day guest of the old-type mountain homes can attest to their particular variety of air conditioning. One man who went hunting in the southern part of West Virginia, staying overnight with his guide, tells about the house, which was so far modernized as to have a thermometer. He said when he woke up in the morning the thermometer registered eighteen above inside the house. When he tried it outside it rose to twenty. So he went outdoors and got dressed.

After that first frontiersman had built his house, there was its furnishing to consider. It was found that hickory was good for chair frames, but white oak was best to split for the seats. A chair seat made of white oak will "wear a pair of britches out settin' on hit afore the chair seat goes." There were the beds and a table and a cupboard, to be fashioned and enduringly put together with maple pegs. Some of this old furniture is beautiful, with the original pale virginity of the pine wood turning slowly golden, and cherry deepening with the years. There was the little rhododendron root table—for the "Bible to set on."

Every self-respecting man made his wife a quilting frame, and there was the dough bowl to hollow out; the red cedar "piggin," with a "hand holt" at the side, to carry water from the spring. There was the broom to make—splitting a white oak stick into ribbons and tying them and spreading them. There were the gourds to hollow out for the soft soap, for the grease to keep the leather door hinges from squeaking.

There were the wooden lasts to be made for the family's shoes—although of course he needed to make only one last for each person. One last did for both feet. There were no rights and lefts to those homemade brogans, square cut from tanned hide. At night the shoe which was to go on the right foot was put where the right foot would step into it in the morning, and the left one was put handy to the left foot, and gradually they wore to shape.

Shoes, however, were something the mountain people could take or leave, evidently. One woman told me that she never had a pair of shoes until she was nineteen. "And then," she remembered merrily, "the first pair I did put on my feet cotched me and throwed me." A man told me that he wore *his* first pair of shoes out from the inside, his feet were that toughened. Some of the old people still resent shoes. "These derned contraptions for the feet that'll make four-toed creatures of mankind yet!" stormed an irate oldster, of a pair that were hurting.

Now that he had his homefolks fixed out, the mountain man had to provide shelter for his stock, although mountain barns are very makeshift affairs. But there was the apple house to put up, and beehives to make; and the sled to contrive, for often the trail to his house was too tortuous, or the creek too tempestuous, for a wagon to travel. The sleds still are simply two oak runners curved at the front end with a frame riding them, and a single tree to hitch the horse to. There were the hoe handles to make, cutting each one to the proper size of each member of the family—for everyone took a row, from the "granny woman" down to the littlest "set-along child." When a piece of especially good bird's-eye maple, or ash, was found, it was laid aside to replace the stock of a gun, come the next rainy day.

When somebody died, some one of the neighbors knocked together a coffin. Once this kindly service was a little previous. Les

Alden got "bad off sick," and someone of the family sent for the coffin maker. The man came, and went right out to the shed and started hammering. He didn't bother to come in and measure, because everybody knew that Les was the longest Alden of the name. But Les, hearing the racket, asked what it was. When he was told he raised up on his elbow and hollered furiously out toward the shed, "Quit that! I hain't dead yet!"

The man who had come to make the coffin was mad. He had walked a long way. "Well, don't send for me next time till you need me!"

The graciously gabled old house on yon side a winding stream and just this side a mountain, yet with enough bottom land in front of it for haystacks to drowse peacefully in the twilight; the high, narrow old house with double porches, the one upstairs latticed in the old southern style, and used as a plunder room, the downstairs one sociable with low-legged homemade chairs; the old log cabins, bespeaking the sturdiness of those builders first to come into the wilderness; even the little plank house built into the side of a mountain, its unpainted sides making one with the wooded heights behind it, with the very smoke from its squat stone chimney drifting out to become a part of the tender distances—all these houses have a quality no others in America quite have. It is a quality that comes of everything about them having been put there by the hearts and heads and hands of the people living in them, and all from material at hand.

Something of that completeness goes into their particular quality of hospitality. Their independence lets them be gracious. There is no more heart-warming greeting in the world than, "Heigh-ho, I'm God-proud to see you." Nor is there a much better farewell than "Come back—."

"Come stay all night," is a familiar and cordial byword. If it's a warm day, you are invited to "draw up a chair, and cool off." If the day is cold, they urge you to put off your parting with, "Best linger up by the fire. That air's stirrin' cool." If their invitation to share a meal with them has an apologetic cast, the apology is purely verbal. "Our food hain't much, but reach out and take yore needs—." The obvious feeling lying behind that prelude is that what is good enough for them is good enough for you.

The natural bearing, as a whole, of the highlander suggests indeed that he is as good as you are, and maybe somewhat better. It is not an arrogant attitude, and certainly not defensive. It is merely a calm assurance of equality that goes deeper than pride, deeper even than thought. It allows them to make that calm scrutiny of the outsider, which sometimes irritates the outsider, and sometimes is badly mistaken for stupidity. They are not gaping. They are merely taking your measure. And if they decide to "confidence" you, their hospitality is very genuine, and often is offered with a dignity and reserve that leave you feeling honored.

On the other hand, of course, your invitation may be one you hesitate to accept. Once I fell in the creek and landed in such an invitation. An angular Amazon who lived up that way happened to come striding up just then, and she fished me out from where I'd fallen in the water trying to get over a high rail fence beside it.

She had been to the store, and had put on a hat for the journey. Even in my dripping condition I looked at her and thought to myself it took more than strength to put on a hat. But she was kind. She insisted on my going in and drying off at her house and having a glass of buttermilk. I looked at the glass, frosted by long and intimate use, which she picked up off the cluttered table and said thank you, but I really didn't care for any buttermilk. She said peremptorily that buttermilk was good for folks. But I didn't have to have any after all, because when she went to get the buttermilk which was in the dishpan, she found that while she was away to the store, the oldest girl had thought it was dishwater and pitched it out the door. Whereupon the annoyed woman picked up the dishpan and whacked the girl over the head with it.

"Ahem," said a disheveled man, appearing in the doorway of the other room. Evidently he had dozed off, and just been awakened by the racket. "But hain't that thunder?"

"No, hit hain't," said the woman shortly. "That's me, bangin' on Clarissa. She's throwed out the buttermilk, and I was a-lookin' to give the company some."

The man scratched his thin hair interestedly. "God-burn certain," he said, "I thought shore that was thunder."

While the social system in the mountains certainly is not stuffy, still it has its definite scale. It hits its high and low, as well as anywhere else. The meal you are invited to share at the opposite pole from dishpan buttermilk, may be served in a big old dining room with the table groaning like the proverbial festive board, and the sideboard loaded with pies and cake and preserved peaches—all prepared from a kitchen with the floor "so clean you could eat off of it."

I remember breakfasts especially in a modern mountain house. (Modern mountain houses, like everything else about the modernization of our forgotten people, keep the best of what is natural to so many of them. The houses being built now are made of local stone and bark shingles—so that they still have, very smartly, a belonging look.)

I remember the shingles that were the same gray as the oak at the side of that particular house in the sun. I remember the freshness of the strawberries from the garden, and the sweetness of the clean homespun table mats and napkins on the handmade table. I remember the way the early sun flooded the breakfast room, and the grace that began the day. There was life to that grace, as though each day were a fresh beginning, full of possibilities and adventures. The grace was for guidance through them, for wisdom to meet them well—given with such lift to it that one expected wonderful things of that day—and so expecting and looking for them, they came, one way or another.

"Logs by the 100"—to make the houses that symbolize the strength and simplicity of a whole people, pointing up their bad and their good with a refreshing lack of veneer.

WORDS AND MUSIC

Margit Ollis age 60 dide July 10 1899 work on farm all of her days

Mountains are like music, the great kind of music that is everything you have ever known about, and something more. They are a powerful music, that rolls up out of the earth. The southern mountains begin their particular theme along the Potomac, quietly, with that quiet swelling out into long full rolls of Kentucky harmony. There is nothing out of line, or out of tune there. Then abruptly—like a stroke of genius, you have the Virginia roughs—mounting and slashing, but just right—nothing else would have done there! And before you can quite regain your composure, the whole thing sweeps together into wild, almighty crescendos—Tennessee and North Carolina pushing their forested lofts up and up and up into that intense green-blue sky! Then, worn out and satisfied, it goes off quietly again, into Alabama and Georgia.

Eight states with music in their earth. Eight states with a people with music in their words.

As a race the people of our southern mountains speak softly. Even their most commonplace remarks somehow are made to sound secret, and of greatest importance. The women especially have low tones, and often plaintively sweet, pitched in a minor key and lilting upward, so that the last word of every sentence is almost sung.

Their phrasing has a rhythm to it, such as "all her days," meaning a lifetime. Then there are: "times I recall when; if happen you pass; enduring the time; the day long; over the ridge and down; I wonder me if; far lands across; the green shadder gum tree; whar all to?"

Sometimes it is an arbitrary accent on the single word that gives the rhythmic effect, as: "agree*ment*, hos*tile*"—the accent placed on whichever part of the word strikes their sense of sound, then the whole stretched out drawlingly to its full length.

They have an instinctive knack with words, somehow bringing out of a limited and ancient vocabulary a wealth of rich idiom. Shapes of phrases repeat themselves and the same sounds re-echo, giving, oddly enough, vividness rather than monotony—as in their use of double words: "down-log; sulphur-match; man-person; flower-thing; mother-woman; storm of rain; tooth-dentist; neighbor-people; ocean-sea; ham-meat; cookin'-pan; belly-empty; biscuit-bread; rifle-gun; ridin'-critter; cow-brute; preacher-man; granny-woman; we-uns; chanty-song."

Adjectives and adverbs are used as though they had plenty of them. "I thought shorely undoubtedly of a sartin hit war so," you will hear, perhaps of a rumor believed in and found in relief not to be true. Or the comment on a girl very slight in stature may be wonderingly, "She's a peart little thing, got plenty of sense, but the least spindlingest little old thing."

Negatives especially mount up. "That boy never done nothin' nohow; I hain't got nary none; I can't get no rest nohow; I never seen no man of no kind do no washin'."

Since the southern mountain people have lived to themselves, a race apart for almost two centuries, their idiom has come to be curiously intense—drawn from their own experiences, and kept fresh in that it is always firsthand. An independent and individualistic people about everything else, it is natural that they should be so in speech, too. Thus, when it suits them to use nouns for verbs, they do—and very effectively. "I didn't fault him for hit; that b'ar'll meat me for a month; chair bottomin' is easy settin' down work; who'll funeralize the corpse?; are you a-fixin' to go squirrelin'?; he hain't much on sweetheartin'; I don't confidence them dogs; that creek turkey-tails out into numerous little forks."

In the same way, if a verb feels better to them as a noun, that's the way they use it. "You can git you one more gittin' of wood out of that pile; I didn't hyear no give-out about hit; listen, all you settin' rounders!"

The same freedom goes for the way adjectives get put into action. "Hit grumbled the old woman, some; he was biggin' and biggin' the story; he went lick-splittin' hit down the road; much (make much over) that dog and see won't he come; come toe-teeterin' in; I didn't do nary a thing to contrary her; hit benasties a man's mind."

And with even more fanciful flux, verbs flow into adjectives: "the travelin'est hosses; the talkin'est woman; the workin'est man; the nothin' doin'dest day; she war just a little set-along child; Jim's the disablest one of the family; hit's a fotched-on hat."

Adverbs too, get their twist: "a person has a rather about whar he'll be buried; I hope yore folks are all gaily."

Southern mountain speech, which is peculiarly pleasing when it is heard, is apt to look crude when anybody attempts to put it down in print. In actuality, however, far from being merely a rude dialect, much of it springs undeniably from the classics. Many expressions are biblical. They use "generation" to mean a certain breed of people just as Moses did when he bemoaned the corrupted children of God as "a perverse and crooked generation."

In the main, however, most of the idiom is a direct carry-over of old English. Queen Elizabeth herself used their "begone! have done with! a sorry fellow; a fere and fellowy man." Out of Chaucer comes their term "feisty," meaning impertinent; "fray" for fight; "gorm" for muss; "pack" for carry. "Mast" is an ancient word for game herbage, and can be heard in the comment of any present-day hunter. The mountain wedding festivities, called the "infare," came from the old prenuptial celebration of the bridegroom. And right out of Shakespeare one of my fifth-grade students in a North Carolina mountain school, reported that somebody in the back of the room was acting the fool by saying, "He's wearin' the bells!"

The lack of gap between Shakespearean times and ours can sometimes be linguistically startling, as when you hear the term "cuckold" used as familiarly as though it were Othello himself mourning, "that cuckold lives in bliss—." Women borrow a "tod-dick" of wool, as they did in *The Winter's Tale.* The past of helped which always is said as "holp" has justification in *King John* when Philip is questioning his legitimacy by declaring, "Sir Robert never holp make this leg—."

Likewise, there is "afeared," from the same redoubtable source; "anticky, harry, misdoubt, rift"; "stout" meaning healthy; "child-ing" meaning to be pregnant; "lay" meaning wager.

"Ary" and "nary" are merely convenient contractions from the classical "e'er a," and "ne'er a." The universal use of "hit" for it, springs from a time before true English itself, being the Anglo-Saxon neuter of "he." And if the fireside and store-front remark in the mountains is sometimes rough, sometimes definitely beyond the pale of polite conversation, so was the fireside conversation of Queen Elizabeth!

The language of the southern mountains, as all etymologists agree, is far more survival than degeneration. However, its particular flavor comes from the curious combination of a manner of speech centuries old and of honorable origin with terms which are rankly out of a raw new country. "Yan side," they twang out, and use strong past tenses like "blowed" and "growed."

Their mispronunciations are lusty: "cha'r, ha'r, b'ar." Sturdy use is made of that "r," often annexing it to a vowel, and even substituting it for the final "s" in "was." Furthermore, they mispronounce at will. "Whar is hit?" someone will ask, and then discover, "Thar hit is." Someone else may choose to rhyme it another way. "Whur is hit? Thur hit is." There is no romantic trace back to ancient terminology in their mispronunciations. They merely mispronounce in whatever way is at hand.

And although the woman of the house may be singing some song whose origin is to be found in the *Percy Reliques*, and singing it as Chaucer mentions it being sung, "entuned in her nose full sweetly"—still, there certainly is nothing classical in the "shucky beans" and "sow belly" and "sass" she is fixing for supper. That is "p'int blank" out of the hills. So are their place names. Mountain place names can be vividly descriptive, but they are obviously inventions of right around home: "Squabble Creek; Morning Star; Pigeon Roost; Troublesome; Wind Ridge; Stand Around; Thousand Sticks; Mud Fork; Cranberry; Sally's Back Bone; Pole Cat Holler; Hell for Sartin."

Both the survival and the earthy freshness of the mountain speech, however, have had their origin and dependence in the peculiar separation which the high lengths of hills have made between mountain people and the world. Now, as modern developments change all that, it is only to be expected that survival and freshness both will be lost in ordinariness. Yet it is apt to go slowly, that combination of the very old, and the very new, because the minor quality is somehow an air which the whole history of mountain people has left to them. The old ballads should go too, as radios and juke-boxes come in with the current tunes—and yet you find the old ballads still being clung to and sung occasionally—for a good reason Shakespeare knew:

> That old and antique song we heard last night;
> Methought it did relieve my passion much,
> More than light airs and recollected terms
> Of these most brisk and giddy-paced times.

So, in a tin-front restaurant in a mountain town growing in cheap quickness to meet the sudden trade going past on the broad new highway, you still can hear a mountain boy, half in jest, half wryly, make a kind of pristine song of the news, "My gal's quit me. I'm about to lock my heart and throw the key away."

Margit Carpenter age 87 1875 dide jun 5 war good womin war good to the pore when she war amind

Abern Jonson age 100.8 dide oc 15 1881 he war farmer and ran forge to mak iron and drank licker his days never war drunk in his days

popelers is springing green apr 1 1901

Jon H. Wiseman 82 dide oc 20 1907 war miler to grind for folks

Brig Coffee age 85 dide apr 7 1910 war deer honter cil 100. 200. 300 deer

Bedford Wiseman age 75 march 1 1910 war farmer and made brandy plenty

Charley Buchanan age 52 dide nov 7 1910 war revenuer for Michel conty

Wm Austin age 80 dide June 6 1912 war farmer hep win mex war

John Wise & Newton Wise & Thomas Wise went to Getsburg for big youn 1913

it snode on Black monton won inch jun 10 1913

Joacob Carpenter took down sick April 1 1919

Alberta Pierson Hannum is indebted to Mrs. Crate Carpenter for the use of the entries here quoted from Jacob Carpenter's diary.

CHAPTER THREE

MEN, MOUNTAINS, AND TREES

by Donald Culross Peattie

The mountain man, in the Southern Appalachians, is not a real mountaineer, as are some of the Swiss living at giddy altitudes; he is a forest man—even when he is also a farmer. He is a hunter born, a natural forest ranger, perennially wise about trees and the ways of woodland life. He lives in a forest home, a log cabin built, for choice, of black locust because it does not decay; his house is shingled with chestnut or oak because they can be split so straight and thin. The logs on his hearth are his only fuel; his ax helves are of ash or hickory, and hickory imparts to his hams, when smoked over its coals, a pungent sweetness. Of finest walnut is the butt of his hunting rifle; indeed, he is laid in a walnut cradle when he is born, and buried in a coffin of black cherry. As a child, he was brought up on sassafras applied internally, and almost anything limber applied externally; his homespun clothes are dyed with butternut, and seeds of buckeye in his pocket bring him luck.

From his front door—in whatever direction he turns—our mountain man has a forest dweller's outlook: forest protects and shuts him in at the same time; it makes him an extreme individualist less interdependent with the rest of society than anyone, even the Indians, in American life. Yet the wall of the woods, still dense and high, has concealed even from himself the retarding results of his isolation. The thick tangles of rhododendron hide his moonshine still; the constant pressure of the woods upon his clearing have shut him in with his clannishness. Mountain people have the forest forever in their heads as well as before their eyes.

What its plumage is to a redbird, so are the trees to the Southern Appalachians. One may see what our mountains would look like, robbed of their forest cover, near Ducktown, Tennessee, where the fumes of the copper smelters have destroyed all vestige of green life. There the mountains are habitation sadder than walls without roof. The rainfall beats directly on the naked earth; all the precious humus, accumulation of millions of years, has been swept away by the surface waters. With the rich biological soil gone, the sterile mineral soil is laid bare. This, too, is vanishing down the ever-growing, irresistible gullies that look like miniature Grand Canyons. Eventually the landscape may be flayed of its flesh of soil; then the rock ribs of the planet will appear—a ghastly skeleton.

Were the same thing to happen to all these mountains, the Southern Appalachians, in a short while as geologic time is reckoned, could be rendered as barren as the mountains of the Mojave without achieving the clear, arid grandeur of the desert ranges. Fortunately, in spite of much wastage and needless destruction of our woods and soils, the Southern Appalachians are still clothed for the most part in shimmering, rustling, sheltering robes of greenery. Probably no other mountain range in the temperate zone is so consistently, so lushly, so variously leafy.

Literally, the trees hold the mountains up, by the roots they send into the soil, and by the infinite, intricate fingers of the moss that they shelter. From the moment that a raindrop strikes the forest soil here it is conserved, sponged up in the great reservoir of the humus layer, until it comes bubbling forth, as needed, from the never-failing springs. Profoundly, too, the forest vegetation modifies the weather and the climate—not perhaps by the direct means implied in the popular belief that forests *attract* rain—but in a subtler, yet more important way.

What this is one can understand if, of a burning August day when the valleys which are stripped of woods are sweltering and thirsting and the eyes are screwed up against the light and the skin is dried by the wind, one steps into a mountain glen, under the shade of hemlock and beech. Here, surely, a waterfall is sending its spray in trailing veils on a breeze of its own making that sets every dainty fern frond, every exquisitely balanced head of meadow rue to trembling. No longer are the eyes seared; the muscles of your face relax, your flesh is grateful in every pore; there can be no one so insensitive that he does not breathe a sigh of relief and smile with delight at the emerald tunnels of the cove.

For the forests are a buffer against excessive upward and downward changes of temperature. They halt winds. They lay the dust. They maintain humidity within tolerable ranges. Thus, in a biological and human sense, they create a climate of their own and regulate the weather.

ABORIGINAL GRANDEUR

Aboriginally the Appalachian forests were vast in extent, clothing the mountains, except for the balds,* from top to bottom. It was the unbroken character of this mountain woodland, and the breadth and density of it, rather than the comparatively gentle slopes themselves, which formed so great an obstacle to the early explorers and settlers. It is still the trees which constitute the greatest challenge to the hiker, climber, and camper. Here one need be no great shakes of an alpinist; one must certainly be wood-wise, something of a ranger.

For these mountain slopes still carry the finest hardwood timber stands in the country, with perhaps twenty million high-quality acres of woodland, from West Virginia to Georgia, about a million and a half of them as virgin as in the days of De Soto. In the val-

* Balds are treeless heathland on isolated summits. It is probable that trees are lacking due to evaporation resulting from altitude and exposure to winds.

The tulip tree is the most impressive in the forest

Looking toward the Tennessee Valley from Pickens Nose

Virgin beech forest, Pisgah National Park

leys between the slopes are found another forty million acres of actual or potential forest land—some of it depleted or abused, some of it in fair or good condition.

The original forest was dense. Lumbermen's records show that on some of the heavily shaded, cool, northern slopes and in deep coves, the virgin forest produced an average of from 1,500 to 50,000 board feet to the acre. Near Looking Glass Rock in North Carolina, 40,000 board feet of tulip poplar to the acre were cut in 1912. Spruce cut on the Great Smokies ran sometimes as high, while an acre of white pine, in Shady Valley, Virginia, once yielded 100,000 board feet. They were choice trees, those wonderful old pines and spruce and poplars; they grew ofttimes in pure stands, arrow-straight of trunk and free of knots, smooth-grained and sound.

Individually the trees of the virgin forest must often have been giants, and today there are still giants in this earth. Most of the trees of the eastern United States, except those indigenous to the flood plains of the Mississippi, reach their maximum height and diameter in the Southern Appalachians. This is especially true of the magnificent forests of the western slopes of the Great Smokies where the moisture-bearing winds from the Gulf of Mexico, which frequently cross the Great Valley of eastern Tennessee quite dry, are forced high over the master chain and so drop their rain on the western slopes. Many people believe that on these densely forested slopes, the precipitation reaches somewhere in the neignborhood of 90 inches a year. Only recently have rain gauges been set on the mountain elevations.

Certain it is that sweet buckeye or horse chestnut are found here up to 125 feet in height, while the tulip tree tops all at as much as nearly 200 feet, in specimen trees, with the beautiful straight boles clear of branches for the first 100 feet. The Canadian hemlock in the Great Smokies reaches a maximum of 100 feet; the chestnut oak is equally tall, and even the cucumber tree soars up, in some of the rich coves, to 90 feet. In the Great Smokies the silverbell is sometimes a forest giant 100 feet high.

Forest trees, as contrasted with field trees, run to height, not girth. Still, there are some massive trees on record. From Highlands come measurements of a Canadian hemlock almost six feet in diameter, of a sweet birch fully six feet thick. In the days before the chestnut blight, chestnuts that were almost eleven feet through were known in the Great Smokies; a yellow birch on Whitetop Mountain was found to be seven feet three inches thick. A mountain laurel in the Great Smokies is reported to be more than six and one-half feet thick in the stem. One glorious white oak had a spread of branches that cast a pool of shade, even at noon, one hundred and thirty-three feet across.

In variety our forests are second to none in North America, and perhaps to none outside the tropics. Neither the Northern Appalachians, nor the Rockies, nor the Cascade-Sierras, nor the Pacific Coast Ranges (all noble mountains in their ways) dare compare themselves with the Southern Appalachians in wealth of tree species. The area embraced in this book, as defined by the editor, is a little more than a quarter that of Colorado. But with our one hundred and forty species of trees, we have about twice as many kinds as that state.

FOREST UPON FOREST

To the beginning student, as to the new visitor even when he is fairly wood-wise, those one hundred and forty species of our mountain trees, and a somewhat higher number of shrubs and woody vines, may well seem as bewildering at first, as the complex mountain system itself. It is the work of several seasons to learn even to name the trees in winter as in summer, in leaf, flower, fruit, bark, twigs, buds, and outline. I certainly cannot tell you how to identify them in these few pages! But when the useful and companionable art of greeting the trees by name is mastered, you learn to see the woods as well as the trees. Interest then centers on the forests, and I use the plural advisedly, for there are not one but many forests here.

They are spoken of as forest *types*—associations of certain species with each other, which are strikingly different in composition and physiognomy from other types. In the warm foothills where the Blue Ridge rises, the "feel" is almost tropical in places; on the highest peaks, where even in summer you may find yourself in the clouds, the "look" is Canadian. A trip by car, indeed, will whisk you through as many life-zones as you would pass in going from central Georgia to central Quebec—all on a mountain road which climbs nearly six thousand feet in perhaps forty miles.

Anyone can understand that trees which grow at sea level on the Gulf of the St. Lawrence would, by reason of climatic preference, be found at three and four thousand feet in the mountains of Pennsylvania and West Virginia, and down here in our latitudes would not occur below five thousand. Thus it is with the red spruce, for instance, that crowns only our highest peaks. In the warm foothills of the Georgia mountains, on the other hand, the climate supports the growth of distinctly southerly species, like the longleaf pine which you see on the coastal plain of the Carolinas, the sunlight glinting like a dazzling star at the heart of each great tassel. In theory, then, the mountains should be banded with zones of trees representing different climates, the zones tilted slightly upward as one follows the mountains southward into warmer regions.

And in general this is what you will find, but in detail the theory is shattered by complex factors. For these mountains are not simple walls or ridges. They are tossed in a congested mass; the axes run in every direction and each axis has been carved by a mature erosion system fed by heavy rainfall. As a result, each range is dissected to show exposure to every quarter of the compass, and there is an astounding difference between the north slope, with its many hours of shadow, its greater humidity, its severer winters, and a southern exposure with conditions corresponding in summer, according to Bowman in his classic work *Forest Physiography*, to those of the tropics at the same season.

There is the further difference between the western slopes of the Appalachians, which catch the moisture-laden winds of the prevailing westerlies, and the eastern slopes which lie in the lee of the westerlies and are correspondingly drier as well as warmer. Add to this the fact that the angle as well as the direction of slope makes an important difference, for the steeper slopes and exposed ridges support a much drier sort of growth (other factors being equal) than the rich sylva which will grow near the foot of a hill, where soil water collects and the soil is not leached of its plant foods. So you may find more southerly trees on top of a ridge, and more northerly trees at the bottom, in some cool cove! Trees characteristic of altitudes between 3,000 and 5,000 feet will creep down in rich glens to the foothills and even out on the piedmont.

It is impossible to draw up for these highlands a vegetation map based simply on altitude. The situation is far more complex than that, and the forest types respond to this complexity, by grouping themselves into more than thirty distinct types, as classified by the Society of American Foresters in 1931. Most of these could only be understood and used by the trained botanist and expert forester. For present purposes it is enough to recognize the four following grand types.

THE SPRUCE-FIR GROVES

What genuine lover of trees and mountains is going to rest, even in the pleasantest flowery valley, when he can see at the summits the somber caps of the spruce and fir groves? He looks longingly at the black, serrated, pagoda-like outlines of these noble trees against the sky or tangled with the clouds; sometimes he can even smell their health-breathing aroma, when the wind comes singing across the gulfs of mountain space. He sees the smooth pale green of the "balds," the subalpine pastures, contrasting sharply with the black of the conifers. And, duty or not, alone or in company, he starts up for the high places. For he feels that he must rest his eyes in the dim emerald naves of these templed woods; he must get the look and the feel of this eerie forest by heart, and revel till he is satisfied in its *Waldeinsamkeit.*

It may seem that in beginning at the top of our mountain forest zones and working downward, I am breaking all rule and reason. But the spruce-fir groves are by far the simplest and easiest to understand in a series of forests so complex that one only begins to feel oriented among them after several years of active study in the field. For the northern visitor, too, the spruce-fir groves have the advantage, as a starting point, of being familiar to anyone who has ever seen the "north woods" of Maine, the Adirondacks, the northern Great Lakes region, or Canada.

Our high mountain woods are in many respects similar to the evergreen north woods, though so limited in area. For balsam and spruce never occur here, in pure, dominant form, below 4,500 feet, and usually not below 5,500. This leaves them only a most restricted area which plots out on a map like a scattered archipelago in a sea of paler green. Yet even this limitation has its advantages, or at least its allure. Some, like myself, find the north woods at times monotonous; in undiluted quantity they are stern, and finally almost suffocating. In the Southern Appalachians where, dark and gleaming, red spruce and balsam fir crown only the loftiest peaks, their rarity, their aloofness, the sweet refreshment of their summer climate, all make them a goal well worth the climb that will quite certainly set you to breathing quick and deep in the thin aromatic atmosphere.

"Pines," these trees are sometimes called, and they are related to pines; like them they bear cones and have evergreen needle foliage. They are unlike pines in bearing their needles singly, not in clusters. Indeed, these are typical Christmas trees familiar to every Northern child. Far darker than any pine woods is the shade cast by balsam and spruce. This is due in part to the dark color of the foliage, a blue-green so deep that it appears black from a little distance and has imparted to the grand Black Mountain Range its name. The depth of the shade is due, too, to the closeness of the needles, the thickness of the boughs, the interlocking canopy of the trees. The trunks stand very close together, closer than those of any other forest type in eastern America. When the trees die they do not easily fall in so densely packed a grove, but are held up in the arms of the other trees; thus this forest type is slow in thinning itself out. The coolness and dampness are perpetual here where the clouds sweep so many days of the year, and this encourages a deep growth of moss and lichens that spread from root to root, that climb high up on the trunks and drip from every dead branch, so that the whole wood seems to be sorrowed over with these delicate growths which themselves conserve and intensify the moisture. Thus everything conspires to give these groves a look of eld—of utmost and venerable antiquity, when as a matter of fact these trees are not, individually, especially long-lived. A child would say it was a "fairy-tale forest," and probably no scientific term, if one could be found, would more deftly express the impression given by this sylvan type.

As this is a chapter on trees, followed by a separate one on wild flowers, I must pass over here the dainty little blooms that peep out through the depths of the moss. Nor can this chapter begin to tell you how to identify all our tree species. Still, every visitor will want to know, if he isn't already wise in these matters, how to distinguish the balsam fir from the red spruce. You can know the spruce by its four-cornered needles, which grow out all around the twig, and never lie flat in one plane. The needles are tipped with little prickles too. And the shining, dark reddish-brown cones, never over one and three-quarters inches long, hang down on the bough. When they fall, they fall entire.

The balsam, by contrast, has flattish needles, never bristle-tipped; on mature boughs they appear to lie all in one horizontal plane—a row of them on each side of the twig. The cones, up to two and one-half inches long, are purplish, with pale green bracts coming out between the scales at maturity, and they always stand erect on the bough. When old, the cone scales fall off separately, leaving an axis standing up like a spike on the branch.

In the trunks of the fir under the bark, there are often big rosin blisters filled with a clear liquid (the balsam of commerce) which the mountain folk have whimsically compared to milk. So they named this the "she-balsam." Thinking perhaps that it needed a mate, and finding the spruce tree, which is devoid of "milk," commonly accompanying it, they named it the "he-balsam"!

These two dominant species may occur in pure stands, but a few deciduous trees are frequently found with them. Such are fire cherry, yellow birch, and serviceberry, mountain holly, beech, rowanberry, striped maple, and mountain maple. Between the two conifers there is a sharp contrast in commercial importance. The balsam, the more beautiful of the two, and beloved for its fragrance, is all but worthless to the sawmill. But red spruce is a good softwood lumber, and has been employed in flooring, for mine props, house construction, and paper pulp, and is prized for the sounding boards of violins.

A railroad was once built almost to the top of Mt. Mitchell to bring down the spruce logs, and there has been much cutting in the past. But this is nearly over, since a large part of the limited area where spruce and balsam occur in the Southern Appalachians has been incorporated in national and state parks. And very properly so. In view of the rarity of this forest type and its precious function in holding the watersheds against erosion, and its value to the people in beauty and recreational charms, no price that could be fetched for these stands in pulp values would ever equal the loss in destroying them. For, unfortunately, the spruce-fir forest does not renew itself readily. When it is clean-cut or burned off, it is replaced by fire cherry, a worthless little weed of a tree under which the seeds of its noble predecessors do not readily germinate.

THE NORTHERN HARDWOOD GROVES

Just below the spruce-fir woods, which are of course evergreen, comes a belt, usually occurring between 3,500 and 5,500 feet altitude, which by contrast is almost wholly naked of leaves in winter. Botanists call these the broad-leaved deciduous trees; the lumberman speaks of them as hardwoods.

The zone of the northern hardwoods is well defined in its upper limit from the conifers, but at its lower limit merges imperceptibly into the zone beneath it by many transitional stages. The occurrence of the northern hardwoods in pure form is "spotty"—irregular and, if it were mapped, would form a thin, wavering, and broken line. Sometimes it is quite absent and the Appalachian zone and the spruce-fir formation practically meet.

The dominant trees in the hardwood belt are sugar maple, as fine as ever came out of Vermont, reaching sometimes a hundred feet in height here, and sweet buckeye or horse chestnut, almost as tall, a magnificent tree with its handsome foliage and spires of yellow flowers followed by the curious seeds. The lovely beech is here distinctly in third place, and the noble white ash, the black cherry valued for its beautiful wood, the yellow birch and the basswood or white linden come next in importance; here and there the silverbell, called "peawood" by the mountain folk, shoulders its way up eighty or a hundred feet, to wave its flowers as high in the forest crown as any. Northern red oak, red maple, and hop hornbeam are frequent here, and so is the curious, flat-topped, dotted haw.

This, above all, is the zone of the filmy leaf, of the light emerald shade that we expect in cool-temperate woodlands. It is a type especially adapted to severe winters and, admittedly, they are severe at this altitude. But it is in autumn that you would know this formation without fail for, from the middle of October to the middle of November, its colors trumpet and shout with orange and garnet and gold.

At high altitudes certain of these trees—the beech, yellow birch, and buckeye, northern red oak, scarlet and white oaks, and the dotted haw—become curiously dwarfed in stature, with thick stems when old, and the wide crowns that trees may develop when they are spaced far apart. They resemble old apple trees in outline, and for this reason the mountain people call them "orchards." In general there are no shrubs or understory trees in these sub-alpine orchards; the flowering herbs and ferns, growing shoulder-high, fill up the "orchards" the way timothy and daisies do in a real orchard. It is curious that the spruce and fir, which go to higher altitudes, show no signs of dwarfing here as they do in the Rockies and Alps and even in the White Mountains of New Hampshire, near timberline. For some reason it is only the broad-leaved deciduous trees that here exhibit this reaction to altitude, and very curious they are, these orchards, but quaint, and pleasant after the dense coniferous groves, reminding one somewhat of the "oak openings" of the Middle West or the "parks" of the Rockies.

Almost every tree among the northern hardwoods is commercially valuable, and if the occurrence of this zone were less irregular and more accessible it would long ago have been cut clean by the lumber trade hungry for good hardwoods. When it is cut, or burned, it usually reproduces itself well, coming up quickly with a fine, even, healthy second growth.

THE APPALACHIAN FOREST FORMATION

The Appalachian forest formation designates the great, typical, original forest complex of our southern mountains. It occurs between 2,000 and 4,000 feet altitude, and hence occupies the great mass of mountain area. Sometimes it runs up to 5,000 feet, and it may frequently descend right down to the piedmont, in favored glens, at only 1,000 feet above sea level.

When you come down out of the restricted world of the spruce-fir woods, through the classic northern hardwoods, and enter the lush and most various zone of the typical Appalachian formation, you pass from simplicity to complexity, from zones that seem to belong to other parts of the country, to a vegetation that belongs exactly where it stands and has stood here for ages while it reached its highest development. It is the best known of all these forest types.

And yet it is the most difficult to define, the most complex to analyze. It includes almost every tree of the northern hardwood zone above it, and a large proportion of the piedmont zone below it, so that its bounds are all but impossible to fix. Yet it is no mere transition between the northern hardwoods and the piedmont forests, though it has sometimes been called the "transition zone." On the contrary, it is *the* aboriginal mountain forest, from which the zones above and below it have probably derived a large share of their woody plants. The Appalachian forest formation contains, too, a large number of species peculiar to itself, like Carolina hemlock, table-mountain pine, and black locust, which give it character.

Some forty-five species of trees—as many as are found in all of Great Britain—crowd into this luxuriant formation. There are at least as many shrubs and woody vines as trees, and ten times as many herbaceous plants. Probably a thousand species could be called typical members of the Appalachian forest proper. It is like passing by old friends on the road without speaking to them, to hasten on here and not discuss the enchanting wild flowers of this forest. But that must wait over to the next chapter, while I endeavor to keep attention on forest structure and forest problems.

This formation is a handsome mixture of deciduous hardwoods

and evergreens. The hardwoods are, except locally, in the majority. In summer their broad filmy leaves give a cool but luminous, not somber, shade. In winter they fall to the ground, enriching a light sweet humus with fresh accumulation of suitable food materials for further plant growth. In early spring they are still naked, or tenderly budded out, for some weeks after genial weather has returned. So at the very season when sunlight is most needed, the hardwoods, no matter how tall and dense their canopy, admit light and warmth. The dark loams absorb it readily, and produce a precocious crop of spring wild flowers. Seedling trees are not necessarily overshadowed in this zone, either, so that the forest is capable of reproducing itself freely and constantly, if not abused. When shade is most needed, in the blazing summer months, it returns abundantly. In autumn, when the leaves fall again, there is a brilliant display of purple and golden wild flowers.

The evergreens take two forms—the needle-leaved, consisting of several pines and two handsome hemlocks, called "spruce pine" by the mountain people, and the broad-leaved evergreens, most of which are shrubs or small understory trees. These last distinctly suggest a tropical flora, or at least a very mild climate. Rhododendron and mountain laurel are the chief of these, and in clear weather when their blades spill and reflect the light, or in winter when they gleam with rain, they shine through almost every prospect. With the pines, they keep the Appalachian formation looking fresh and green all winter. Combined with the deciduous hardwoods which look so tender when budding out in spring, and flame so gorgeously in fall, they make a forest formation of endless variety and loveliness.

These woods excel in what are vividly if not scientifically called flowering trees. True, all our trees, in strict botanical interpretation, have flowers. But the flowers of conifers and of the nut trees like oak and hickory, birch and beech, are inconspicuous; we think of these as primarily timber trees, and noble ones. The Appalachians boast an enchanting display of trees with showy blossoms. Some, like the tulip tree with its great petals resembling full-blown red and yellow tulips, the magnolia with blooms like water lilies, the buckeye with its golden candelabras, the black locust with its drooping clusters of flowers like some white wisteria's, are tall foresters. Others, like dogwood, with wide-eyed starry white bracts, the redbud with fanciful little magenta butterflies of bloom that burst from the naked wood in earliest spring, the silverbell, the sourwood, the fringe bush, and the mountain laurel, are understory trees. Gaily they light up the sober aisles of the timber trees. In all North America and Europe there is no sylva so flowery as this one. Truly, this is a forest which has its wild flowers not only at the foot of its trees, but in the tops of them.

As an instance of this, I recollect gazing down once, in July, from the slopes of Mt. Mitchell at the coves of the Craggies, upon the whole forest, far as eye could see, tossing with the creamy blooms of the chestnut, which in those days was king of the cove hardwoods. They were so many, the chestnuts, and each crown bore such a myriad of long shining catkins, that as the wind threshed those woods the whole sea of waving leaves seemed breaking into whitecaps. It was a sight one would not have beheld by looking up under the woodland canopy; only by gazing down, from the vantage point of a hawk, did one see this grand primeval treetop flowering. In the right place, and the right season, one may similarly see the mountainsides stormed by the blithe hosts of mountain laurel, dogwood, and redbud.

THE PIEDMONT WOODS

Washing right up to the base of the mountains, climbing the foothills sometimes up to two thousand feet, extending in long tongues up the mountain valleys, and seated broadly and firmly on the Asheville plateau, is a forest typical of the central counties of the Carolinas, Georgia, and Virginia. It merges imperceptibly into the Appalachian formation, sharing with it hosts of species, having the same attractive combination of evergreens and hardwoods, timber trees and flowering trees. It differs in a number of ways; it is usually a much drier sylvan setting, earlier to leaf out and flower in spring, hotter in summer, less lush, with fewer very tall trees. Predominantly it is composed of many types of oak, much good hickory, and shortleaf and scrub pine, with plenty of such fine trees as tulip tree and red maple, but lacking sugar maple and the lovely sweet birch with its fragrant satiny red bark, lacking—except where it merges with the Appalachian type—the noble hemlocks and the classic-looking rhododendron with pink, rose, and white blooms.

Much of the piedmont forestation is what country people call scrub woods. Perhaps I am making it sound too unattractive. It is not so except where it has been ruthlessly burned, overgrazed, and cut over. In virgin form it is a handsome type and boasts some lovely and valuable trees not typical of our other forest zones, like the persimmon, the red birch, "Christmas" holly, and the sweet gum with its shining, star-shaped leaves. Spring, summer, and autumn, the wild flowers troop through these woods. Where the piedmont and Appalachian forests mingle, as in the warm foothills of the Blue Ridge, a flora of unsurpassed beauty and richness can be found.

FOREST SUCCESSION AFTER FARMING

Both the piedmont and the Appalachian woods have suffered heavy inroads at the hands of man. The mountain farms are chiefly located here, and while, of course, it is only right and to be expected that trees will have to go when they stand on soil that will yield higher returns from agriculture, it is entirely wrong that they should be cut from slopes too steep or soils too thin or infertile to support a permanent paying farm. In such places the returns on the forest, even though slight in cash, are incalculably valuable in soil conservation and maintenance of stream flow. Yet injudicious deforestation has gone on for a century or more in these zones, with the result, of course, that the farm, as soon as its brief first fertility has been exhausted and heavy erosion sets in, is abandoned and the mountain farmer, moving on, cuts down another tract of woods.

This acknowledgment of mistaken forest management, however, does not mean the automatic restoration of the forest. After abandonment of a farm, there is a tedious cycle of worthless successive growths to be gone through before a first-class forest can be restored. In the first year after abandonment there is a one-year stage when horseweed and finger grass predominate; the next year ragweed and heather aster, appropriately called povertyweed in some places, take over. The third year you get broom sedge or beard grass. Then comes the scrub or Virginia pine, a weed of a tree, which slowly takes over from broom sedge, and in about ten years the first hardwoods make their appearance, most of them small species like dogwood. In seventy-five years, first-class forest is just making its appearance.

Truly, lands mistakenly cleared for farming are more destructive to the total economy than the worst fires, and every bit as bad as the poorest lumbering practice.

FOREST FIRES

Forest fires in the Southern Appalachians are of shocking frequency. Millions of acres have been worn down by repeated burning to a point where not only the trees but the biological layers of the soil are gravely depleted. More than two thousand serious forest fires a year rage in these priceless woods and, according to the Forest Service, ninety-nine per cent are man-made, most of them of an incendiary nature. That is to say that they were started with deliberate intention, not necessarily malicious, perhaps to clear a piece of land or to improve the browse. For mountain farmers, having few natural pastures, expect to graze their cattle on the forests. This the woods can support without damage, but in order to hasten out the growth of new shoots in spring the farmer often burns off the winter's dead leaves and shoots. True, this does quicken the coming of greenery—providing that the fire does not get out of hand and burn down the whole forest—a risk too likely to become reality, and regarded with entirely too much resignation. Crown fires, so much feared for their destruction of mountain homes and even lives, are rare. But a slow, thorough, deep-burning ground fire is very wasteful, for it eats out the humus, and destroys the valuable ground cover, too. When new seeds fall, it is in soil unfitted to nurture them.

Many man-made fires are inadvertent, or, more exactly, due to carelessness in burning off brush. Careless logging methods cause fires by leaving a vast matchstick pile of slash which goes up like tinder from any spark, as soon as it has dried. Practically every bit of this loss is preventable.

LOGGING—YESTERDAY AND TOMORROW

The forests constitute the greatest single natural resource of the Southern Appalachians, a self-renewing resource if properly conserved. The hunting which the mountain man so dearly loves, the herb industry, the tourist trade, and even the water power depend, ultimately, on the maintenance of the forest. This does not mean that the timber should not be cut. Except in the national and state parks and on vital watersheds, it is only right and sensible to treat the forest as a lumber crop. It is a crop in which all the mountain dwellers can share, for by far the greatest part of our woods is in private ownership; indeed, almost every mountaineer is a landowner and a tenacious one, and almost all own trees, either farm woodlots or else great forest tracts.

But instead of treating the trees as a crop, their owners too often considered them a mine. True, heavy lumbering was a long time in beginning, for the lack of railroads, or even good cart roads until the seventies of the last century, made our timber inaccessible, and there then was still plenty of lumber, both hardwood and softwood, to be had in the northern states. Today, with the northeastern and Great Lakes forests far past their production prime, the Southern Appalachians possess the most promising stand of hardwoods in America. They are close to the center of the wood-consuming provinces, and with the advent of the portable sawmill there are few stands in the wildest parts of our mountains that are not potentially accessible.

The cut of timber trees here has gone through various stages, successively deleterious. At first, about sixty years ago, only the most precious cabinet woods were culled—walnut, cherry, and magnolia, with a selection of the choicest construction timber from yellow poplar (lumberman's name for tulip tree) and white pine and basswood. The mills did not bother with logs less than twenty inches thick at the small end! In a decade, they were glad to get logs twenty-four inches at the stump end. Even so, the lumberman could still select nothing but perfectly clear poles containing at least three hundred and fifty board feet.

By 1905, it is said, the finest cabinet woods and the longest, soundest construction timber had been so culled that white oak and chestnut, once despised, were being taken, and very slender logs of those. Today the average grade of lumber has been lowered as much as forty per cent of what was acceptable in 1905; and markets have developed for one species after another—black and scarlet and chestnut oak, chestnut, and sugar maple, birch, beech, black gum, and hemlock—which were scornfully passed over by the early loggers.

Formerly enough timber was left standing to justify reworking cut-over areas for pulp and tannin extract. But such woods have been reworked time and again, sometimes eight times in the last half century. Probably two billion, two hundred and fifty million board feet of Southern Appalachian lumber is being cut annually.

The result has been that all the finest trees, and most valuable species, have been pulled out of the forest as if they were objectionable weeds, while the species of little commercial value, like dogwood, have been left to multiply. The only trees that were certain to be spared were superannuated specimens, usually full of disease and decay and taking up far more than their share of the light and soil moisture. This is selective logging with a vengeance! By comparison, clean-cutting of the hardwood forest is wiser practice. For it gives all the seedlings, of all kinds of trees, an equal chance to come up in a swift, uniform, healthy growth. Indeed such second growth is worth more to the owner and the miller than many a virgin forest with its too large proportion of superannuated and seedling trees.

Forest-fire prevention and sound logging practice could, in most places, restore the full timber resources of the Southern Appalachians. The production of this resource is a matter that concerns not only the owners but the whole country, for everyone, whether he realizes it or not, is a heavy consumer of forest products, and he pays a price that is directly influenced by diminished quality and quantity, wood waste, and mismanagement.

CHAPTER FOUR

BLUE RIDGE WILD FLOWERS

by Donald Culross Peattie

THE APPALACHIAN PLANT TYPE

The Appalachians may be low as mountains go but adventure for the plantsmen in them is high. True, they lack certain types of mountain vegetation, as for instance that of the arctic-alpine zone which is in popular opinion typified by edelweiss. Yet neither in the Alps nor on the Riviera, nor in California or New England, have I seen anything more superb than the summits of the Black Mountain Range of North Carolina ablaze from end to end with thousands of acres of purple rhododendron. There are no more beautiful flowers than the many species of trillium found in the Appalachians, almost every one with a different and delicious fragrance, yet each unlike any odor in the world, so that there is no describing them to those who have never smelled them. Certainly there is no odder flower on any tropic isle than that of our wild gingers—"monkey-jugs" some mountain folk call them—each with its little jug-shaped calyx half buried in the earth and hidden under its mottled leaf.

Now, to those who have never seen them, trillium and bloodroot and pinesaps are unimaginable plants. So too is strawberry shrub, with its dark red nipple-form flowers (called "bubby-blossoms" by the mountain folk) and its strange odor, something like fermenting strawberries. In all the world there is nothing exactly like our superb locust shrubs, that gardeners sometimes call rose acacia, species of *Robinia* with great rose-purple butterfly-shaped flowers in pendant trusses that look too big for their twigs. Unique too is galax. Characteristically Appalachian are our dainty species of bluet in the spring, our striking sorts of turtlehead in autumn, some purple and some white.

All this is but a way of saying that many, and often the most characteristic, of our mountain plants belong to a distinctive flora, the Appalachian, one of the great floral provinces of the earth. The influence of the Appalachian flora is felt far; it reaches Canada and Florida and the prairie states. But the point of its greatest concentration, the center of its distribution, its very capital, is in the Southern Appalachians. Here you have it in its most nearly pure form, with perhaps some two hundred species, out of about two thousand, endemic—that is, native to and wholly confined to the Southern Appalachians only, as defined in the strictest sense. The further off you go from the Southern Appalachians, the less there is of this flora, and the more, on its periphery, it becomes diluted by, and finally yields place wholly to, contiguous floras. These are the circumpolar flora on the north, the Great Plains flora on the west and, on the south, the subtropical flora of the southern coastal plain.

Perhaps it is not possible to characterize the Appalachian flora in any single, simple way, for there is nothing simple or single about it. It is very large, it grows under the most various conditions of altitude, temperature, moisture and soil. Yet one can say that certain families are superbly represented in the Southern Appalachians. Take, for instance, the lily family (in the widest sense) with sixty native species in our area, almost a fourth of them endemics. Or the orchid family, of which our region has, for an area in the temperate zone, a fine showing. More than fifty ferns (a group that always lends to any plant landscape an air of coolness and bespeaks a well-tempered environment) are found in these mountains. Probably no other region of the same extent has so many kinds of violets—or such beautiful ones as the long-spurred and the pansy-like crowfoot. The Southern Appalachians form one of the world's most interesting centers for the study of the magnificent heath family, to which belong such favorites as rhododendron, azalea, and trailing arbutus.

GREEN MANSIONS OF APPALACHIA

So, under the shelter of pervading woods grows a richly various vegetation which runs to pellucid or filmy leaves, often of the compound or dissected type familiar in the fronds of maidenhair fern. The flowers represent, as a matter of fact, an astonishingly large number of families—far greater than in all of Europe, or all of our western states—proof, perhaps, of the geological antiquity of our flora. In common they have, botanically speaking, little enough. But, dropping the standards of science for those of sense impression, one might remember Appalachian wild flowers as seldom big, gaudy or resplendent, but rather like most forest flowers they are delicate, fresh-looking, and fragrant.

Indeed the fragrance of an Appalachian year deserves, at the hands of some science not yet conceived, a thorough treatment. There is no measure for a smell, and there is no way of describing one until it is known. But Napoleon is said to have stated that were he set down blindfold on his native Corsica he would have known the place by the odor of the *maquis*, the dense scrub that covers so much Mediterranean land. William Beebe has testified to the many bad smells of much of the vegetation of the Galápagos Islands. Robert Louis Stevenson refers to the "graveyard odor" of certain fog-swept groves near Monterey, California. And, though I could not very well prove it, it has always seemed to me that the Southern Appalachians have an unusually large number of intensely fragrant flowers, of aromatic leaves and barks. It may be that the moisture of the air here, coupled with the warmth, helps to bring plant fragrances to our attention. Certain it is that from the beginning of spring to the end of winter, the very air and earth smell deliciously. Nor are all the odors due to our flowers. One must add the pervading aroma of sun-baked pine needles and the shade-steeped smell of ferns and lichens and fungi.

Indeed, some of these humbler plants contribute much to the harmony and wealth of the Appalachian vegetation and give it much of its velvet depth and green unity. It is said by those who know that in no other part of the country are there so many kinds of mosses as in the Southern Appalachians, many of them unique, others with surprising affinities in distant parts of the world. Though so slight in commercial importance, our mosses are nevertheless economically vital in the job they perform of acting as soil and moisture conservators. There are few good Appalachian landscapes that are not richly clothed by these ancient and delicate plants which beautify all that they touch. It is not possible here to do justice to the fascinating fungi of our region. Many are strangely beautiful, some subtle in color, some as showy as flowers, some ghostly. The abundance of fungi in any region is largely conditioned by the abundance of rainfall. With our heavy precipitation it is natural that the fungus growth should be great. There are handsome shaggy bear's-heads, and delicate little coral fungi. There are superb great brackets and an endless variety of bright-colored boleti. Many are parasitic upon our trees; others are saprophytes, which merely turn back to mold the dead wood in the forest, and form tremulous rimes upon every old twig. Others seem to enter into mutually dependent relations with our greatest forest trees. Indeed, some of the commonest and most attractive toadstools are merely the transitory fructifications above ground of an elaborate perennial system of "spawn" below ground, which not only intertwines with the great tree roots, but in some cases penetrates far and high into the tissues of the trees themselves.

Obviously the total plant life of the Southern Appalachians is then not made up solely of trees and wild flowers. It is extremely rich in the "lower" plants, mosses, fungi, and ferns. The whole forms a flora of the greatest complexity and fascination and all of it in a state of delicately balanced mutual adjustment. It is a flora, indeed, in which one can scarcely conceive of a weed if by that we mean a violently aggressive, discordant, unbalancing sort of species—not at least while the vegetation remains virgin. As an illustration of this there is the story of the mountain woman who visited Asheville for the first time and saw some dandelions on a lawn. She asked of the owners, and obtained, permission to gather some of the attractive seeds of this exotic rarity, in order to sow them around her door at home!

NINETY-FIVE MILLION YEARS OF FLOWERING

Since land life first appeared anywhere on the North American continent, there has been plant life on the Southern Appalachians. At least, as those mountains are defined in this book to mean the great igneous and metamorphic rocks uplifted from the Roanoke Water Gap to northeastern Georgia, and excluding the sedimentary limestone folds and furrows of the Central and Western Appalachians, it is true to say that almost no portion of our mountains has ever been under the sea since any life first appeared here. For three hundred and fifty million years roots have been thrusting in these rocks, leaves have been falling upon other fallen leaves, sweetening the soil. It is truly a solemn thought that the plant life we see today, necessarily descended from that which grew here so long ago, has a pedigree literally older than the hills! In fact, the first Appalachians came long after the plants; they arose and were worn away after a hundred million years or so, and have arisen again, all without interrupting the peaceful evolution of plant life in this place.

Indeed, it has been suggested that the first of the flowering plants above the rank of conifers originated here, in the period between the first and the present Appalachians, in the Cretaceous some ninety-five million years ago. This theory may astonish some, but the enthusiasts for the Southern Appalachians will find no whit surprising the thought that the higher flowering plants (which botanists call angiosperms) may have found this spot a congenial cradle, and from this point spread over the world, displacing conifers and ferns from their seat of kingship. All of the species of those days, of course, have vanished with the vicissitudes of time, but a mountain man, if he could be transported back to the woods of Tertiary times in the Appalachians, would name on sight many familiar forms—magnolias, tulip trees, sassafras, sycamores, sweet gums, beeches, oaks. True, they would not be identical with modern species, but they were doubtless the ancestors of those we see today. Perhaps they were slowly carried up on the backs of the present Appalachians, as the mountains rose in the Tertiary.

Now when the Tertiary was drawing to a close, and the dawn of geologic modernity began, about a million years ago, great glaciers plowed down from Canada, like bull-dozers. They destroyed all life over large areas. And the harsh climate of the Pleistocene killed off many of the semitropical plants that had flourished here in the genial, lush times of the Tertiary. Thus, though the Southern Appalachians were far beyond the rim of the glaciers, we lost many of our species. These mountains, however, became the refuge of such plants as could survive, and when at last the ice retreated, it was from this sanctuary that much of the reforestation of eastern North America came.

In Europe the glaciers had been equally devastating, both directly and indirectly. The tree flora of all Europe was reduced to about eighty-five species. In our own western states a great change had taken place too; the hardwoods had been largely driven out, and in the much more arid climate of the west today it is chiefly the conifers that survive. The fossil record of herbaceous plants is much poorer than that of trees, but probably the changes amongst the wild flowers were as great or greater.

ORIENTAL AND APPALACHIAN KINSHIPS

But in eastern Asia, as in southeastern North America, many of the old Tertiary types of plants had survived—with the curious result that the Appalachian flora has some startling resemblances to that of China and Japan. For instance, the tulip tree, the loftiest forester in the eastern United States and one of our most beautiful and typical Appalachian types, no longer grows, as it did in Tertiary times, in Europe only three thousand miles across the ocean. Nor does it grow today in California, only two thousand miles across the continent. But *nine* thousand miles away in China is found a tree so closely like ours that the differences are little more than pedantic. It may be somewhat startling to think that the Mayflower or trailing arbutus, pride of the pilgrim's land (though it is really an Appalachian type that always seems to me to grow a bit unwillingly in New England) is practically identical with a similar wild flower in Japan. But the fact is that Virginia creeper, trumpet creeper, Carolina jessamine, wild hydrangea, sassafras, persimmon, and witch hazel have their counterparts in eastern Asia, but in vain would you seek them in Europe or the western United States. The same is true of such familiar wild flowers as jack-in-the-pulpit, Dutchman's-breeches, pipsissewa, wintergreen, shooting star, and many others. It is true too of ferns like our dainty little walking fern, the stately cinnamon fern, our maidenhair and the ostrich fern.

A human consequence of this unlikely kinship is strikingly illustrated in Dr. David Fairchild's charming book, *The World Was My Garden*, where this veteran plant introducer tells how he invited Madam Fuji, granddaughter of Prince Ito of Japan, to see on his estate near Washington, D. C. his Japanese flowering cherries; secretly he was planning to offer her a delicious dish of a Japanese vegetable which he was growing there. But on the way his car had a puncture and the lady wandered into the roadside woods. Suddenly she exclaimed: "Mitsuba, my favorite vegetable!" It was the same which Dr. Fairchild had carefully introduced from Japan, and was so proud of being able to proffer. It was honewort, a native American plant. Yet the Japanese species is absolutely identical. "The only difference was," Dr. Fairchild confesses, "that in Japan it was a favorite vegetable while in America no one knew even that it was good to eat."

This kinship of the oriental and Appalachian floras has not proved to be a matter of purely theoretic interest to the botanist who takes a global outlook upon his subject. That kinship is linked to the strange story of shortia, the flower lost for a hundred years in these mountains, and it is bound intimately into the causes of the once celebrated ginseng trade which has made much colorful history in these mountains, when the descendants of Confucius became the customers of the descendants of the Scotch-Irish pioneers of North Carolina and Tennessee! But both the stories of shortia and of ginseng are linked with the name of a gallant French adventurer and ardent plantsman. And so I must turn back the pages of scientific history and tell you something of the life of André Michaux.

ANDRÉ MICHAUX EXPLORES THE MOUNTAINS

There came to Charleston, South Carolina, in 1781 André Michaux, the most eminent botanist who had ever reached these shores from Europe. He was then forty years old, a widower with a son of about seventeen, François André, who accompanied him on most of his trips, and he had been trained by the great Bernard de Jussieu at the Jardin des Plantes in Paris. His mission was to collect for His Majesty Louis XVI the finest flowers and trees of the New World, to be acclimatized at Rambouillet and ultimately to be set out at Versailles. Already he had been to Persia and the shores of the Caspian; now he had come to Charleston to establish an acclimatization garden near what is now Ten Mile Station. Nor did he come empty-handed. He brought with him many flowers of the Old World as a gift to the New; perhaps the most memorable of all was that beautiful fernlike tree with fragrant blossoms, Albizzia, which Southern people call "mimosa tree."

When you are in Charleston, or anywhere in the Carolina "low country" the Appalachians are as out of mind as they are out of sight; there is no hint of their cool breath in the soft heavy air on which the Spanish moss sways dreamily and the mockingbird sails and sings. There is no memory of the speed and song of the mountain creeks, that have laved the roots of rhododendron and spruce, left in the meandering, wide, brown rivers with their black borders of tidal mud. And from the wide-spaced groves of live oaks, the heavy splendor of magnolias, the longleaf pines and thc palmettos, one would never guess that not three hundred miles away there rose steep groves of balsam with their fragrant crowns in the clouds.

But it was primarily to find those mountains and their rare plants that Michaux set out in June for the up-country. Fortunately we possess Michaux's diary of that journey, and of many that followed it. May I be forgiven if I quote from the longer account of his life in my book about the great naturalists, *Green Laurels?*

"The original manuscript is no more than a small pocket diary, dog's-eared with travel, stained, they say, with salt water and bear's grease; stained, too, like most explorers' logs with loneliness and weariness. It was written on his knee, by the flickering of his camp fires. It is fragmentary—full half of it lost by shipwreck—and it ends abruptly, as your journal would do if, unconscious that life will not thus go on forever, warm-blooded, full of the impact of living, you were suddenly to die. . . . Michaux's extant diary begins as he sets off for the mountains with his son and a train of horses. . . .

"At last, out of the still blazing monotony of the piedmont pine woods in the heavy southern June, rose the first trembling mirage of the mountains—the Blue Ridge uplifting a thousand-mile wall of granite, and beyond it, written in a gray dreamy scrawl upon the sky, the Great Smokies, the Craggies, and the Balsams. The travelers were now arrived at the frontier village of Seneca, on the borders of the Cherokee Nation—one of those vile hamlets where two different races meet for the exchange of their characteristic cheaper wares, their national forms of deceit and immemorial vices. But above this rubbish heap rose the mountains. The sound of the Tugaloo and the Keowee, plunging into each other in a perpetual collision, rose above the harsh raven voices of the Indians bargaining for blankets and rum, and petticoats for their wenches, in exchange for their services as guides in the peaks where no naturalist but eccentric William Bartram had ever before adventured. And when the Frenchman and the boy staggered up wearily from feasting upon bear's grease and the strange, wild sweet potato of the Carolinas, they could step out into the night and smell the wind from the mountains blowing fresh and damp, smelling of balsam and resin. The man thought of the morrow, and what strange treasures, never touched before, never suspected, might be in those mountain forests—a resin as precious as camphor, a flower of future fashion more fair than the rose, or a bark to rival quinine of Peru.

"And in the morning the saddle rose under the travelers with the first swells of ground; the great rhododendrons closed about them—and the mountain journey was begun. For those who have seen the Alps or the Rockies, the Appalachians are not likely, as mountains, to stir the heart. They are, rather, a forest upon a high-rolling floor, and in all the continent, in all the world, I believe, there is no such hardwood or deciduous forest as this. All the beauty of the Appalachians is forest beauty; one feels it marching over the hills, filling the valleys, leaving nothing bleak, nothing eroded, nothing arid. Everywhere the murmur of leaves, the trickling or the rushing of water; and overhead, above this father and son, the roar of the wild bees in the June blossoms of the sour gum tree and the chestnut.

"Nor is the forest all kindly. Even today in the country post-offices placards such as these are exhibited: Hunter lost: seen last six months ago south of Bryson City. Woman lost crossing the Balsam range on foot. Children lost, back of Sam Knob, in rhododendron tangles (where the forest floor has never seen the sun in jungles of thorny smilax). Even the birds, wrote Michaux, will not sojourn or sing there:

"June 1st. We continued, still having the river first on our right, then on our left; we had to pass over great boulders, straddle monstrous trees fallen across the jungle of shrubbery, where one could scarcely see where to go on account of the density of the thickets. Lofty peaks towered above us, and the obscurity that a rain-dark sky produced seemed to envelope us in a sombre night. This trouble and confusion was increased by the noise of waterfalls and the crashing on the rocks of the river that we had to ford up to our knees. The savages tore ahead through these streams afoot, or ran along the logs, while the young man and I had horses to guide, so that at last we were forced to dismount, and one of us had always to run ahead to see what had become of them, for there are no trails in those places except those made by bears and occasionally by Indians. I was constantly afraid of treading on snakes, but terrified when I had to ride my horse across the stream on a rotting log covered with crumbling bark and slippery vegetation that had grown upon it.

"After hours of this they arrived exhausted in a little valley, one of those tender, tranquil meadow pockets amid gloomy peaks where, in the midst of so much wilderness, gay, shivering flowers lean on the lip of torrents suddenly quiet, running smooth over the white quartz rocks and the fragments of mica and garnet and gold in the dark sand. In such spots grow bluets darker blue than the sea, and yellow stemless violets. . . . And here the weary travelers rested, dining upon wild strawberries and the coldest pure water that ever Michaux had drunk. A shower swept out of the hills, passed by, and in the twilight, I think, the thrush, solitary priest, must have praised beauty.

"When at last Charleston saw Michaux again it was at the head of a pack train laden down with hundreds of plants—packets of seeds, frail flowers in moss, and shrubs and young trees balled in earth, swaying and joggling to the gate of the garden, looking bewildered and unnatural in this lowland heat and glare."

The next year Michaux again set out for the mountains, but this time in autumn, in order to gather seeds, and to lift roots and bulbs when they are least liable to damage. Once again we find him approaching the steep defiles and frowning ridges of the Toxaway country in which so long ago De Soto had become entangled, but this time it is winter, with icy rains, short and dark days, penetrating winds. Once again let us hear him describe the scene:

"The roads became more difficult as we approached the headwaters of the Keowee on the 8th of December, 1788. . . . Two miles before arriving there I recognized the *Magnolia montana* which has been named *M. cordata* or *auriculata* by Bartram. There was in this place a little cabin inhabited by a family of Cherokee Indians. We stopped there to camp and I ran off to make some investigations. I gathered a new low woody plant with saw-toothed leaves creeping on the mountain at a short distance from the river. The weather changed and it rained all night. Although we were in the shelter of a great Strobus pine our clothing and our covers were soaked. About the middle of the night I went to the cabin of the Indians, which could scarcely hold the family composed of eight persons, men and women. There were besides six big dogs who added to the filth of this apartment and to its inconveniences. The fire was placed in the middle without any opening in the top of the cabin to let the smoke out; there were plenty of holes, however, to let the rain through the roof of this house. An Indian came to take my place by the fire and offered me his bed which was a bear's skin. But finally, the rain having stopped, and annoyed by the dogs which kept biting each other continually to keep their place by the fire, I returned to the camp.

"This place which is called the source of the Keowee is incorrectly so indicated. It is the junction of two other rivers or large torrents which unite at this place and which is known only as the forks of the Keowee.

"On December 11 it froze hard and the air was clear and keen. I noticed a chain of high mountains which extended from west to east and where the frost was little felt in places exposed to the sun. I gathered a *Juniperus* (*repens*) which I had not yet seen in the southern part of the United States but it must be noted that I saw on these mountains several trees of the northern regions such as *Betula nigra*, *Cornus alternifolia*, *Pinus Strobus*, *Abies*, Spruce, etc. We crossed a space of about three miles in the midst of *Rhododendron maximum*."

Michaux made many other trips in the Appalachians (as well as to Florida, to Lake Mistassini in Canada, and out on the prairies of Illinois, then unexplored). He ascended Grandfather and Roan Mountains, Yellow Mountain and Table Rock and traversed the Linville Gorge. Often he crossed to Tennessee, to Kentucky, and crossed back again. He stopped with "a Mr. Andrew Jackson," and he turns up in George Washington's diary as a guest at Mount Vernon. Thomas Jefferson wished to send him to the Pacific, upon the journey subsequently taken by Lewis and Clark, but the French government interfered. Thus Michaux became a well-known character of the frontier. Trappers and Indian chiefs, planters and farmers, got to know him and had plants ready to show him, and passed him on with letters. On the summit of Grandfather Mountain, he records with naïve pleasure, he sang (under the mistaken impression that this was the highest peak in the Appalachians) the Marseillaise, and shouted "Vive l'Amérique et la République Française! Vive la liberté!"

"When he left America he had no expectation that he would never see it again. But the ship 'Ophir' bore him away under ill omens, and off the coast of Holland she went aground and lay on her beam ends. Michaux, all his cargo lost, was washed ashore unconscious on the beach at Egmont. But in Paris honors awaited him, and his diary ends abruptly in the full flood of dinners and visits of state. The republic hastened him off on a new venture, dispatching him in the Baudin expedition for ultimate Oceania. On the way Michaux demanded to be put ashore at Madagascar. He foresaw new worlds to conquer, fierce tropic splendors to make his own. Instead, the great black island claimed him, and he was brought out of the mountains, dead of fever."

SHORTIA, THE LOST FLOWER

Michaux's specimens were carefully studied and named by the French botanists, but no one could make anything of one strange little leaf and pod—just a fragment. It carried no notes except the statement that it came from the "high mountains of Carolina" and it gathered dust for half a century until young Dr. Asa Gray and John Torrey came to Paris, preparatory to writing his great *A Flora of North America*, to see all American type specimens in Europe.

"I have discovered a new genus," he records on April 8, 1839, "in Michaux's herbarium—at the end, among the *plantae ignotae*. It is from that great unknown region, the high mountains of North Carolina. We have the fruit, with the persistent calyx and style, but no flowers, and a guess that I made about its affinities has been amply borne out on examination. . . . I claim the right of a discoverer to affix the name. So I say, as this is a good North American genus and comes from near Kentucky, it shall be christened *Shortia*." Dr. Charles Wilkins Short was a fine pioneer botanist of the Bluegrass State. So shortia was described in botanical manuals of the time, always with the baffling statement: *flowers unknown*. In the meantime Dr. Gray had set out at the first possible moment after his return to America, in the summer of 1840, to search for it. He made his headquarters at Jefferson, in Ashe County, North Carolina, and searched far and wide—all in vain. Evidently he did not connect the reference in Michaux's diary to the "little shrub with scalloped leaves," with the fragment in the Paris herbarium. He could have no idea that he was more than one hundred miles from Michaux's original station or type locality, nor that he was hunting for it in the wrong season and at the wrong altitude.

"Year after year I have hunted for that plant!" Gray was to write later. "And I grew sorrowful at having named after Dr. Short a plant that nobody could find. So conspicuous for its absence had this rarity become, that friends of ours botanizing in the mountains two years ago, were accosted with the question— 'Found shortia yet?'—from people who had seen our anxious search for it."

In the meantime Dr. Gray had discovered in an old Japanese herbal the picture of a plant that unmistakably was a shortia, and so there at last he beheld a picture, at least, of the flowers. They might not be identical with those of the lost American species, but they could not be far different. So Dr. Gray's prediction which he had made for the form of the flower, based on the structure of the seed pod, was borne out. Shortia, it was evident, must be a member of the same family as galax.

The search caught the fancy of young Charles Sprague Sargent of Brookline, Massachusetts, the future director of the Arnold Arboretum and America's greatest authority on trees. He turned back to Michaux's original diary and at last he detected in the portion of it already quoted, the resemblance to the fragmentary specimen Gray had seen in Paris. Let me quote, taken up exactly where I broke off a few pages back, the passage in the Frenchman's diary, which at last set Sargent off on a quite different track from that taken by all previous searchers:

Dec. 11 . . . I came back to camp with my guide at the head of the Keowee and gathered a large quantity of the low woody plants with the saw-toothed leaves that I found the day I arrived. I did not see it on any other mountain. The Indians of the place told me that the leaves had a good taste when chewed and the odor was agreeable when they were crushed, which I found to be the case.

A typical chimney top in laurel season

Catawba Rhododendron in bloom in the National Park

The glory of the Rhododendron at Craggy Gardens

Shortia Galaupolia

Trillium

The Black Cohosh

Goat's Beard

Directions for finding this plant:

The head of the Keowee is the junction of two considerable torrents which flow from cascades from the high mountains. This junction is made in a little plain which was formerly a city or village of the Cherokees. In descending to the junction of the two torrents, having the river at the left and the high mountains which look to the north on the right, one finds at about thirty to fifty paces from the confluence a little path formed by the Indian hunters. Continuing in this direction one arrives at last at the mountains where one finds this little shrub which covers the soil along with *Epigaea repens*. [Trailing arbutus]

So in the autumn of 1886, just ninety-eight years after Michaux had written the passage above, Sargent found himself in the Toxaway country, with its steep-gabled high ridges drenched much of the time in rains, and its plunging stream valleys perpetually shaded by dense rhododendron thickets. "Would I were with you," wrote the aged Dr. Gray. "I can only say, Crown yourself with glory by discovering the original habitat of *Shortia* which we will believe Michaux found near where *Magnolia cordata* came from in that first expedition." * Gray's letter arrived in the evening mail, just as the botanists were emptying out their vascula after the day's collecting. Dr. Sargent produced a strange leaf and passed it over to one of his companions with a query. "Why, that's shortia, of course," was the joking answer—which proved no joke at all.

Perhaps I can best describe where, after a century, shortia was found again, by a reference to my own notes, for the day that I discovered shortia for myself was like that when Sargent came upon it, torrentially rainy. I had walked all the way from Tryon to Toxaway in fine weather. Now I was soaked to the skin by a downpour and driven to take shelter in a mountain farmhouse. My host showed the mountain man's disposition to talk to strangers so long as he and not they asked the questions, and as mountain people seldom walk for the sake of exercise or adventure, I was

* It was really Michaux's second expedition to the mountains.

forced to give a complete account of myself. Diffidently I brought out my search for a rare flower. I had no reason to think that my host knew the Latin names of plants.

"I don't suppose you know of a flower around here called shortia?" I assumed.

Even the smallest of his children from the other side of the stove chorused a scornful, "Of course we know shortia!"

Why, boasted my host, he guessed he had more shortia on his land than anybody else in the country, "and there didn't many people got any, because it was the durndest rare flower God ever made."

My host invited me freely to take all of his shortia I wanted—which was very little—and gave me minute directions for finding the trail (perhaps the same that Michaux followed, almost certainly so, indeed). The rain having momentarily abated, I set out according to directions, expecting to have a steep ascent, and found myself going down, and down . . . and *down*.

According to my map I must now be down to about fifteen hundred feet, and well inside South Carolina. I realized at last how Gray and others were misled by Michaux's note "High mountains of Carolina." He didn't say *on* the high mountains. He meant to say *among* the high mountains. High they certainly loomed in this dark and gloomy place, dominated by the crashing of Horsepasture Creek as it plunges toward the piedmont, above which tumult I could hear the growling of another storm approaching. There was not a flower anywhere this early in the year and under the eternal shade of the rhododendron leaves. The heavy forest was utterly silent and lonely, and I could hear another downpour coming through the woods, with a sizzling sound, and see the veil of rain water trailing swiftly toward me.

And then, suddenly, right under my feet, spreading far as I could see under the rhododendron, growing on the steep bank with leaves of galax and partridgeberry, I beheld the long-sought-for little flower, its round leaves beginning to curtsy, and its frail sweet bells to swing under the first pelting of the rain. I set a trowel under a plant of it, and just as the rain smote my face, I lifted from the sour soil a living *Shortia galacifolia.*

I like to remember that Dr. Gray lived to hold, too, in his hands the blossoms of shortia, sent him from North Carolina. His many searches for it resulted in the discovery of hosts of other new species in our mountains. And it is probable that his discovery in the Japanese herbal of another kind of shortia, so far away across the world, stimulated him to make the pioneering discovery that the floras of eastern Asia and eastern North America are cousins descended from Tertiary ancestors.

THE DOCTRINE OF SIGNATURES

With the rediscovery of shortia, the strange story of the Asiatic-Appalachian floral kinships is still not exhausted. It has never been more practically demonstrated than in the colorful story of the ginseng trade. But before I tell of it I must explain, first, why the Chinese esteem ginseng so much, and to do so one must first understand the ancient "doctrine of signatures" which is at the root of almost all primitive medicine.

Put in its simplest form, this doctrine would hold, for instance, that to cure cardiac trouble one must seek a plant with a heart-shaped leaf. Hence Shakespeare's name of heart's-ease for the violet. To cure hepatic ailments, find a liver-shaped leaf. Thus do we get the name hepatica for a common spring wild flower. "In brewing medicines, look for an herb the same shape as the organ you want to cure," one mountain woman is quoted as saying, in that excellent book, *Cabins in the Laurel*, by Muriel E. Sheppard.

The Cherokees were ardent adherents of the doctrine. Thus a little orchid, the rattlesnake plantain, with net-veined leaves, looks enough like a snakeskin to suggest that it may be a "rattlesnake-master" or cure for snake bites. Another plant, the black cohosh, has a spike of button-like seed-pods, like an uplifted rattlesnake tail. So it too was deemed sovereign against the venom of the serpent. The mountain folk, having a deep respect for rattlesnakes, put credence in a whole list of other antidotes, mostly based on the doctrine of signatures. They are convinced, too, that their Indian predecessors here knew a great deal more than they told about the good points in the native flora—which indeed they did. It is remarkable that almost a third of the plants used in Cherokee medicine have held a place in the official *United States Pharmacopeia*, although only about half of these are employed for the same ills for which the Cherokees relied on them. Yet even a sixteen-per-cent agreement between the red medicine man and the white one is tribute to the Indians' centuries of experimentation, resulting in the beginnings of a genuine science of materia medica.

So the mountain people might not smile at the Cherokee belief that the tight-sticking burr of wild comfrey is a signature for a love potion boiled from the root—to make a lover stick to you. According to a statement I have read, a decoction of the root is still boiled in these mountains by some women and administered to husbands as a "manhood" medicine. The Cherokee woman ate plants with milky juice to keep her breasts full for her sucklings. And the old wives of the mountains today are not averse to taking, sometimes, a dose of squawroot for "female complaints," or of giving their teething children a little papooseroot.

The desideratum of all the ancient herbalists, just like the patent-medicine manufacturer of today, was a panacea, something that will cure anything that ails you. And what would the "signature" for that be? Why, a man-shaped root, of course. In Europe this was generally supposed to be the mandrake (an Old World member of the nightshade or potato family, quite unlike our American mandrake or May apple). With its bifurcated root, it sometimes remarkably reproduced also the head, arms and other external organs of a man, or, again, of a woman. Plainly this was an herb of the most powerful and desirable "vertues," as the herbalists said, and in order to keep the trade in it to themselves they beset its extraction with many difficulties. It was declared so dangerous that one who touched it might die. Hence it had to be encircled first with a chain of iron and then dragged out by dogs! It grew, according to some, only under gallows where it was fed upon human decay; according to others it "will give a great shreeke at the digging up." Besides curing "everything," it was thought by some to be sovereign in certain "loving matters, too full of scurrilitie to set forth in print, which I forbeare to speake of," says old Gerard primly.

THE 'SANG DIGGERS

Now if our ancestors of Shakespeare's time believed in this sort of thing (even though Gerard himself was skeptical) it is not surprising that the Chinese had similar faith in one of their plants which they called jen-shen or root of life. A member of the English ivy family, it is rather an inconspicuous plant, growing about eight to fifteen inches high and producing three leaf-stalks at the summit of the stem; each of these bears five leaflets, arranged radially, like the fingers of the hand. And from the triple fork of the leaf-stalks arises the slender little flower-stalk bearing a tight head of six to twenty little greenish flowers, followed in autumn by bright red berries. Such are the outward and visible signs of the underground parts that for thousands of years the Celestials have held in almost holy awe. For the root is a spindle-shaped affair having a manlike or womanlike form and, sometimes as in the case of mandrake, the semblance of head, arms, legs and the like. To the Chinese this root bears the supreme signature and must be fit to cure every ill and prolong life. Mixed with the powdered antlers of a buck, it is also believed by the hopeful to be a sovereign aphrodisiac. And though I must draw over its further specific effects the veil of reticence, like Gerard, it is plain that such a root would be in high demand. When we consider how many Chinese have lived in China since the doctrine of signatures was first accepted, we can readily see how jen-shen has been uprooted from every last nook and cranny of the Flowery Kingdom.

European traders soon became aware of the exorbitant prices paid for jen-shen. But when they asked their own herbalists for the root, there was none to be found on the whole continent. Then, in 1715, jen-shen, or ginseng as we call it, was discovered in Canada. For it was another of the ancient Tertiary types that grows only in eastern Asia and eastern North America. And naturally such a plant would be found abundantly in the Southern Appalachians. It is said that it was Michaux who taught the mountain folk how to recognize it, when to collect it and how to prepare it and find a market for it. Indeed, the first American ship ever to set out to engage directly in the Chinese trade was the "Empress of China," which sailed in 1784 for Macao with a load of ginseng to exchange for tea, ginger, silk and camphor. The American species proved acceptable to the herbalists of Cathay, and so was begun the colorful trade which was to enjoy more than a century of profit. Thus grew up here in the mountains a special profession, that of the 'sang diggers.

The Indians too have engaged in 'sang digging, at times. In 1877, for instance, the price paid them by the wholesalers was fifty cents a pound—or equivalent to three days' wages. It is notable that in the ancient Cherokee "magic formulas," ginseng root had always been reckoned as of human form and called "great man" or "little man," though the name of the plant as a whole, in Cherokee, is Atalikuli, meaning "it climbs the mountain." The Cherokees employed it for headaches, cramps and female complaints.

The retail price of ginseng in America has fluctuated, going as high as twelve dollars a pound, and when war breaks communications, there is sometimes no market for it. But though nobody ever grew rich out of 'sang, many a mountain family has been kept from starvation by it, for after all Nature produces it; it costs nothing in cash to harvest it, and though much skill is required to dry it properly, this too involves little outlay. It must be dug in autumn for if collected at any other season it shrinks more on drying and, because appearance is everything under the doctrine of signatures, this would impair the market value.

'Sang digging is an essentially nomadic affair, for the diggers must range far over the mountains and into the uttermost depths of the forest to find their quarry. So whole families may be engaged in the hunt; they work fast because there is just the one season and an immense territory must be covered in it. A mountain man once described to me a party of 'sang diggers. He was no timid soul himself, but: "They was the most terrifying people I ever see," he confessed. "I was over in the Balsams, near the Pink Beds, when I see them coming down through the woods—men and women with eyes that didn't seem to see nothing, and their clothes all in tatters, and their hair all lank and falling down on their shoulders. They humped along through the woods like b'ars, muttering to themselves all the time, and stooping, and digging, and cursing and humping on and digging again."

I can't say if all 'sang diggers were like this; the only mountain people I have met in the 'sang business today were growing their own, as a crop—a slow process (with a seven-year wait for maturity!) and woefully subject to theft. I must confess indeed that I have seldom in all my wanderings in the Southern Appalachians seen any ginseng. It is more plentiful in my experience in the northern suburbs of Chicago! The 'sang diggers seem to have worked themselves out of a job, like their Chinese brothers.

A CLIMB UP MT. MITCHELL

Perhaps I can most fittingly close these rambling pages on the mountain wild flowers with the notes that I made upon a climb to the top of Mt. Mitchell. I find that even to read over to myself the names of the glorious plants I encountered that long summer day, brings back all the zest of that scramble, with its heart-lifting views. Certainly I never had a more botanically instructive day in the field, for to climb any of our high peaks is to pass from the warm temperate zone of the splendid passionflower to the Canadian zone where the white chalice of the mountain oxalis peeps from the moss. One obtains thus a cross-section of the whole of Southern Appalachian vegetation. And while not every mountain plant can be seen on the Black Mountain Range, it is, after all, our highest.

A friend and I motored from Tryon on July 9 to Black Mountain—a spot most people remember as a momentary halt on that superb train ride from Marion to Asheville, where the track snakes its way up and over the divide and may be seen looping far below you. But Black Mountain has an interest for botanists. For here died in 1818 an excellent English collector, John Lyon. Out of the somber peaks of the Black Mountain Range, so named for its dark covering of spruce and balsam, Lyon brought many of the rarest and loveliest plants of the Carolina mountains. In this town he was laid low with his last illness. A friend, it is said, held him up that he might look out of the window at the great dark billowing mountains he had loved so long, and with their outlines burned on his retina, he closed his eyes.

We passed the early part of the night in a mountain hostelry. As we had no camping equipment to spend the night on Mt. Mitchell, we must start early if we were to get back by nightfall from a climb to the summit—6,711 feet—and a round-trip hike of almost forty miles. So we dressed shivering in the cold mountain air at the cheery hour of three, and by four had struck a long stride for Montreat. It is a settlement sunk in a deep gorge, dominated by the roar of a mountain stream, but it has a splendid Appalachian type forest overhead that, too leafy now in midsummer, made the settlement seem gloomy and damp. But there was stately white alder in flower to light the way, and almost every rotting stump was covered with the pallid little frogspike orchid. The first shafts of sunlight caught the great pink flowers of rose acacia.

A thousand feet above Montreat, on the slopes of Pinnacle Mountain, we met with the brilliant gold spires of Aaron's-rod, one more of the east-Asia and southeastern-American "splits," with great golden butterfly-like blooms, and handsome, clear bright-green foliage like that of an ash tree. There were not many other flowers here, but the forest cover was superb, and up we climbed under tulip tree and chestnut oak, mountain magnolia, dogwood, and silverbell. There was not a conifer to be seen.

It was at about four thousand feet that we saw the first of the flowering raspberry or raspberry rose, looking like a dark red *Rosa rugosa* or Japan rose of our gardens. The great, lush rose-purple petals, and the big three-lobed leaves, sometimes a foot across, were rather like some garden shrub—startling in the loneliness and wildness of this place, and strangely glowing in the deep shade of the primeval forest. We tried some of the big raspberry-like fruits, but they were insipid—and we were thirsty as the day grew warmer and we struck the old logging railroad. This has since been turned into an easy-graded highway making it possible for the laziest to reach the summits. But walking ties is not a lazy man's gait at any time. The first ten minutes aren't so bad; after that it's a question of endurance in the face of torture. After an hour of it we decided to go back to mountaineering again though we had now lost the trail, and scrambled up another thousand feet until in mid-morning, breathing fast, but still fresh and zestful, we flung ourselves down in a saddle-shaped meadow near the summit of Pinnacle Mountain. It was carpeted deep in mosses, the common little polytrichum which makes miniature "Black Forests," the curly broom moss and spongy beds of sphagnum, the "sheet moss" of the nurserymen who use it to ball the roots of trees and shrubs. All this was fed by a slow seepage of clear water that seemed to be slipping down the hillside in a broad film. Here on this Parnassian slope we flung ourselves down to rest, and cooled our wrists and calmed our pulses, enjoying a view of a fair share of all western North Carolina, with Pisgah tossing up a blue cone-shaped peak on the faint horizon.

Here mingled flowers coming up from the lowlands and stopping at approximately this altitude, with more distinctly montane species descending from the higher slopes and marking a lower limit in this meadow. The splendid Canada lily was abundant all over this meadow, and the curious big flypoison lit up the sward with flecks of white. There was a lilac fleck here and there from the downy horsemint, and a brilliant lilac-purple display from that splendid orchid, the fairyfringe. The mountain sundrops were as gold as we remembered buttercups to have been in our childhood. And everywhere sprang the exquisite mountain bluet which is not forget-me-not blue like the common kind, but a deep, almost a gentian blue—one of the daintiest mountain flowers I remember having seen anywhere, the high meadows of the Alps not excepted. The Southern Appalachians, indeed, are the center of distribution for bluets, as they are for trillium, azalea, wild ginger, and many another clan of plants which find their greatest expression here.

Not content with this mixture of colors, Nature plunged boldly ahead with her effects to mingle vermilion with lilac, by adding everywhere the shooting stars of the fire pink, which is about as "pink" as the dress parade uniforms at Buckingham Palace. In this meadow we saw the last of the dark leathery flowers of urnvine, of galax and cow wheat, St.-John's-wort and meadow rue. Lowland plants, they could climb no higher. We said farewell here, too, to the flame azalea, surely one of the world's most splendid flowers, with its orange-yellow, honey-yellow, and flame-red corollas—sometimes all three combinations on the same bush.

Still anxious to avoid the tie-walking on the log railroad, we decided to cut up through the dense thickets of Catawba rhododendron, which my mountain friends insist is the only "true" rhododendron, for they assert that the great-leaved common kind is laurel, while what I call mountain laurel they will call ivy. Some, indeed, wish to call the Catawba rhododendron "blue laurel," though its glorious flowers, in great heads, are purple to my eyes. When they light up hundreds of thousands of mountaintop acres in earliest summer you realize that no name for them expresses their breath-taking splendor. But this shrub was out of flower now, and within five minutes of struggling to line-buck, or creep under, or wriggle through, or swim over, this intricate growth, we could find no names sufficiently harsh for it. I understood now how it is possible in winter, when the weather can be intensely severe here, for persons to become entangled in this scrub and never get out. I saw how so many men were found dead on the brambles around the Sleeping Beauty's castle, and it seemed a question what maiden could be worth it.

Mountain folk call this growth a "bald"—meaning that compared with the densely forested peaks, the knobs covered with Catawba rhododendron appear close-cropped. Nothing is so deceptive as appearances! The "heath balds," as botanists call them because most of the associated shrubs like mountain laurel, blueberry, and minniebush are of the heath family like rhododendron itself, can only be compared to the *macchia* of the Mediterranean, the chaparral of California, and the *Krummholz* of the Alps, or the "lashorn thickets" of dwarf spruce on high mountains of Virginia, all of which are practically impenetrable growths of scrub.

The loss incurred by one mile of heath bald traversed was one gold watch, one pair of gold cuff-links, one fountain pen, one hour of valuable daylight and two tempers. The flowers that consented to grow in the hateful shade of the rhododendron, in the thin and very sour peat, were few. The oddest of them was a little orchid, the twayblade, which I would certainly never have seen under its deep carpet of moss if I had not been wriggling like a copperhead on my stomach at the time.

Presently the logging railroad caught up with us again, and I hailed its accursed ladder of torment with joy, and gladly racked my limbs on the ties once more. Mt. Mitchell was now in sight, though it did not seem to me a bit higher than the Black Brothers to the north, and indeed it has never been settled beyond dispute that they are not higher than their more famous neighbor. The view across to the Craggy Range was superb, and far to the north peaks rolled up the sky in a thin blue line that culminated in a sudden peak that was probably old Grandfather Mountain.

Spruce and balsam enclosed us now, with mountain ash the principal deciduous tree. The look and feel of the whole world about us was now really montane, though not alpine, for none of the Southern Appalachians, situated so far south as they are, ever break into a genuinely arctic-alpine flora. The railroad ended abruptly in a logging camp, apparently deserted. While we were hunting for a trail to the summit of old Mitchell, two fellow human beings appeared, a barefoot young woman and a child at her breast. With sweet gravity she received our salutations, and walked a way with us to show us the trail, changed the child over to the other side, and when we looked back once, she waved the baby's hand at us in salute. Above the lumber camp the forest is in virgin condition. The air was spiced with the delicious aroma of balsam and everywhere, covering every bit of soil like a carpet, clothing the dead logs of balsam (though seldom of spruce), covering the ancient boulders, swathing the tree butts, and climbing the trunks to the top, ran the mosses, and their strange kin the liverworts, and those most mysterious and elfin creations of all the plant kingdom, the lichens. Never anywhere have I seen mosses so beautiful except among the California redwoods. Outstanding are two mosses which, though I had resolved to use no scientific names, I can, for lack of common ones only call by their botanical monickers of *Hylocomium splendens* and *Hypnum crista-castrense*, a shining filigree that blanketed the soil and the standing boles. Rocks showed a soft sage-green pervading sheet of sphagnum. Some trees had as many as a dozen kinds of moss and eight or nine liverworts growing together. The lichens, on the tree limbs as on the soil and rocks, curled and dripped—beard lichen, reindeer moss, pyxie lichen and many others I had not the time nor skill to recognize.

Deep in among the lycopods or club mosses grew the mountain oxalis, looking exquisitely dewy and fresh; everywhere the big poisonous leaves of hellebore were ranked, and the brilliant red berries of trillium stood boldly erect. Rosebells and balsambells rose out of the moss. And still in flower, reminding one of spring in the foothills, the mountain saxifrage first discovered by Michaux tossed the spray of its precise and dainty petals. The most brilliant flower in bloom was a great lavender-purple turtlehead, *Chelone Lyoni*, named, of course, for John Lyon who died at Black Mountain.

When we climbed the observation tower at the very summit, a cloud rolled in and spoiled the view; in a moment we were enveloped in it; our shirts, wet with perspiration, became icy sheets, and we fled the place, as indeed Nature intended man to do. One could easily imagine how intensely cold must be the winters here, for an isolated peak at 6,711 feet will have a vastly severer climate than an extensive plateau at the same elevation. One could see, too, how it came that Elisha Mitchell, in a cloud cap on his mountain, came to fall from a precipice to his death here in 1857. That fall followed his greatest pride. For many years this Connecticut Yankee of a Southern Presbyterian minister had carried on a feud with Thomas Lanier Clingman (who lived to discover diamonds in these mountains, and to become a general in the Confederate Army), as to which is the highest mountain in all the Appalachian system. Dr. Mitchell had just established by measurement the official height of his preferred mountain when he met his death. His body is buried on the top of his mountain. Clingman is immortalized by the name of the highest peak in the Great Smokies.

CHAPTER FIVE

ADVENTURES AMONG THE MOUNTAIN CRAFTSMEN

by Ralph Erskine

A PERSONAL RECORD

My first sight of a craftsman of the Carolina mountains came when I was a child of six. He made such a vivid impression on me that it seems as though I can recall every element of the incident, the feathery mimosa trees beneath which he stood, arching over to the wide veranda of the old Mills Plantation house, my mother's quick dash indoors to get her sketching materials. He was a very old man, unbelievably ragged, and he carried on his back a fishtrap he had made of white-oak splints. The trap was a long cone which doubled back into itself like an old-time fly-trap. It was designed to be anchored in a stream with bait placed beyond the aperture of the inner cone. The fish could swim in easily to get the bait, but once through the inner cone they could never find their way out again. Probably this primitive trap and the art of weaving it was a survival from one of man's earliest inventions. And, strange to say, in this year of Our Lord, 1943, I found the remnants of just such a trap rotting among the reeds on the river bank.

Years later I sent a New England Windsor chair to Uncle Jim Gosnell, the chair-maker, and asked him to copy it for me. I heard nothing from him. Then one day during a Christmas vacation from college I rode out to see him. He was at work at his home-made lathe in his open-sided cabin-chair shop. His lathe was as primitive as those used in ancient Egypt, nothing but a springy pole fastened to the beams of his cabin so that a rope tied to the end of the pole could be given a turn around the billet of wood he wished to fashion. The other end of the rope was tied to a treadle which hung a few inches from the floor. When Uncle Jim stepped on the treadle the billet whirled toward him and he touched it with his gouge and the chips flew. When he lifted his foot the spring-pole pulled the rope up again, reversing the motion of the billet.

He had made his gouge out of an old file at the blacksmith shop. His only other tools were an ax, handsaw, brace and bit, and a drawknife. With these he fashioned the best chairs of any man in our part of the mountains. Near by was a wood fire around which thin slabs of green hickory were drying. He had bent them over a straight stick, alternating them on one side and the other with two outside parallel sticks over which their ends were caught and held in place by their own pressure. These were the back slats for his chairs. Sets of well-turned rungs were also stacked around the fire to dry. But the chair posts of fresh-cut green wood were carefully kept away from it. Uncle Jim's only glue was the green wood of the posts shrinking around the tenons of the bone-dry, well-shrunk rungs and back slats. When the chair was driven together he put little pegs through the posts and tenons. This was the universal method of joinery of all the chair-makers of the mountains and the only change in it today is the use of angle irons and screws at the joints by those who purchase their wood from the mills and are too hurried to go out and get the green wood as heretofore.

"Why haven't you made me my Windsor chair?" I asked Uncle Jim. I could see my own chair hanging on a peg in his shop.

"Wal, you see, that thar cheer my wife's a-settin' in a-churnin'? I been gittin' forty cents fer hit the last forty years and I just cain't make out. I gotta git fifty cents. Ef I wuz to make that thar cheer o' yourn I couldn't make out." Yet when I offered to sell for him all the hand-fashioned Windsors he could make for $8 each, he was so angered by the profligacy of the "furriners" up north that he turned away from my model in disgust.

When I started my own shop in the mountains to make chairs and chests Uncle Jim was one of the first men I employed. My power-driven lathe had been installed and Wayne Creasman, a youth trained at Mrs. Vanderbilt's Biltmore Industries, was at work at it. Uncle Jim came in to see us and his eyes sparkled as he saw the thin shavings curl away from Wayne's smoothly turning billet. He watched for a minute, then asked timidly, "Might I take a turn at that thar thing?"

"Of course," I said and showed him how to set a square between the head and tail blocks.

Uncle Jim selected the biggest gouge there was and looked it over approvingly. He fixed his steel-rimmed glasses firmly on his nose and planted his feet squarely in front of the whirling billet as though for a mighty effort. Then he glanced over his shoulder at me apprehensively.

"I hain't said I kin turn hit."

But when he touched his gouge to the wood and felt the chips pelt his glasses and saw them fly over his shoulder his tenseness eased and he slid the chisel back and forth on the steel guard till the wood was smooth and round. Then he threw back his shoulders in triumph.

"Give me two days at that thar thing and there hain't no man kin beat me." And he was about right.

It was through Uncle Jim that I learned the meaning of the ancient trade-term "rodman." I had heard it from some Scotch cabinetmakers applied to the draftsman who draws the details of construction and lays out the work for the men, and I had run across it up in Pullman, Illinois, where I had seen all the joinery of the woodwork of a Pullman car drawn on a long, clear board which was called "the rod."

After Uncle Jim had been with me a number of months I noticed that when I gave him the dimensions for a new chair he would take out his two-foot rule and look at it knowingly while we discussed the size of the seat and height of back. But pretty soon he would come back bringing a chair and a four-cornered rod and his jackknife.

"I don't rightly ricollect what you said," he would say as he set the chair before me. Then I would go over it again and when I held my rule against the chair to show him a dimension he quickly placed his rod beside it and made a notch with his knife. Thus he would get from me each detail of spacing for rungs and slats and size of seat, all told by notches cut in the four corners of his rod. At last it dawned on me—Uncle Jim couldn't read a two-foot rule but he was a true "rodman."

At the turn of the century mountain crafts were as yet uninfluenced by tourist trade. The chair-makers worked in the main for their own people. When they made up their stock they peddled it from door to door and traded what they could at the store for tobacco, snuff, salt, cloth, and other "needcessities." The same held true with the men and women who wove baskets of willow twigs, splints, and sometimes honeysuckle vines. The large melon baskets were often works of art with splints graduated in size according to the curves. In making the splints alone much skill and labor was involved, starting with the search for the right young white oaks and hickories, splitting out the long billets and shaping them with a drawknife. Then came careful splitting of the splints with a handknife, inching them down with the grain of the wood, and last the scraping of the splints with bits of broken glass. The weaving of baskets was done by many members of the family, sitting on the porch in rest hours when it was too hot to work in the fields or by the fire on long rainy days of winter. Today, as in all the mountain crafts, the old-time weavers are dying out and youth, in spite of many efforts by schools and social workers to foster the crafts, is loath to spend long hours at such labor.

In the early 1900's pottery was made by the mountain people for the mountain people. There were no modern shapes and beautiful glazes such as are now made for the tourist trade. The only "jugtown" I knew at that time was over at Gowansville in South Carolina, close to Dark Corner, where there was a good demand for jugs which a corncob fits for a stopper and a ring is made to hitch your thumb in when you swing it up to rest on your elbow to pour or to drink. A farmer owned the clay pits, built the kiln in the side of a hill, cut the green oak wood for firing, and supplied the dry pine "lightwood" to get a roaring blaze. Two potter's wheels housed in a log shed were near by. The potters were itinerant "turners" who mixed the clay and kneaded it, and slapped the lumps on the wheels as they kicked them around with their bare feet. It was not a winter occupation. They made their own slip-glaze of powdered shards, clay and white-oak ashes. They knew nothing of colors. The day I was there both the men at the wheels were named Sneider.

"Brothers?" I asked.

"No sir," said one of them. "We're not related but I reckon we're some kin. Ye cain't find a Sneider who don't turn." And I suppose they believed it. To them pottery-making was a family affair in which the secrets of the potter's "grips" were handed down from father to son.

The men made the pottery and the farmer carted it around to his neighbors and the settlements and sold it—the potters and the farmer halved the proceeds. Five cents a quart was the price regardless of shape, a gallon jug, twenty cents, a two-quart pitcher, ten cents. The color was natural burnt red with bottle-green venations where the glaze melted and ran down. All shapes were purely utilitarian except some funny little pigs for the children which whistled when you blew on their snouts. Civilization pressed close around these simple craftsmen but as yet it had not touched them.

Today pottery-making in the mountain area has progressed to a fine art. It may well become a recognized locality for many wares. For years I have regarded the dishes made by Mr. and Mrs. Ernest A. Hilton as ideal accessories in early American settings. They have been much photographed and written about and their wares would be eagerly sought by many large shops in the North if these two aged people could get adequate assistance and could guarantee deliveries. They have built excellent kilns by the roadside on the highway between Marion and Asheville. Many of their forms were taken direct from old pieces brought by Mr. Hilton's people from "across the water," and they have continued the firm glazes of natural fawn color with cobalt-blue rims and blue knobs on bean-pot and casserole covers. The pitchers have spouts made by gently pinching in the sides when the clay is soft. The sizes vary with the shrinking according to their nearness to the fire.

The late O. L. Bachelder exerted a profound influence on all the mountain potters. Crowning sixty years of achievement in ceramics, this man who had carried his churns and crocks around in the mountains and sold them to farmers and stores, built his Omar Khayyam Art Pottery at Candler near Asheville. In 1919 he received the Logan Medal in an applied art exhibition at the Art Institute of Chicago. Paul St. Gaudens says of him, "Bachelder's pottery had a timeless quality. His vases would be superior examples of throwing and glazing in any age or country."

"Old Bach's" friend, Walter B. Stephen, who built the Pisgah Forest Kilns on the old highway between Asheville and Hendersonville, told about Bachelder's death.

"Bachelder was buried in a high location alone. He did not want to be buried in a graveyard. He had no minister, but a woman whom he had befriended read the Sermon on the Mount, the only part of the Scriptures in which he took any stock. He was very kind to people in trouble, the sick, and animals."

One cannot but be impressed by a visit to the Pisgah Forest Pottery, impressed by the beauty of the forms in vases and the brilliance of the turquoise blues. Stephen, the owner, wrote me the other day requesting help in locating a certain lady who had asked him to experiment with Chinese ox-blood reds. He wanted to report progress but had no real success; this is not strange, for that color is reputed to be the most difficult in the world to get and gold is required in the glaze. The war has cut his work to the bone with no people motoring to his door, nor does he seem too happy about the future of his peaceful art.

Wood-carving is a recent art in the highlands, largely an outgrowth from craft schools. Dogwood flowers and naturalistic ornament are everywhere a bit too obvious and romantic from the standpoint of good applied design. Miss Vance and Miss Yale, of the Tryon Toymakers, gave a fine impetus toward sound decoration in carving. Their pupil, Frank Arthur, has achieved a good record in his special order commissions. Of late there has been a vogue for little farm animals whittled out of wood. For the most part they are smoothed and polished to a modernistic slickness. But the character figures carved by young Tom Brown of the Pleasant Hill Academy in Tennessee are different. In them every tool mark counts. They are vibrant with life and motion in their performance of the daily chores and pastimes.

The best weavers of wool and cotton coverlets I knew were Zanie Pitman and Mrs. Tallant. They had no idea that they possessed a valuable skill. They were merely weaving for their home folks and to get a bit of cash now and then from the few "furriners" who came to their valley.

The memory of man is short. Zanie Pitman, sitting at her loom, weaving patterns in blue and white coverlets the names of which told her own history, knew nothing of her own or their origins. Whig Rose! What were whigs and tories to her or what did she know of Wars of the Roses? Virginia Trouble! A complicated design which spoke of the weary journeys of her people through the wilderness of Virginia till they gave up the struggle at the foot of Tryon Mountain! I asked her if she knew anything about it. She shook her head. Then I wanted to know how she had learned to weave these patterns. "They come from Gran'maw's book o' trompin's," meaning the dots and dashes on page after page of a dog-eared notebook that told when to "tromp" the treadles of her loom in designs first recorded in England, then in Ireland, and with the last entries in Virginia.

At the moment "Miss" Zanie had some fine wool homespun on her loom. The warp was pale green and the woof, or "fillin'," red-brown. As I remember it she said she dyed the one with willow bark and the other came from hickory or perhaps madder root. Her dye-pot was an iron kettle down by the spring. She said the wool cloth was "dimity" for winter sheets. On looking up the word dimity I found she had used it in its most ancient meaning, two threads criss-crossing, from the Greek *dis* meaning twice and *mitos* meaning thread of the warp. I bought some of the "wool sheets." For years they kept us warm in the shooting seasons in the north woods and were often used as light summer blankets.

Today aniline dyes have for the most part supplanted those made from indigo and the various simples from which true vegetable dyes were compounded. The ancient skill is kept alive by many purists who are now practicing weaving arts of the finest quality. It is more than a nostalgic hobby of romantic antiquarians. But the thousands of hooked rugs and the coarse weaving done by the roadsides are dyed with commercial dyes. The mountain highways are dotted with shacks where the country poor eke out a pitiful living making hooked rugs of burlap and stocking rings which they snip from the waste of the hosiery mills and loop together. These are dyed in garish colors and worked up in designs which are for the most part pretty terrible—fit accessories to go with the plaster-of-Paris dogs and horses arrayed on northern stands. But buyers come along and the people themselves luxuriate in their new emergence from the silence of hidden fastnesses to places in the stream of life where folks are always passing to be stared at.

Although Granny Pritchard, spinning wool yarn on her "high wheel" in her cabin down in Tryon "hunting country," is representative of the last survivors who carry on as part of their home economy, the many schools throughout the mountains and their related weave shops are not only rescuing this valuable craft from a threatened oblivion but are making the mountain area a producing district which should have a bright future. The people are the same stock as those who have for hundreds of years made the highlands of Scotland the source of the finest woolens in the world. Under the tutelage of Berea, Penland, Pleasant Hill, Brasstown, Biltmore, Asheville, Tryon, Cherokee and Crossnore, hundreds of looms are thwacking away all through the mountains.

Geneva Turner, caddy on the golf course, when promised a new winter coat if she would stop swearing and chewing tobacco, said, " 'Tain't wuth it." I asked Geneva the other day why she no longer caddied.

"I'm workin' at the weave shop."

"How do you like it?"

"I like it fine."

The products of these shops are gaining markets all over the country. The looms now hold wool, silk, linen, cotton, and from them come coverlets, shawls, wool throws like those woven by the *habitants* in Canada, scarves, men's wool ties, baby robes of delicate softness, draperies, tablecloths, luncheon sets, and excellent homespuns for men's suits and women's skirts. Their workmanship is top quality.

The craft school at Penland deserves special mention. Begun by two devoted teachers, Lucy and Rufus Morgan, in 1914, it now has a fine central building for the crafts. It is built on an eminence overlooking a lovely valley. I counted car licenses from twenty-six states parked on its wide terrace one afternoon. Delightful little work sheds are tucked behind laurel thickets and you hear the merry sound of hammers on metal and see old and young working together, people from the neighborhood learning how to earn a livelihood along with strangers who have discovered that life has new meanings when you learn to use your hands. Last time I was there I saw a withered little old mountain woman, neat as a pin and bright as a button, teaching a white-haired gentleman from the North how to spin flax. Again and again the thread that seemed to feed itself so evenly from the spindle of fiber to her nimble fingers grew thin and broke when he took it up. There were many implications in that picture.

Among the crafts milling of grain should not be omitted. Many people from far away obtain from some particular mill fresh-ground whole-wheat and water-ground meal. One owner of a chain of restaurants has purchased an old mill at Flat Rock to supply his ovens. A similar opportunity exists in the mountain areas, but John Reddin voices certain queries. A year or two ago his mill was stopped for the first time in a hundred years by a strange ruling of Government which required of each farmer an affidavit regarding the use of every pound of wheat flour ground from his grain. It frightened the farmers to death. John Reddin said:

"Seems like every time the Guvmint tries to help us little fellers they pushes us down."

John has been a good miller all his life, but he has gone to farming. He and his buxom wife have raised thirteen healthy children and now all his sons are off to the wars. It is too bad that the regulations about reporting wages for Social Security taxes and such things are drying up the ancient sources of fresh-ground grain at a time when values of vitamins and minerals are being emphasized as never before. John holds his hand in the flaky stream with pride as he points out how cool it is as it comes from the slowly turning stones. He says modern high-speed mills heat the grain, that the fats of the germ are removed from commercial flour because it must be made for long-time storage. Yes, those vital power traps of solar energy are now no longer helping the mountain poor as they once did. Even in the village stores of the mountains bakery bread has taken the place of locally milled flour which only a few years ago was a main staple of trade.

There are and have been isolated examples of extraordinary craftsmanship in the mountains. There were the Bechtlers, who from 1831 to 1840, at Rutherfordton, North Carolina, made their own dies and minted gold coins for the people. They built the first "plank" house (house made of hewn timbers instead of the usual full, round logs). It was at Gilbertville where, fifty years earlier, John Sevier and his Over-Mountain Men had joined the troops from Virginia and marched against the British at Kings Mountain. According to the records kept by the old mint at Charlotte, the Bechtlers coined $3,625,840.00 in pure Carolina gold. In addition to that they made jewelry for the mountain people and even contrived fowling pieces and guns which were inlaid with gold. I have seen the great stone wheels they hewed out of granite for crushing the gold quartz, now lying among the alders down by Cathey's Creek where they say the Bechtler mines once were.

Another example of exotic craftsmanship in the mountains which is thriving today and might well lead to something in the future is the gem-cutting by the village miller of Hawk, North Carolina. A year or two ago when I was in California I chanced to meet a famous geologist and told him that I had kept my eyes open as I motored west for interesting gem stones and asked him where I could best find them. His reply was:

"You say you live in the mountains of western North Carolina? Well, go right back home again. True rubies and sapphires have been found there and many semiprecious stones such as garnet, amethyst, aquamarine, zircon, tourmaline, peridot, beryl, topaz, rutilated and reticulated quartz, and hiddenite, a sea-green stone of great beauty found in Alexander County."

Alexander County is near where Roby Buchanan lives, and it was these very stones which so appealed to him as a boy that he found ways and means of learning how to cut and polish them. If you really want to scramble out of civilization and get a strange thrill, climb up to Hawk, above and beyond the Penland School of Handicrafts, on a narrow mountain road beyond Bakersville. There, in a tiny mill with overshot wheel, you will find youthful, mild-mannered, blue-eyed Roby Buchanan who grinds the meal for his neighbors and cuts Carolina gem-stones as perfectly as a Dutch lapidary. His machine is of his own contriving.

His mill stands so close to the road there is barely room to park your car. Across the way is a rocky cornfield and to the rear a wooden race holds in scant control a boisterous stream which spouts from many a crack and hole on its way to his mill wheel. You could put the whole building in a fair-sized living room. His sign, *Local Gems Cut to Order,* means just what it says. Inside the door is his grain mill and to the right in a tiny room is his lapidary equipment. Roby is not a talker. If you persevere you can get this shy craftsman to show you each step in gem-cutting, both cabochon and faceting, ending up with a delightful array of jewels spread out on a bed of cotton, sparkling in the sunlight.

Gem-cutting should be a "natural" in the mountains, worked in conjunction with the making of metal dishes, trays, and vases of the craft schools. Even though "costume jewelry" made of plastics has spoiled the market for inexpensive hand-made jewelry, the matrices of these stones and those crystals in which flaws catch the light are ideal for incorporation in box lids and such, after the manner of the Chinese and Italian craftsmen.

It must be admitted that many heartaches attend the efforts of those who devote their lives to helping the mountain folk. For the most part the handicrafts are carried on by the very poor and needy. One of them said, "We just live from hand to mouth and sometimes the hand don't quite reach the mouth." An old man had brought me a supply of hand-split hickory spindles for my Windsor chairs. He took his money in speechless gratitude and went out and climbed into his wagon. He got almost up to the highway when I saw him stop, tie his mule to a swinging limb and slosh back through mud and rain. He opened my door and stood there turning his hat in embarrassment. "I don't reckon you can rightly understand what it means to an old man like me to get fifteen dollars in the dead o' winter." He had come all the way back to say it.

Such people are well deserving. One of them said to a friend of mine who is alive with outgoing charm, "Your house sits mighty easy. You won't never meet a stranger." * And there is often a gentle poetry about their phrases such as, "The smoke is lazing up today. Hit's goin' to rain." Or shrewd perception in this about a person who does good and then talks about it, "She does, but she undoes."

THE CRAFTS TRAIL

An excellent beginning of a guild for highland crafts was made by Miss Frances L. Goodrich in 1908. She had built up a co-operative selling organization called Allanstand in Asheville. In 1931 she gave this property to the Southern Highland Handicraft Guild, an organization of her promotion which now numbers among its members twenty-nine producing centers. It is primarily an educational organization composed of those schools and shops which

* A compliment to the friend on her outgoing, kindly ways. All who meet her will feel her friendliness and never be ill at ease like a stranger.

have achieved stability and stand for quality. If one were free to browse around in the highlands in search of fundamentals, certainly to do so under their auspices would provide a wealth of experience and delightful association impossible to discover in any other way. And in these days of restricted travel one could pick at random any of these centers, drop a card of inquiry in the box and get a prompt reply about places to stay and opportunities to do war work that would absolve the most scrupulous of charges of selfishness in seeking a vacation.

Many of the stations of the Guild are outside our territory, as at Berea, Hindman, Ary, Pine Mountain, all in Kentucky, and Bris, Virginia. If one starts the trail at Norris, Tennessee, where a great variety of Guild articles are, a side trip should be made to Pleasant Hill where Tom Brown makes his carved figures and other workers produce dolls, and wood-turned specialties.

At Russellville, Tennessee, to the northeast on highway U. S. 11E, Sarah Dougherty guides the people in making bags, zipper purses, fine towels, and luncheon sets.

The most spectacular trip, probably, in the entire mountain region is the climb to Gatlinburg, Tennessee, and on over the pass at Newfound Gap where Clingmans Dome is close to the south, with the deeps of Nantahala National Forest below us to the east. Gatlinburg, Tennessee, hangs high on the western slope of the Great Smoky Mountains. It is famous for a museum of Cherokee Indian relics; the Arrowcraft Shop has hand weavings and crafts, and Woodcrafters and Carvers offer furniture, patterns, and metal work. Cherokee, North Carolina, is down the mountain in the Cherokee Indian Reservation. Here the Indian School makes braided rugs, baskets, wood carvings, Indian dolls.

On the way to Brasstown, North Carolina, our trail passes through the wild boar and bear country of Lake Santeetlah to a place you won't hurry past if you like folks as well as what they make. We who live in the mountains are apt to know some enterprising young farmer who has attended the John C. Campbell Folk School at Brasstown, which emphasizes vegetable-dyed weaving, carved animals, ironwork, and promotes the old-time music and folk dancing. Certain festivals are well worth inquiring about.

From Brasstown we wind eastward, climbing up to Franklin and on up a deep gorge where rushing torrents of good trout waters lie below us all the way to Highlands, the highest town in the mountains. Now we head for Tryon in our crafts search, through the tiny village of Cashiers, North Carolina, where the Cabin Quilters make small articles, sunbonnets, quilts. The road winds over high passes where timid drivers cringe at breath-taking views, down to Brevard, through Hendersonville to Tryon.

Tryon, North Carolina, is not a Guild Center but it has long been one of the recognized crafts sections of the mountains. There in 1912 Miss Mary Large began the Mountain Industries. Trained at Hull House, Chicago, she taught a large group of basket-makers and chair-makers better lines and methods. Miss Large's star pupil was "Miss" Salley Cathey who organized the Blue Ridge Weavers and has been an inspiration and a source of livelihood to many old-time weavers, chair-makers, and potters in the mountains round about. From her shop are sent high-quality handicrafts to all parts of the country. Also in Tryon, the Appalachian Hand Weavers produce excellent homespuns from which particularly good wool ties are made and many hand-woven cotton rugs that are sold to crafts shops all over the country.

The trail of crafts now turns north to Asheville, the home of the Southern Highland Handicraft Guild and a center whose importance cannot be exaggerated. As we near the city we come to the Spinning Wheel, a charming group of buildings devoted to choice craftsmanship in handmade furniture, weavings, pewter, wood-carving. We have already passed the Brown Pottery near-by, where Valor Ware, copies of French cooking utensils, are made with unglazed exteriors of terra-cotta color and high gloss interiors of chocolate-colored fireproof texture, very smart and handled by smart shops in the large cities. The Brown children are the sixth generation of potters. For the past eighteen years Davis P. Brown has specialized in garden pottery at Arden, which is the post-office address of his pottery.

Pisgah Forest Pottery is on the old Asheville-Hendersonville highway. We have already mentioned the art pottery of Mr. Stephen. His cameo ware is like that made in England by Wedgwood. He qualifies as the dean of artist potters in the mountains. At near-by Candler another artist potter is Mr. T. Throckmorton. Stuart Nye, R.F.D. 2, out of Asheville, makes hand-wrought silver, jewelry, copper. Swannanoa, almost a part of Asheville, has a handicraft producer.

Heading north through Burnsville we come to the most inspiring crafts center in the mountains, the Penland School of Handicrafts. Here you may join a class in metal-work, learn to weave, to spin flax on a low wheel or wool yarn on a high wheel, hammer copper and pewter into trays and dishes, turn on the potter's wheel, model figures of clay and fire them with colored glazes in the kilns, carve in wood. "Miss" Lucy Morgan carries on a great tradition and is vibrant with enthusiasm and deeply versed in understanding of the mountain people. The Morgans gave encouragement to Roby Buchanan in his gem-cutting and there is not a home industry or household craftsman who has ever turned to them for help and not received it in full measure. Penland is not a place to skim over. There you may dig deep in folklore and get your fill of human interest stories.

Spruce Pine, North Carolina, is on our way north. Here is a forge accredited to Williamsburg, Virginia, from which you may obtain the "Williamsburg Designs" in wrought iron. If you want articles for building, latches and locks, a wrought railing for your stairs, they will be designed and made for you. You may have butterfly hinges, rat-tail hinges, H. & L. hinges, all made by hand in the old-time way, and with old-time implements.

Follow U. S. 221 to Crossnore, where we enter the Linville-Blowing Rock country, land of beautiful summer estates and gorgeous scenery. But Crossnore School knows little enough of financial affluence. Here Dr. Mary M. Sloop and her physician husband have for years befriended the poorest of the poor, children for whom the state provides no institutions, the offspring of parents who cannot take care of their own. But the place is alive with activity in every department of building, farming, teaching, printing, weaving, rug-making. The story of how this work has been carried on is beyond belief—the building and equipment of a stone hospital, dormitories constructed by the people round about, little by little, and by the pupils themselves—who took down and transported old mountain cabins for weave shops and work rooms.

On and up to a high pass close to the Blue Ridge Parkway is Boone and the Watauga Industries for metal-work, weaving, wood-work. Now we take a long stage north to lovely Charlottesville, Virginia, the last Guild Center of this itinerary.

Our trail of crafts has necessarily skipped many makers, for there is hardly a hamlet in the whole area without a producer of some object of interest. And why is this so? Ask yourself as you journey through the mountains, "Were I to settle here how could I earn a living?" The irrefutable answer would come instantly, "Impossible! Unless I could summon some special aptitude and produce something salable in the world outside." Well, that's the way it is with the mountain people. They want to live where they live and these home crafts are the sole source of cash for many of them.

CHAPTER SIX

FOLK BALLAD AND CAROL*

by John Jacob Niles

For many a year past, the southern mountains have been all things to all men. This land of contrasts has been home to a stalwart group of people, most of them descendants of pioneer settlers; it has been a bonanza to coal operators and prospectors; it has been a fertile field of exploration to the man in search of folk songs, and often an infertile field of operation to the man who plows the land for a living. It has drawn the merely curious, and, in even larger numbers, it has attracted those anxious to improve the lot of the mountain people—drawn them from far and near, from the cities of the southern states and, likewise, from the more populous centers above the Mason-Dixon line. It has acquired disproportionate fame as a land of free gun-play and water-clear whisky dispensed in Mason jars; and it has amazed an outside world already inured to its sins by fabulous displays of religious aberration—by its fire-eating preachers, its snake-handlers, its hysterical revivals. As Tolstoy has said of Russia, we may say of the southern mountains: ". . . who can cut thee in a single swathe, who can bind thee in a single sheaf?"

The railroad train, the incandescent electric light, the radio set,

* Mr. Niles insists, and rightly, that the discussion of the ballad cannot be confined to the area of this book.

the sewing machine, the reaper-and-binder, the electric incubator and brooder, the county high school and the county agent, the black-top and the concrete highway, the coal-tipple and the chain grocery store—all these things have come to the southern mountains. Slowly perhaps, in small measure and at great pains. All these evidences of modern civilization have come (and in some places have even gone), but the southern mountains are still essentially the same inexorable mountains, still possessing the same mysterious quality, a magic kind of majesty, a brooding, almost sullen stillness, that has been broken only slightly and at the outer fringes.

The visitor from the outside world hears of mountaineers dancing the running-set, singing the folk ballad, producing hand-woven coverlets, but unless he is willing to go to some pains, and ride the dim back roads, his penetration will be shallow, he will see the sordid outer fringe—the deserted coal-tipple, the burned-out logging camp, the eroded mountain cornfield, the artificial mountain made of slag, on which not even ragweed will grow. These are the things one encounters on the fringes, and they are not unlike the newspaper stories of our family and political wars (the word "feud" is used more often by writers in the outside world).

I do not say that life in the remote coves and valleys of our southern mountains is at its fullest. I do believe it is fuller than it was some years ago. There was a low point in the cultural life of the mountain people, and it came about because these people were deceived by the glaze and the shine, the glitter and weak fineness of store-bought articles, and the apparent advantages of citified music and dancing. Some of this yearning for what then appeared so desirable is caught in the folk song "If I Had a Ribbon-Bow"—a latter-day folk song, but with an exquisite tune. The time is definitely set by the first verse:

> And when he goes to Frankfort, a-loggin' on the rise,
> He'll bring me back with his own hands, a very pretty prize . . .

The night before the barbecue the clan begins to gather

Granny Pritchard, one of the few surviving users of the high spinning wheel

Examples of weaving, pewter, and silver

And the girl's longing for city life finds expression in the verse following:

> Then I'd live in Frankfort, where all the lawin' goes,
> I'd lark about them settlemints, and wear them furrin' clothes . . .

All this, if she but had a ribbon-bow to bind her hair.

The local product, and particularly the folk music, were in for hard times. For many years now, the ballads had been under attack by the kind of religionists who go in for hellfire-and-damnation. Many a dulcimer and many a guitar had been laid away as instruments of the devil. And now, from the outside world, came newer, brighter things. The ballad, once denounced as sinful, was to be laughed down as silly. But there was a change in the making.

Never shall I forget Mrs. Nolan of Pine Mountain (Harlan County, Kentucky) and her reminiscences covering the fall and ultimate disappearance of hand-fashioned articles for daily use, and then the happy cultural renaissance which began twenty-five years ago and is today restoring handcrafts and effective home-making to their rightful position.

Mrs. Nolan's grandmother had said that the decline in the popularity of fine homemade articles began just after the War Between the States. By 1875 it was in full swing. People were ashamed to appear in homemade clothes, or to be caught singing "old-time" music. Store-bought articles from Knoxville, Cincinnati, and Louisville were displayed at every crossroads. Revivalists from the North brought in books full of jerry-built hymns, hymns motivated by the most obvious and poorly harmonized tunes, hymns confusing sentimentality with worship, hymns that have since become more humorous than reverential. The local general store rose in importance, and the task of supplying these emporiums created a hauling problem of the first magnitude. One storekeeper drove sixty-five miles through rocky creek-beds to the nearest railroad terminal to buy the latest high-buttoned coats and tightest-bottomed trousers, and then drove his buggy back over the same sixty-five miles to his little store. China dishes, tin pots, city-made leathern articles, notions, frills and finery—to be used or worn—were bought by backwoods men and women who had so recently been accustomed to linsey-woolsey, to shoes made from home-cured hides, to handmade tools, to earthenware cups and saucers, to salt-glaze tableware that offered many things in place of city shine—and not the least of these, the delightful irregularities.

Mrs. Nolan says that it was "this way" for quite a long while. The flax-hackle, the wool cards, the spinning wheel, the weaving loom, and the hand cotton-ginney were relegated to the barn loft or the attic of the cabin. And the men went forth into the fields in blue denim overalls and seldom, if ever, appeared in their fine handwoven linen shirts.

But the mountain school came, and even though it was often hampered—even stringhaltered—by religious ideas, it brought with it an old idea made new by new voices and "fotch-on" enthusiasm. In many cases, the founders of the mountain schools were women, and in most cases they were women who believed in the simple homely virtues. These women had a surprisingly high sense of art values. They not only condoned folk dancing, they even made it part of their regular course of study. True it is that they varnished the running-set a bit by calling it a "play-party game" as a sop to the local preachers and to those northern contributors who thought dancing *per se* was a device of the devil. Presently prizes were offered in ballad and folk-song singing, fiddle contests were encouraged, the shape-note singers were received with open arms, homemade articles for wear and use were declared beautiful.

The teachers in the mountain schools asked about the spinning wheels. They wanted to know what had happened to the looms. Their own costumes were reminiscent of clothes worn by peasants the world over. If the truth must be told, many of the so-called peasant dresses worn by the early mountain teachers came from

Denmark, Norway, Sweden, Finland, etc., and had been purchased at considerable cost. But they served as a reminder that hand-crafted articles could be beautiful, and those who wore them declared that they some day would be stylish.

Before long, the spinning wheels and the weaving looms came out of hiding. They were a symbol. With them came all the fabulous paraphernalia of folk craft—the hackle, the wool cards, the leather-curing vats, the wood-carving tools, the madder-bed once overgrown with weeds, the dye-flower bag, the foul-smelling indigo pot, the hand forge and the great leathern bellows. Young craftsmen had to be developed, and old ones who had almost lost the art had to be retaught. A market for the output had to be discovered, new designs had to be created, and the entire movement had to wait upon a change in the tastes of the city public—the ultimate consumers. All this took years to accomplish, but once accomplished, it was only a short step to Madison Avenue, New York, N. Y. Following the custom long prevalent in Stockholm, Helsinki, and Copenhagen, the finest shops began to offer carved ducks and wild turkeys of burl-apple (apple wood having a knot or swirl in the grain), summer and winter weaving, homespun cloth, and hand-turned tableware. And Berea, Pine Mountain, Hindman, Brasstown, Carr's Creek, Carcassonne and Gatlinburg rose in importance; and Bybee, Jugtown, Pisgah Forest and scores of others became terms known all the way from the Southern Appalachian Mountains to Marshall Field's in Chicago, and to Saks-Fifth Avenue, and to Wanamaker's.

Yes, Mrs. Nolan has seen a revolution, and so have I, and so have many others who have observed the changes in the daily life of the southern mountain folk. Still I say that life in the remote coves and valleys is not at its fullest, but such as it is, it has made a noble contribution to the sum-total of our national culture.

Like many timeless and completely sincere contributions, the contribution of the southern mountaineer was made, and is being made, quite unconsciously. The contribution to the art of folk craft was part of a desire for economic improvement. The weaver whose family has an annual cash income of less than one hundred dollars has more than art for motivation when she sits down at her loom. The dance caller at Gatlinburg, Tennessee, who knows his running set so well, provides entertainment, relaxation, and vigorous exercise for summer visitors—and, by so doing, increases his own income. The man who carves tiny walnut ducks is a sculptor, indeed—and thanks to his skill, and the patience of his wife who polishes them, he is also a fellow with the extra cash to build better living quarters for himself and his stock, to fence his fields and to buy good seeds and fertilizers. Here we see art and culture as the handmaidens of a better rural life. And this problem of a better rural life is nowhere more acute than in the southern mountains.

It is, however, in the field of music that the southern mountaineer has made his greatest contribution. And the music for which he will be remembered in centuries to come is the music he sings to motivate the Anglo-American ballad, carol, and folk song.

At this point I think I should say very definitely that relatively few of the total population of the southern mountains, or the nearby lowlands, sing the ballads, carols, and folk songs for which the entire population is given credit; and that these few will also sing many tunes and ditties of little or no value, and positively no permanence. Far be it from me to add support to those investigators who would give the impression that every mountain man speaks Elizabethan English and sings in the modal scales. The people of our mountains have too often been pictured as unrealistically as the shepherds and shepherdesses in a sixteenth-century pastoral romance. This falsification is all the more unfortunate because it is also unnecessary: the ballads, folk songs, and carols of the southern mountains will stand or fall on their own merit. They have stood for centuries, and the chances are that they will stand for centuries to come, for the very simple and obvious reasons that they are motivated by excellent tunes, couched in powerfully poetic verses, and, historically, are part of our Anglo-American cultural inheritance.

In the early part of the nineteenth century, when the southern mountains were being settled, singing represented both a means of emotional expression and of recreation. This singing could be compared in no way to the performance of the self-conscious, highly trained individual artist; it was the singing of a person who had inherited both his method and his material from a father whose forebears had only recently come from the British Isles. Here, I believe, is a positive example of the importance of inheritance in the cultural development of a people. From generation to generation the process is an accumulative one. Legend, lore, music, unwritten history, family relations, the traditions and methods of folk crafters, folk dances—all this fabulous material is passed on with individual additions and deletions, not following any uniform plan, varying considerably from time to time, but finally resulting in an almost pure national type of expression.

For lack of a better title, we have called the inherited musical material of the southern mountaineer the Anglo-American folk ballad and carol. Its important characteristics are the excellence of the tunes and verses and the durability of the songs themselves. Many of the ballads can be traced to Elizabethan and pre-Elizabethan sources; most of the carols have their antecedents in the fifteenth century—the Golden Age of carol music. And these two characteristics of excellence and permanency are closely related, for it is hard to believe that music could endure in oral tradition through centuries of time without some intrinsic qualities to recommend it.

In ancient times, all forms of folk music had to withstand the Church, for although the Church did finally give her grudging consent both to the mystery play and the carol, nice pious people continued to look upon ballad-singing with suspicion. And then came Oliver Cromwell and his so-called Commonwealth. That was a dark and bloody ground for art, particularly the art of carol music. But the ballad and the carol carried on, were even enriched by vicissitude. They are still carrying on, and are becoming more widely known and more widely used, in spite of such botherments as the dusty efforts of old-fashioned educators and the sometimes doubtful benefits of educational broadcasting.

But our Anglo-American ballads, folk songs, and carols did not spring from the southern mountains. They found safe asylum in our mountains, but they came here from far places: our own backwoods people would say: "From a far piece . . . from the far furrin world." They were brought to this country from the British Isles, and, in more or less fragmentary form, they can be found up and down our land even unto this day. In such Kentucky areas as the Purchase, the Pennyrile, the Bluegrass country and the mountains in Virginia and West Virginia, in both the Carolinas, in Georgia, Alabama and Tennessee; in the New England States, the Ozark Mountains, Texas, Indiana, Ohio, and Pennsylvania, in fact almost everywhere east of the Rockies, and even in the back alleys of our great cities. For the folk song is art, and as such, quoting James McNeill Whistler, "No hovel is safe from it, and no prince can depend upon it."

It is the common error of the enthusiast to expect to find a folk singer sitting beside every elderberry bush. Would that it were as easy as that! I think I can say from many years of field experience that the native folk singer and his song are as elusive as most valuable things usually prove to be. But if the native singer, once found, is approached with tact and understanding, he readily becomes cooperative. Frankness is absolutely necessary. You must declare your business quickly, for a man who appears to be looking for information without saying precisely what he hopes to find, is quite likely to be mistaken for a revenue agent.

Only twice in thirty-six years of folklore collecting have I resorted to paying money for the privilege of taking down a folk song, though I must admit using chewing tobacco, drinking whisky, bacon, fat-back, lard, string, cotton gloves, cornmeal, wheat-flour, almanacs, corncob pipes, aspirin, soda, garden seeds and other blandishments too numerous to mention, as polite bribes. In almost every case, the end justified the means, for the singer was supplied with some merchandise vital to his daily life and the great public was supplied with the folk song they might have lost.

Most of the important ballad, folk song, and folk carol collections from American sources have been made during the twentieth century. Until just forty-odd years ago, the few Americans who had troubled themselves with the study of the ballad thought that the United States was a rather barren field. In the latter half of the nineteenth century, when Francis J. Child was working on his *English and Scottish Popular Ballads* (Houghton Mifflin, Boston, 1882-1898), he reported seventeen so-called British ballad survivals in the United States. Mr. Child had made no studied attempt to collect these ballad survivals in America. He only noted them incidentally. The following list, quoted from a now rare U. S. Department of the Interior publication entitled "Special Inquiry, November, 1913" will give the reader an idea of the geographical distribution of these 17 ballads:

2 survivals from Maine
2 from New Hampshire
10 from Massachusetts
5 from New York
1 from Pennsylvania
1 from Maryland
4 from Virginia
4 from North Carolina
1 from South Carolina

Some of these are duplicates, the total of different titles being seventeen. A great many men and women have collected folk songs in the United States since Professor Child made the above statement. Some carried the traditional black notebook and pencil, others carried a mechanical recording device, and some even added the weight of a camera to photograph the singers.

Looking back over the results of this labor of love, one is astounded at the vastness of the gathered store. One publication from the state of Maine, *British Ballads from Maine*, by Phillips Barry, Fannie H. Eckstorm and Mary W. Smyth, contains 64 British and Scottish survivals, not to mention 30 additional fragments which Mr. Barry is pleased to call "traces and jury-texts." This book represents years of effort on the part of the three authors who labored in a state where Professor Child thought one might discover two survivals.

The most remarkable collection of American folk balladry, however, was made by an Englishman named Cecil J. Sharp. This collection was assembled in 1916, 1917, and 1918. Sharp was materially assisted by Mrs. Olive Dame Campbell. In fact, if Mrs. Campbell had not convinced the gouty Mr. Sharp that this material existed in the Southern Appalachian mountains, he would have gone back to England empty-handed and sorely disappointed. This vast collection contains 45 English and Scottish survivals (and many versions thereof) in addition to 229 other titles under the heading of folk songs, folk hymns, nursery rhymes, jigs, and play-party games. It came from 2 counties in West Virginia, 11 counties in Virginia, 7 counties in North Carolina, 3 counties in Tennessee, and 11 counties in Kentucky. One of these Kentucky counties was Fayette, in the heart of the Bluegrass country.

Francis J. Child's published collection of English and Scottish popular ballads is exactly what it claims to be—a collection of the folk balladry of England and Scotland collected and edited by Mr. Child from such existing manuscripts as Bishop Percy's Papers, the Kinloch MSS, the Harris MS, and many others. Professor Child numbered his ballad collection from No. 1 to No. 305, and these numerical designations have become so well established in the field of ballad study that today any balladry in the Anglo-Saxon world that is worthy of the term is indicated by the same Child designations. They are simply called Child ballads or are indicated, for example, as Bonny Barbara Allen, Child No. 84. My own folk song collection, coming entirely from oral tradition, contains 54 Child ballads and an uncounted mass of folk love songs, work songs, soldiers' songs, sailors' songs, gambling songs, fiddle tunes, Negro spirituals, and nursery rhymes. Most important, to my mind, is the collection of carols—not for its size (there are less than twenty titles), but for the excellence of the tunes and the antiquity and poetic quality of the texts. Important, too, because until recently it was supposed that the carol, fifteenth-century in origin and Catholic in inspiration, had been lost to the tradition of Protestant America.

My collection, a small portion of which has been published and put on records, has been made over a period of thirty-six years. It started out as a few penciled notes in high-school copybooks, heavily interlarded with sentimental diary notes. My earliest "informants" were my father, who sang ballads, and the Negroes of Louisville's "Cabbage Patch," who sang spirituals at the famed Cabbage Patch Revivals—and at whose expense, incidentally, I learned the trick of musical shorthand. In those long-ago times, I surely did not know the value of the material I so casually wrote down; I was rather like the man who handles a lethal weapon, not knowing that it's loaded. But when I did finally discover the power and the value of the charge, I began to make a map of the places where this material was found. Now, more than a quarter of a century later, I believe I can say that in the southern mountains, more important English and Scottish ballads are known to more people than in any other region. And when I say known, I mean well known—known so thoroughly as to be singable and sung.

In the beginning, the true poetry of the people—the ballad, the carol, and the folk song—was intended to appeal to the ear, not as other poetry which must be read before the mind's ear can hear it. The poetry of the people was sung, and today, if it is to serve its purpose, it must still be sung. For the ballad verses represent only a portion of the ballad, the other and very important part being the tunes. These tunes, however, need not be constant. In fact, they are not constant; they vary from county to county, from state to state, and—even more widely—from the homeland in England to their transplanted home here in the New World. The verses, too, may vary in certain details, certain omissions or additions, but the essence of the tale to be told is usually found even though submerged under local variations. (Be it said here that every statement on the subject of balladry should be tempered to include the exceptions—the most notable one in this connection being the ballad titled "The Lass of Roch Royal," the original of which runs into thirty-odd verses—whereas the American versions are usually content with three verses lifted from the middle of the text, to make a delightful little love song known as "Who's Goin' to Shoe Your Pretty Little Foot?")

The English and Scottish originals of what we now call Child ballads were no doubt known to a great majority of the people who came to this country from the British Isles in the seventeenth century. But the delights of the printed page, the concert hall (such as it was), the theater, and the urban life of populated communities were stiff competition for such things as "Barbary Ellen" and "Little Mattie Groves," for "The Seven Joys of Mary" and the Eucharistic carol, "Down in Yon Forest." The pioneer ancestors who lived in the then struggling little cities had schoolhouses near by. They may not have been the kind of schools we have today, but they taught the three R's, and the city population was able to read newspapers and books.

Already ballad and carol singing was beginning to be looked upon as "old fogy," and we find the objective and impersonal poetry of the masses (the folk ballad and carol) slowly giving way before something new, something brassy, something almost inexorable. It was the kind of literature in which the individual was accented. "Paper and printer's ink had long since set up a kind of privacy for both the author and his public. The confidential and sentimental poet, full of his own dignity, went abroad and made friends with all men."

Careful records of the early settlements in the Southern Appalachian Mountains were surely not kept. But it appears likely that the first settlers were as well taught as the brothers and cousins they left in the eastern lowlands when they set forth toward new lands. But when they settled in the southern mountains, in isolated coves and valleys, there were fewer schools for their children, and a higher percentage of people grew up who could neither read nor write. These people, armed with a kind of leisure born of an easy-going disposition and a peculiar scorn of worldly riches which seemed as unattainable as they were unnecessary, used the method of oral transmission to retain the lore and the legend of their English and Scottish ancestors and, incidentally, proved quite conclusively that education and culture are not interchangeable terms.

The problem of racial inheritance has supplied the basis for many an acrimonious discussion. Internationalists will propose a world-wide concept of cultures, while the nationalist will demand that the student or the citizen must start with his own national cultural inheritance—and then, if he has the scope and the capacity, move on to an international point of view. Many educators today are beginning to believe that at a very early age, students should be given an opportunity to come into their racial inheritance through the study and ultimately the possession of the cultural achievements of the past. If we agree that music and literature are among these achievements, then "the folk songs and the folk ballads of the race to which these young people belong, or the nation whose language they speak" would naturally seem to be required study. It is too bad that all the young people in the United States cannot learn the ballad and the carol from their parents. It is comforting, however, to think that at this very moment many of them are learning this folklore from their schoolmasters.

The carol "I Wonder as I Wander Out Under the Sky," which I collected in Murphy, North Carolina, during the summer of 1933, is a case in point. In ten brief years it has become common property in many of the high schools in the United States. "I Wonder as I Wander" came from the singing of a young woman who said her name was Annie Morgan and who passed herself off as the daughter of some evangelists who traveled in western North Carolina and northern Georgia. In Murphy, where they had set themselves up in the public square, they were rated as an A-1 nuisance, and had been requested to move out when I happened upon Annie Morgan and her delightful carol. I have never found anything just like it anywhere else. Nor have I found anything remotely like it in my research in libraries here and abroad. At first, I did not expect much of it. But the public knew better. It is definitely not a hymn. It has nothing whatever to do with the sentimental evangelical hymns of the past fifty years. Tune and text place it unmistakably in the best carol tradition. In the most direct and poetic terms, it asks a question that has troubled theologians for centuries past:

> I wonder as I wander out under the sky
> How Jesus our Saviour did come for to die
> For poor on'ry people like you and like I . . .
> I wonder as I wander out under the sky.

There are about thirty such carols extant in North America, many of which stem directly from the Golden Age of carol music—the fifteenth century. If you want to trace the ancestry of the carol "Sing We the Virgin Mary," you have but to turn to the *Oxford Book of English Verse*. There you will find an anonymous fifteenth-century carol with the first line: "I sing of a maiden that is makeles." Compare this verse from the American version:

> So silent came our Jesus
> Unto his sweet Mary,
> As dew of April falleth
> On flower so tenderly

with the third verse of the English original:

> He came al so still
> To his mother's bour,
> As dew in April
> That falleth on the flour.

These carols must not be confused with the equally fine Negro spirituals or the little-known shape-note hymns. The sale of shape-note hymnbooks has represented an important source of income to many a publisher south of the Mason-Dixon line. None of this material was ever passed on as were the ballads and carols—that is, by oral transmission. To be a shape-note singer, one had to be able to read and write. One also had to be able to read music, because shape-note hymns are almost invariably written in four or six parts. I think I can say that with a few exceptions, the best native folk singers of the older generation whom I have encountered were unable to read or write. They were inordinately interested in my process of writing down the words and tunes of their precious ballads. It looked like chicken tracks to them. Today, as I look back over these twenty-five-year-old manuscripts, it looks like chicken tracks to me. Fortunately, I have long since learned the tunes, and most of them have either been reduced to published music or recorded on bronze for mechanical reproduction.

"The Maid Freed from the Gallows" (Child No. 95), "The Wife of Usher's Well" (Child No. 79), five ballads concerning Robin Hood, "The Unquiet Grave" (Child No. 78), "Lord Lovel" (Child No. 75), "Dives and Lazarus" (Child No. 56), "The Cruel

Mother" (Child No. 20), "Edward" (Child No. 13), "Lord Randal" (Child No. 12), "Earl Brand" (Child No. 7), "The False Knight Upon the Road" (Child No. 3), "Sir Patrick Spens" (Child No. 58), and forty-five others make up the bulk of the Southern Appalachian ballad collection.

My personal choice of the most important ballad in our mountains is one titled "Little Mattie Groves." In the Child collection it is known as "Little Musgrave and Lady Barnard" and is indicated as No. 81. My text, taken down from the singing of a man I met at Allanstand, North Carolina (and who later spent a day with me in Asheville), runs into twenty-six verses. The tune is as dramatic as a battle cry; the text is not as complete as one from eastern Virginia, and some of the verses do not rhyme. But for a ballad seeming to involve people living at the time of Henry VIII and one quoted in Beaumont and Fletcher's play, "The Knight of the Burning Pestle" (about 1611)—for such an antique, I think the North Carolina version is quite thrilling. At least, I have found it so in performance hundreds of times, all over the English-speaking world.

The best-liked and most widely known ballad is "Barbary Ellen" (Child No. 84)—more sentimental than dramatic. Once while visiting Jackson (Breathitt County), Kentucky, I asked an auditorium full of high-school students how many knew "Barbary Ellen." Every hand went up. And I dare say that if there were five hundred students present, there would be five hundred variations of text and tune. The variations would be slight, but they would be important to the individual singer. The weak notes in the melodic line would be emphasized, and in many cases the gapped scale would be used. (By gapped scale, I mean a scale with certain notes left out entirely.)

As great an authority as Cecil Sharp admits there is neither accurate nor reliable evidence on the scales used by folk singers in England during the eighteenth century. It may have taken these people a hundred years to advance to the present use of the seven-note scale. If this is true—and Mr. Sharp admits that it is only a supposition—then it is easy to see how the mountain singers of today are inclined to the use of the gapped scale in imitation of their ancestors who were, in turn, contemporaries of the eighteenth-century English singers.

Any discussion of modality in folk music is the spark that inevitably sets off a barrage of acrimonious comment from musicologists. I have been studying modal music for twenty-five years, and if I manage to live another quarter of a century, I may be able to come to some sound conclusions on the subject. Meanwhile, suffice it to say that many of the tunes that motivate the ballads and carols are indeed modal tunes. And if the "gentle reader" wants to know what modal music is, and why it is, and he is not so "gentle" but that he can take steep climbing, I would suggest a quiet perusal of some of the volumes listed at the back of this book.

The carol and the folk song are perhaps more easily understood and more easily managed in three-, four-, or five-part arrangement than the ballad, and for this reason, they have been more widely used by children in the grades and young people in our high schools. Twenty-five years from now these people will be in their early maturity, some will even be approaching middle life. They will represent the first generation in the United States to have been exposed to a studied program of Anglo-American musical culture. If this program had been initiated earlier in the century, the young men fighting for democracy would have as good an understanding of their cultural traditions as they seem to have of their social and political inheritance.

The folk carol, being concerned with the "birth, youth, life, crucifixion and ascension of Jesus Christ," can be used as nursery music for tiny children. In fact, children of three years and up will not only listen to the carols with great interest, but will try to sing them. "Jesus, Jesus, Rest Your Head," coming out of Hardin

County, Kentucky, "See Jesus the Saviour Asleep in the Manger," from Index, Kentucky, "The Seven Joys of Mary" (fifteenth-century in origin, and known in quite a few communities throughout the southern mountains), "The Ten Commandments" (portions of which seem to stem from the Orthodox Jewish service), "The Twelve Days of Christmas," and "Sing We the Virgin Mary"—these and many others are great favorites with children barely able to talk.

In some mountain communities made up of very strongly Protestant people, the carols are looked upon with disfavor because of the emphasis they place on the Virgin Mary. I shall always remember the itinerant singing-master whom I picked up on a dusty road in Tennessee, who rewarded me for my small kindness by singing the carol "Jesus the Christ is Born." But, having sung it, he was greatly worried lest his name be connected with such popish stuff. This verse, especially, troubled him for its reference to the "Queen of Heaven":

> For in this lowly guise
> The Son of God do sleep,
> And see the Queen of Heaven kneel,
> Her faithful vigil keep.

And then there was the Holiness preacher in North Carolina, who sang me one dull hymn right after another all through a blisteringly hot afternoon—and finally, when I had almost given up hope, began to sing: "Down in yon forest be a hall, Sing May, Queen May, Sing Mary . . ." My hands trembled so that I could hardly set down the notes, for I knew that here was a carol that had been recorded only once before in modern times, by Ralph Vaughan Williams in England. And here it was, in the fastness of the North Carolina mountains, making a second appearance. I had never encountered it before in this country, nor, to my knowledge, has anyone encountered it since except in its published form or on records.

But the Holiness preacher who sang it made light of it, and thought ill of me for preferring such doubtful material to a good old rousing hymn.

At times, some of these mountain people have even accused me of being "popish" for singing the carols or trying to teach them. My explanation is simple. First, the carol almost invariably possesses fine, deeply moving music; second, the verses are simple, direct, and poetic in the best sense of the word; and, finally, the carols have been loved and sung by so many generations of our ancestors who never thought of them as belonging to any particular sect or creed that they have now become perfect examples of impersonal, objective folk expression, possessing a reverential quality that is inescapable. All this explanation, however, is just explanation and nothing more, for I humbly stand with the great English authority, Cecil Sharp, who said: "I am not here to defend the idea of folk music, folklore, or inherited folk culture; I am here to declare it."

The term folk song covers a wide field. It includes nursery rhymes like the Elizabethan lampoon titled "The Strange Marriage of Mr. Frog and Miss Mouse," love songs, humorous songs, songs of mighty men like John Henry and Paul Bunyan, songs that sing of great railway disasters, the winning of the West, strikes, mining disasters, and—up to date—the New Deal Administration. Family wars provide perfect material for the maker of modern folk songs. Some of these even get onto ballad sheets and are sold by itinerant fiddlers and street-corner singers on court days or at political speakings. The song concerning the Martin-Tolliver feud (fought out at Morehead, Kentucky) found its way onto a ballad sheet, and in the larger mountain towns of Tennessee and Georgia, Negro banjoists and singers will offer printed sheets of spirituals and sermons. No one can ever keep up with the folk song, because by the time the catalogue is written, new numbers will have been created. The music of these songs cannot compare in any way with the tunes of the ballads and carols. Nor is it up to us either to compare them or evaluate them. That is the task of time. Two hundred years from now the best of these latter-day songs may still be remembered; the others will have been happily forgotten.

In the backwoods of the mountains—in the really isolated places—many of the singers will possess a so-called "ballet" book. This will be a store-bought blank book containing hand-written verses of the ballads, carols, and folk songs known in the family. The tunes are not written down. These ballet-books are usually kept by younger members of the family, who have had the happy opportunity to attend school. The books will also contain sentimental poems clipped from printed sources, pinned or pasted onto the blank pages.

The mountain singers of today rarely use the dulcimer, the three-, four-, six-, or eight-string instrument once traditional in this region. There are, however, some dulcimer-makers in the mountains of Virginia and Kentucky. They make a few instruments each year. James Edward Thomas, who lived near Bath, Kentucky (1850-1933), claims to have made as many as 1,200 dulcimers in his lifetime. At least, he was numbering his instruments above the 1,200-mark at the time of his death. Being a dulcimer-maker myself, I am naturally interested in my fellow craftsmen. In my lifetime, I have known five of these men personally. In every case they were inordinately proud of their work, and in every case but one, they were unable to perform convincingly on the instruments they made. I make dulcimers entirely for my own use (twenty-six in the last ten years), and I use them for accompanying the voice. I do not recommend the dulcimer for playing the melodic line. I also believe that the quality of dulcimer tone is improved by using the fingers to pluck or strum the strings instead of twanging them with the traditional turkey's quill.

The most widely used instrument in the southern mountains today is the violin—known almost exclusively as the fiddle. Mail-order houses have inexpensive fiddles—case, bow, rosin, extra strings, and instruction book complete. Many of these bright brassy things even bear a counterfeit of the name of the world's greatest maker of violins, Antonio Stradivarius, with the date, 1721, affixed. I have been given the opportunity of buying countless "Strads" for almost any sum I would pay.

Many of the mountain fiddlers tune the instrument in their own unique way, and some play with the head of the instrument down and the back of the fiddle resting against the player's stomach. Gourd fiddles were once in general use in the mountains. Some examples may still be seen in various museums—notably the one at Pine Mountain Settlement School. Banjos and guitars were also made and used by men who either sang or provided music for dancing. Today, however, "fotch-on," store-bought instruments are the rule. One coal-mine operator in Breathitt County told me that many a young man has come to him for work, and quit as soon as he had saved up enough money to buy a "city guitar" or a "Chicago banjo."

Not all the ballad, carol, and folk song music coming out of the Southern Appalachians is good enough to stand the test of time. Much of the latter-day material is written far from the mountains and is intended for the early-morning radio ear. But the existence of this poor material should cause no undue alarm. It is safe to say that when our classic ballads were young, they had many contemporaries of lesser worth whose names we no longer even know. But our classic ballads and carols became classics only in due time and season, and as such they have remained, generation after generation, and now thanks to a renaissance in public taste and a new spirit of national consciousness, these Anglo-American classics are leaving the dusty shelves of the libraries and finding their way into the hearts of the American public.

Our researchers and scholarly folklorists have done well, but trained as they are to be interested in scholarly volumes of findings, with pages of cross references, they have perhaps spent too much time in academic discussions of such matters as the individual or communal composition of the ballad, or the exact meaning of the word ballad, or the definition of the folk song, and so forth. When I hear fifteen hundred high school children doing a superb performance of a four-part version of the carol "I Wonder as I Wander," these academic problems seem unimportant. I know then that the folk music of the United States is returning to the people, that the dust is being brushed off it, that no matter how it was originally conceived, no matter where it came from, no matter who dug it up, no matter who arranged it in singable form and caused it to be published, its beauties and its advantages are at long last becoming apparent to the masses. And the masses, right or wrong, usually have their way.

The people of the southern mountains have made a noble contribution to our national culture. And the schoolteachers of the United States are slowly bringing this contribution to the youth of our country as part of their cultural inheritance. Hundreds of years from now, these mountains will still stand, silent brooding masses. The slag-piles will be overgrown, the boom-towns forgotten, the coal-tipples tumbled into dust, and the family wars fought out and forgotten—but, if the present trend prevails, the folk music of today, much of which is now four centuries old, will prevail then and will be as precious to the masses in that far future time as it is to a relatively few students and enthusiasts today.

CHAPTER SEVEN

WHAT ABOUT THE CLIMATE?

by Ralph Erskine

EVERY MONTH HAS ITS CHARM

Climate and the pull of the Southern Appalachians have determined the kind of people who live in these mountains and have molded their ways of life from the days when the first settlers followed the lure of free land to the present moment when a new economic force is bringing a new kind of influx and making close neighbors of humble mountain folk and well-to-do city sophisticates. These latter are buying hide-outs and building homes with feverish haste as though impelled by migratory instinct, like lemmings scampering from some impending catastrophe.

The climate in our area is to all intents and purposes uniform; with local variations of frost pockets, thermal belts, and wet and dry areas which are caused by the mountains themselves. The north and south lines of latitude are only one hundred miles apart and the east and west diagonal parallels are barely eighty miles from each other.

In the heights are forests of balsam, spruce, and white pine. Once there was a magnificent growth of wild cherry which was slaughtered in the days of wooden Pullmans and cherry-trimmed trolley cars. Recently some culling was done in Pisgah National Forest and I saw boards of cherry twenty feet long and thirty inches wide. I have seen photographs of these virgin cherry forests, unbelievable trees growing as straight and smooth as tulip trees. But their existence must have been kept pretty much of a secret, because I find no reference to them in any of the standard books of horticulture. In the mountains you see all the northern hardwoods in abundance and to them are added at the various altitudes an astonishing array of flowering trees and shrubs such as azaleas (pink, lemon, and flame), laurel of a size and profusion unknown in the North, silverbell, dogwood, the purple Judas tree or redbud, and the cucumber magnolia or cucumber tree: these I name because they put on a show each spring which makes even the uninformed stop and look. And above the tree line on Craggy Mountain, forty miles north of Asheville, is a concentration of purple rhododendron growing out of a carpet of lush grass in which bluets and grass flowers tell us that at that elevation the climate is about the same as in New England. The United States Government has built a road and provided a wide parking space from which you can make the climb up to the Craggy Gardens without too much exertion.

Climate, caused chiefly by altitude, drew the people of Charleston and the rice plantations to the mountains almost on the heels of the retreating Cherokees. On a wide plateau where the waters divide and flow south to the Atlantic and west to rivers emptying into the Gulf they founded one of the first summer resorts in the country and called it Flat Rock in honor of a spectacular outcropping of smooth, igneous rock which covers many acres. The average elevation here is 2,200 feet. If you place a ruler on the cities of Charleston and Columbia it will parallel the Savannah River, which is the boundary between South Carolina and Georgia, and point directly at Flat Rock, twenty miles over the border of North Carolina. Here, on the upland nearest to their seacoast homes, the wealthy planters and citizens of Charleston laid out large estates with long avenues of white pine planted formally on either side. The houses were unpretentious but comfortable, with high ceilings, and furnished with a combination of pieces made by journeyman craftsmen and now and then with some choice bit brought by wagon from the coast. Their servants built their place of worship, St. John's-in-the-Wilderness, of native stone, and were proud of their own gallery in it and their own voice in its government. Long before railroads were dreamt of, as soon as azaleas and dogwood announced the beginning of summer, the chariots of the Rhetts and the Ravenels, the Barings and the Mannigaults labored up through the gorges above Greenville and Travelers Rest. These "pleasure" vehicles were weighty affairs with closed bodies hung on leather straps and steps which let down when doors were opened. Extra horses helped to drag them up the steeps. While ladies, children, and the aged rocked over the roads in them, gentlemen rode horses which for blood lines were the pride of the country. Supplies were carried in covered wagons. Old letters and newspapers constantly refer to the pleasures of life up on the Flat Rock plateau where cattle and horses thrived on good green pastures and farming was a pleasing avocation because nature had provided lime deposits in an otherwise micaceous soil. Fresh-ground whole grain came from slow-turning stones of many water wheels. A cool spring-house near each dwelling kept milk and foods sweet. The fragrance of pine was good to smell as young folks rode along shaded paths and every eminence had a reward of distant peaks beyond the French Broad Valley where shapely Pisgah, only twenty miles away, drew all eyes to a focus. The long summers passed in peace and contentment for these people of the low country, and their children and their children's children have loved it through all the generations since.

If you journey west from Flat Rock up the French Broad Valley to Brevard you pass through rich bottom lands in which the river winds about with no more current than enough to make a canoe trip *down* to Asheville (although that city is due north) a pleasant summer excursion. Here the elevation is still 2,200 feet on the average and the climate is at least ten degrees cooler than at the 1,000 foot level. In the old days the farmers raised their own flax from which they spun and wove the coarse linen cloth for their grain sacks. You pass substantial farmhouses of stone and hewn logs covered with clapboarding and again long avenues of white pine give a clue regarding the age of the settlements. Many streams keep the air "conditioned." The region is ideal for boys' and girls' camps. Swimming pools are easy to construct and small lakes for power or for pleasure are hidden in the hills. Village stores are filled with fishing tackle and expensive tapered lines and flies for trout casting and fascinating lures for bass are evidence enough of what men think about.

Always as you travel westward the beginning of the coastal plain is barely ten miles south of you, just over a line of densely forested pointed hills on your left, and on your right the high peaks of Pisgah National Forest keep tempting you to turn aside to see the famous "pink beds" of mountain laurel and fish the streams that tumble crystal-clear, draining thousands on thousands of acres of unbroken forest. Here in summer in the Brevard section the nights are cooled by the "draw" of air flowing down the valleys. July is the hottest month, yet the average temperature then is only 72.4 degrees. In winter now and then a fall of snow is heavy enough to give a day or two of skiing on the slopes, but snows generally melt within the week and although the January low for the past thirty years has been twelve degrees below zero, the average temperature in winter is well above freezing. Even when a long succession of nights occurs when exposed pipes and radiators would freeze, each day by noon the long fingers of hoarfrost which thrust out from the banks of road cuts have melted and dropped their crust of dirt as one more contribution to the endless process of erosion. The coldest month is January, in which the average temperature is about 37 degrees.

Should we continue our journey beyond Brevard we must choose between a high climb ahead or leaving the mountains by an abrupt turn to the south over a wide ridge to Caesars Head. Here when November has whipped the leaves from the hardwoods you can turn aside in a gentle valley and go gunning for quail and woodcock—that is, if ever the season is opened again for those cocky little migratory birds. And if you climb up around Rich Mountain on your left you may think your dog has come to a point on a covey of quail and then get the thrill of thrills when a ruffed grouse roars up.

All this land is in Transylvania County, a district which is said to have furnished many of the Over-Mountain men who fought with John Sevier in his battles with the Cherokees and against the British in the Battle of Kings Mountain. I had an amusing experience there. I was eager to learn whether stories of the deeds of old are told at the firesides by the descendants of men who took part in them. I asked Farmer Hogshead (pronounced Hogsed) whether his people had fought in the Revolution. He looked puzzled.

"You mean that old war . . . that big old war when we freed the Yankees?" he asked.

I had my answer. Mountain isolation had done a thorough job.

Journeying straight ahead to the west from Brevard—as straight as a frightened black snake, twisting up a stony gulch—you come to the highest town of any size in the entire mountain region, Highlands. Here, strange to say, in spite of a rise of 1,200 feet in forty miles there is only a slight drop in average temperature. This is due to our having penetrated an area of excessive rainfall which we will discuss later on. But at this 3,000-foot level we have again come to one of the earliest summer resorts in this country. Again we find the famous names of Charleston and at High Hampton —a charming country club on the estate of a brother of General Wade Hampton—we are reminded of that famous family of

Columbia and the days when the Hampton "Red Shirts" rid the South forever of the pestilential "carpetbag" invasion.

Now, when superb roads engineered to easy grades feed the nooks and corners of this higher plateau, you marvel at the temerity of the families in days gone by who made the annual trek to the dizzy heights overlooking the coastal plain and built comfortable homes, laid out gardens bordered with English boxwood and clipped hedges of intermingled hemlock and rhododendron so far from civilization. The answer is that the contrasts of these cool heights with the fever ridden rice lands were all-compelling, the rewards for the arduous journeys were more than generous, and the people understood the arts of husbandry whereby they were able to live a self-contained existence on the fertile benches where streams wander lazily through level meadows before taking the plunge over the mountain rim.

Today these settlements have been augmented by many families from northern states who have made the discovery that here the summer climate possesses certain qualities of uniform coolness combined with an invigorating lightness of the air. Moreover the rewards of good comradeship have been attractive because it happens that there is a chain of universities and colleges in South Carolina and Georgia lying not far distant whose faculty members find this a convenient and inexpensive locality in which to escape the heat of the piedmont. It would be easy to get lost in theories when speculating about the kinds of people for whom the mountains have an appeal and what the effect of the selectivity of heights and rugged ways is in giving character to the communities. It should therefore be enough to remind ourselves that this matter of comradeship of kindred people is important.

It is obviously impossible for us to give the attention that we have paid to Flat Rock and Highlands to the numerous other summer resorts which have grown up all the way from the Virginia border to the Georgia line. The two oldest will have to serve as examples of how elevation and climate operate as a sole cause of existence. Follow the Blue Ridge Parkway from Roaring Gap in the North through the National Forests past Blowing Rock, Linville, and Little Switzerland to Asheville, and you tap hundreds of them. Then circle around over a maze of highways and you find settlements where the mountains have called to generations of dwellers in the lowlands. At Montreat there is a community whose common bond is that they are all Presbyterians—descendants of the Scotch who settled many coast counties. High in a romantic gorge they have built a large stone inn, substantial conference buildings, a swimming pool and playgrounds. The organization is designed to give wholesome activities to young people while parents enjoy the companionship of lifelong friends. Near by is Black Mountain, where a school of modernists in education labors to work out their advanced theories in untrammeled isolation. And then there is Biltmore, fabulous estate where in the early nineties George Vanderbilt reared for himself an unbelievable monument of stone in the form of a French château, filled with tapestries and garnished with ancient sculptures, set on an eminence above the French Broad River where he could look out over sixty thousand acres including Mt. Pisgah itself—all free of any visible habitation. Standing on his terrace where Egyptian lotus planted in formal basins perfumed the night air, he could gaze as far as his eyes could see to where the stars touched the mountains and say, "All this is mine." It was climate and the mountains that had drawn him to this spot outdoing anything he had seen in a world of travels. He did well, for he assembled in one convenient package, title clear, the first great stretch of forest land which the Government acquired in what is now a whole region of national forests. And he began the first scientific study of forestry made in the United States.

At Roaring Gap (elevation 3,500 feet) just below the Virginia border, a place little known to tourists, climate and elevation have called to the industrialists in busy cities which lie almost in the shadow of the mountain wall. Here they enjoy a settled way of life in well-constructed, smartly-decorated houses, a sophisticated country club hotel, a well-groomed golf course. Sitting on a close-cropped lawn where the whole world to the east and south is spread out before you in the hot, blue haze of summer, a covey of Chukor partridge imported from India run out from a laurel thicket and look you over with fearless inquisitiveness. Keen young men who bear the names of those who first settled the land and now run the industries—Haynes, Chatham, Calhoun—saunter up. They take as a matter of course the fact that minutes rather than hours are needed for them to climb from the blistering heat of city pavements to wide spaces where there is rarely a night when at least one wool throw is not a comfort.

Go southwest across the state from Roaring Gap to Brasstown, near the Georgia line, and you come to a place where consecrated souls have devoted their lives to teaching mountain boys and girls how to make the most of their mountain farms, how to recapture their ancient ballads and songs, how to keep alive their folk dances, and how to preserve their old-time crafts. All the region that lies between the north and south mountain parallels is dotted with settlements, each one of which has come into being because of the allure of climate and altitude, and each presents its own special claim to our interest.

Yes, the whole mountain region is an inspiring place and it would take many chapters to tell the stories of it. How each summer the population of such towns as Asheville and Hendersonville is doubled, and thousands of car licenses from Florida, Alabama, and all the Gulf states appear. In a brief tour one June to see the purple rhododendron on Craggy Mountain, thirty miles north of Asheville, I counted automobiles from twenty-eight states and Canada. And there are golf courses scattered over the whole area with bent-grass greens which testify not only to the spirit of play of the people but to the startling difference of cool, moist nights in the highlands as compared with the sere summer fairways of the piedmont at the one thousand-foot level, where only Bermuda grass can stand the blistering July and August sun.

In all the long summer a million streams and waterfalls cool the air in the mountains so that each night in the valleys there is a "draw"—a steady wind such as one feels when standing in the bow of a ship. It is the cool air flowing down to the lowlands to replace the heated columns rising above sun-baked cotton fields.

The Great Smoky Mountains are at the southwest tip of our area. They lie half in East Tennessee and half in the westernmost part of North Carolina. Between them and the Pisgah Range of the Blue Ridge is a deep, fertile valley drained by the Pigeon River, which flows north to Newport, Tennessee, and by the Little Tennessee River which flows west to Deals Gap where it drops from an elevation of 2,200 feet down into the Mississippi Valley. Here are the last remnants of the Cherokee Indians on the small reservation which was left to them after that last disgraceful episode of expulsion from their primeval hunting grounds. You see them standing by the roadside selling gaudy little toy bows and arrows. A kind of shame comes over you when you remember the horror and the dread their great-great-grandfathers inspired and how the white folks "took to fort" at mere mention of their name.

The beautiful little town of Waynesville, thirty miles due west of Asheville, is the center of a famous apple district and wherever the forests have been removed lush grass grows to the topmost ridges. Here again plenty of lime in the soil combined with steady rainfall and cool nights makes for good pasture ranges. Lowlanders send their horses up there for the summer. The temperature records for the past thirty-five years are almost identical with those of the French Broad Valley. A number of industries of national importance have been attracted to this locality because of constant water power, evenness of climate, and abundance of forest resources and mineral deposits. The eastern slopes of the Smokies shed their snows as rapidly as their sister peaks of the Blue Ridge to the east, but the western slopes, which hang directly above and due south of Knoxville, hold their snowfalls, above the five thousand-foot level, for weeks at a time.

The western wall of the Great Smoky Mountains is so steep that Government highways have demanded the best engineering brains to construct reasonable grades for automobiles. The climb from Gatlinburg, a charming little resort which clings to the cliffs above Knoxville, up to Newfound Gap (elevation 5,045 feet), just north of Clingmans Dome (elevation 6,642 feet), even doubles back on itself and the road makes a turn through a tunnel so that you find yourself looking down on the spot where you were a few minutes before; and you see at a glance why it is that references to climate and elevation on the western side of the mountains are of little practical value to all except the most venturesome mountain climbers.

But the Great Smokies are the mecca for campers and mountain climbers. It is strange that we hear so little conversation among adults about scaling this peak and that. The sport seems confined to excursions from the boys' and girls' camps which exist in surprising numbers all the way from the neighborhood of Flat Rock and Hendersonville through the mountains up into Virginia. Authorities estimate that this boy-and-girl summer population may reach five thousand in a normal year. Parents and relatives of the children have made the discovery that they can use the camp facilities—there are riding horses, trucks to carry food and blankets after the camp sessions are ended, and plans for de luxe excursions up into the little-known camp grounds. This is a tip worth knowing about for any riding enthusiasts who would like a spectacular change from western dude ranching at a fraction of the cost. The climate in September and October is ideal. It is a period of minimum rainfall. Insect pests have gone. Hardwoods flaunt a glory of color unmatched even in New England, for in this district in addition to oaks, maples, and beech trees there are the sourwoods which turn to flaming ruby, and black gums and dogwood offer their own special bouquets of green shading to burnt sienna and copper. Government stations have been constructed with every convenience a camper could wish for: stone grilles, protected springs, proper sanitation, privacy. And everywhere there is the sound of rushing waters.

Looking into the long future it is easy to believe that this combination of temperate to warm climate with the maximum elevation to be found anywhere on the eastern seaboard will endear itself to untold thousands of nature lovers. Here are scores of peaks more than five thousand feet high; twenty of them rise more than six thousand feet above sea level, with Mt. Mitchell in Yancey County, in the center of the area, topping them all at 6,684 feet. Spring brings all the shy ground flowers associated with New England. June puts on a garden show unmatched east of Oregon, of rhododendron and giant laurel lining the parkways at the three thousand-foot level. Summer offers a complete escape from the heat of the coastal plain and the shimmering Mississippi Valley. And fall brings a period of sparkling nights and brilliant days. Even if winter drives all tourists back to their labors in the lowlands, it sends out special invitations to all sportsmen.

FISHING AND HUNTING ARE POSSIBLE THROUGHOUT THE YEAR

Since the first whites came into the mountains every man and boy has known that all work and daily chores lead up to but one thing—to go out with gun and dog. In such a population it would be folly even for the Federal Government to fail to make some provision for hunting on its lands. Accordingly in the national forests within the borders of North Carolina the Federal Government has turned over to the state the management and regulating of hunting and fishing. The work is well done. Bass fishing is unexcelled. A glance at the recreation maps will show you that at no time are you more than ten or fifteen miles away from some deep mountain lake where boats and live bait can be obtained. A detailed description of regulations regarding trout-fishing will illustrate how such sport is handled. The whole mountain district is divided into four areas of the government-owned lands, and outline maps naming streams, highways, and mountains are mimeographed on the backs of sheets the faces of which are devoted to lists of the open dates on named streams according to each area. These sheets together with all other data pertaining to fishing and hunting are furnished gratis by the North Carolina Division of Game and Inland Fisheries at Asheville.

Farthest north is the Boone area in the neighborhood of Blowing Rock and Linville, North Carolina. The streams are bold with many falls and deep pools. Grouse-shooting is excellent here, but this is not the best area for deer and bear and there are none of the wild boars of Russian lineage referred to elsewhere in these pages. The Mt. Mitchell area comes next. Streams flow down deep gorges to rivers like the Toe, which have long stretches comparatively free of shore thickets for good fly-casting. This area is renowned for large bear and deer as well as for grouse and small game. Inns near by are open the year round in Burnsville and Spruce Pine. The new Blue Ridge Parkway leads into the heart of the fishing grounds. No government-controlled trout areas exist from here to a point south and west of Asheville, a distance of about fifty miles. From here due west to Waynesville and south to Brevard are the two areas named Pisgah Game Preserve and Sherwood Wildlife Management Area which lie in a rough triangle of which these three towns are the apexes. Each year the streams which are open for trout fishing in each of these four areas are specified and dates are named for each stream. In 1943 the trout season extended from May 8 to August 31. You

A sportsman's paradise

The storm attacks Mt. Mitchell

pay a dollar a day for fishing or small-game shooting within these regulated areas. This is in addition to your regular county or state license. The stations where these fees are paid are clearly stated on each date sheet and are conveniently located in each area. Out-of-state residents must, of course, take out a nonresident license, but this is not too much of a burden if you are an angler and love the mountains well enough to come to them for an outing. A kindly fisherman I once knew had the right of it. He was wont to say as he cast his fly, "This is one-quarter of it." Then he would look around to where laurel nodded above the pool or up at the tapering hemlocks and add with an inclusive gesture, "This is three-quarters of it."

Formal bear hunts on government-owned lands are staged many times a winter and conducted according to strict regulations. But there are also many other hunts on privately-owned lands which only the initiates attend. The meeting place may be at some large barn where the huntsmen gather around an all-night fire to gorge on fried chicken, swap stories, and perhaps pass a flask or two of the Mason jar variety. After a few winks of sleep in a hayloft, long before dawn, the hunters are sent to their stations on this ridge and that at certain crossings where the "b'ar uses." These stations are often miles apart and some hunters may get a sight of the bear or they may not. Skilled men handle the hounds. From the villages you hear them baying and hear the men's halloos now deep in the valleys far away or perhaps on precipitous heights above you. The hunt may last for days and the bag turn out to be a bear or two weighing anywhere from three hundred to over five hundred pounds.

There is generally good quail-shooting over all mountain farms. On the side of Roan Mountain, near the central part of the Tennessee line, there is a beech forest where grouse aplenty feed on the mast. Grouse are called pheasant by the natives. Here, for those who can take it, is probably the best grouse-shooting south of the

Canadian border, but it is little known to sportsmen. Perhaps the ground is too rough and the accommodations too primitive. Yet the thunderous fellows get up with the same heart-thumping roar that thrills sportsmen from Maine to Minnesota and they put a bush between themselves and the huntsman as skillfully as though schooled by constant practice.

In Pisgah National Forest deer have become so plentiful that the authorities try to regulate their population from year to year by stating the number they would like to have killed and deciding the number of formal hunts accordingly. Deer and bear and wild boar are hunted according to a schedule of dates for the various areas where they abound. You pay a small fee for a two-day hunt and send it in to the same bureau as for the trout-fishing together with your application. This is the "check-in-check-out" system. After you receive your assignment you meet with the other sportsmen at the specified place and check in. When you make a kill, either bear or deer, you check out at once. Experienced guides are in charge of the hunts and you meet kindred spirits from many parts of the country.

But of all the sports in the mountains, that of wild-boar-hunting in the Nantahala National Forest in the heart of the Great Smoky Mountains is the most thrilling and the most exhausting. When November leaves lie brown and deep in the woods around Lake Santeetlah near Robbinsville, fifteen miles from the westernmost mountains and in the southwestern point of our area, ten hunts are held under the auspices of the Santeetlah Co-operative Wildlife Area. It seems that a wealthy Englishman back in 1912 imported wild boars from Russia and turned them loose on Hoopers Bald, near what is now called Joyce Kilmer Memorial Forest. Drawings from among the applicants for these hunts are made by the North Carolina Division of Game and Inland Fisheries at Asheville, and twenty-five hunters are assigned to each hunt.

The sportsmen assemble before daybreak. Local residents supply trained hounds of the common Carolina breed and handle them, four or five brace to the hunt. When the dogs pick up a scent the drivers know by the terrain where to station the hunters. The hounds are loosed and the hunt is on. The quarry is a fierce, shaggy beast with wicked tusks, quick as lightning and weighing anywhere from 225 to 300 pounds. They say that the ruler of Santeetlah is a great blue fellow with long, needle-sharp tusks who weighs around 440 pounds and is big as a heifer. It is the voice of the hounds that tells the hunters whether to stay put or run at breakneck speed through laurel thickets, up rocky heights, or plunge across streams in pursuit. The chase generally lasts all day and is a test of stamina to the last instant when any one of the sportsmen may have to face the boar as he fights his way out of the ring of hounds and makes his last charge. A number of dogs are wounded in each hunt. Most men prefer the 30-30 rifle. All carry side arms in case a rifle jams. Some hunt with cameras and now and then a true Nimrod hunts with bow and arrows. But it is the most dangerous sport on the eastern seaboard and no one without a strong body and alert mind should take part in it.

SOME CLIMATIC DETAILS

Only a romanticist believes that the mountains are a place for remunerative agriculture as compared with the easier operations on even less fertile soil in the lowlands. Of course, there are mountain districts which enjoy exceptional advantages in soil and climate which are favorable for specialty crops such as grapes and apples, peonies and narcissus—things which often command good prices but the marketing and culture of which entails specialized knowledge and technical skill. In such crops altitude is of great importance and a careful study of exact location should be made because it often happens in the mountains that a shift of a few hundred feet may avoid a frost pocket and secure the advantages of a thermal belt. It is noticeable that most successful operations in grape culture or horticulture are conducted by some outsider or a vintner from France or the Rhine and that very few of our native descendants of the original Anglo-Saxon immigrants ever step aside from their ancient struggle for a bare subsistence from corn and vegetables.

Climate in our mountain area is not like anything else in the country. It is well worth the special study our United States Government has given it. For four years accurate records were kept and observations made by responsible, trained men in fifteen key locations scattered over the area we have been considering. At each location four or five sets of recording instruments, housed in well-made cabinets, were placed on southeastern exposures at different elevations within a span which permitted the observer to walk from one cabinet to another to take his readings. The findings revealed interesting evidence, often of a startling nature, which were published by the U. S. Department of Agriculture. They made a volume of over one hundred pages and are replete with photographs of the stations, maps, charts, and tables of statistics about temperature, rainfall, frost and snow, and wise comment on almost everything man may want to know when he sets about selecting land and building for himself a home where he can grow fruits and produce in the mountains.

To get an idea of climatic conditions over the whole area in which the fifteen sets of stations were established we might select the farthest north and highest, the farthest south, a central location, and that at the lowest elevation, and set down the most significant of the statistics for each. Here they are:

Linville. Farthest north and highest elevation, 3,800 feet. In the shadow of Grandfather Mountain (5,964 feet); famous for honey made from the flowers of American lindens; significant location for the district comprising Roaring Gap, Blowing Rock, Linville Falls. Rainfall, 62.72 inches. Snowfall, 24.8 inches. Days with more than 1/100 inch of rainfall, 96. Average July and August temperature, 65.6 degrees. Average January and February temperature, 30.9 degrees. Highest recorded temperature, 87 degrees. Lowest recorded temperature, —16 degrees. Growing season from first to last killing frost, 150 days.

Highlands. Farthest south and wettest. Elevation, 3,350 feet. Rainfall, 81.73 inches. Snowfall, 18.1 inches. Days with more than 1/100 inch of rainfall, 121. Average July and August temperature, 66.1 degrees. Average January and February temperature, 34.9 degrees. Highest recorded temperature, 87 degrees. Lowest recorded temperature, —19 degrees. Growing season from first to last killing frost, 157 days.

Asheville. Central location and intermediate elevation. Elevation, 2,253 feet. Figures are significant for surrounding area, including Biltmore south to Hendersonville and Flat Rock. The most populous and industrious district of the mountains and the driest in the entire state of North Carolina so far as actual rainfall is concerned. Rainfall, 40.37 inches. Snowfall, 10.9 inches. Days with more than 1/100 inch of rain, 133. Average July and August temperature, 71.7 degrees. Average January and February temperature, 38.7 degrees. Highest recorded temperature, 96 degrees. Lowest recorded temperature, —6 degrees. Growing season from first to last killing frost, 193 days.

Tryon. Lowest elevation, in the thermal belt grape district. Elevation on Trade Street 1,075 feet, and at the lowest station of the Government observation location, 950 feet. Rainfall, 57.77 inches. Snowfall, 7.5 inches. Days with more than 1/100 inch of rain, 117. Average July and August temperature, 76.3 degrees. Average January and February temperature, 43 degrees. Highest recorded temperature, 105 degrees. Lowest recorded temperature, —3 degrees. Growing season from first to last killing frost, 194 days.

Many freaks of climate and strange anomalies occur in the mountains. For example, observe the days when rain fell in Asheville, which is in the heart of the driest county in the state—133. Now look at the same category for Highlands in the heart of the wettest district east of the Rockies—only 121. Evidently maximum precipitation in a year does not necessarily imply the greatest number of days when more than 1/100 inch of rain falls. It is interesting to learn that three spectacular downpours have occurred in Asheville during the last thirty-three years at approximately ten-year intervals. In May, 1909, 2.70 inches of rain fell in two hours. In October, 1918, 2.73 inches fell in two hours. In September, 1929, 1.86 inches fell in two hours.

Snowfall in a year has been 39 inches at Banner Elk while only five miles away at Linville the figure stands at 24 inches. Also note that the wettest and the driest counties in the state adjoin each other, namely in the Highlands and the Asheville districts. In Macon County it is 81.73 average inches per year. In adjoining Jackson County it is only 43.96 inches.

Here is the explanation of the tremendous precipitation in the Highlands district. Winds, like invading bombers, load up with moisture in the Southwest Atlantic and the Gulf and take off for the North. The bombers meet no fighter resistance to speak of until they attempt to sail over the mountain formations that rise in a jagged wall where the Appalachian system begins in the tumbled masses of the Blue Ridge and the Great Smoky Mountains. But where Brush Mountain (4,200 feet) and Satulah Mountain (4,560 feet) guard the pass at the cornering of Georgia and South Carolina with North Carolina the moisture-laden winds hit the first water-cooled air pockets. There the bombers are forced to throw out a cloud screen as they thrust ahead. But in a few minutes they are met by the ack-ack resistance of still colder air currents which hover over the countless streams and waterfalls at Highlands, where Whiteside Mountain (4,930 feet) rears his head, and right behind him are Hogback Mountain (4,950 feet), Wayah Bald (5,336 feet), Black Knob (6,273 feet), Tennessee Bald (5,622 feet), Cold Mountain (6,000 feet), Water Rock Mountain (6,480 feet), and Mount Pisgah (5,749 feet)—all of them within a radius of only twenty miles. What a tangled cluster! The bomber winds have opened their bomb bays long before they reach them and they are forced to fly on in scattered formations comparatively empty handed. That is why the Highlands stations recorded the greatest precipitation east of the Rockies. But this phenomenon is merely a cause of wonder in our kindly region as compared with the harshness of desert on one side of a range and forests on the other out on the West Coast.

But what of the sunny days—days when we draw in our breath and say, "This is typical Asheville" or "Linville" or "Tryon weather?" If I have emphasized rain and frost and snow in my statistics it is that for some reason they seem to be the rare exception. All who have lived in and loved this wilderness of mountain peaks and fertile pockets have long agreed that it is the Land of the Sky. And all its contrasts of crashing storms and rolling thunder with flashing nights and brilliant days, of lazy clouds and blue mist fragrant with wood smoke at evening are sublimated into old Mr. Pittman's conviction as he let his eyes travel up the mountainside from his cabin door, "I reckon this is the finest country in all the world."

Among the strange vagaries of climate which the government studies revealed, special attention is paid to the subject of thermal belts. These are sheltered bands where over a long period there is a distinct lessening of wide ranges of temperature as compared with contiguous territory. Examples are the vineyards along the sides of Tryon and Warrior Mountains, where Nature first showed the way with a marked belt of ancient wild vines, black and python-like, that twisted and tossed among the tulip trees and oaks.

Even a casual observer can see a difference in springtime along this belt where the hardwoods put out their new leaves quite definitely in advance of those either above or below it. Also in winter this belt is most plainly visible in a frost line. On January 28, 1943, although a long night of rain had flooded the valley, the upper thermal line along the whole length of Tryon Mountain and the Warriors was plainly marked in glistening white above dun slopes. This line corresponded exactly with the upper border of the vineyards planted by a Kentucky gentleman, Mr. W. T. Lindsay, more than fifty years ago. With the first direct beams of the sun the glory flashed for a brief half hour, then faded to drab winter branches and dripping rocks.

The government reports are careful to make clear that the thermal qualities are revealed in the averages and that the days free from storms are those when the most startling variations of temperature in the belt area from those above and below it are most evident. For example, the morning of January 21, 1943 dawned clear and still—a perfect day for quail-shooting off in the Green River district at the end of Tryon Mountain. Dr. John Preston lives near the foot of the Lindsay Vineyards. When he called me to see if I could go gunning with him his thermometer read seventeen degrees while mine, only three-quarters of a mile away, read twelve degrees, and twenty minutes later, when we reached "Shorty" MacDonald's at Mills Spring eight miles to the southeast, *his* thermometer showed only five degrees above zero. These observations by conscientious amateurs are at least significant of the settled opinion of the residents of the district. But a sad denouement in this year of war when fruits and vegetables are of supreme importance is that on Friday, the sixteenth of April, killing winds of cold swept down from the north and all the young grapes shriveled on the vines and hundreds of thousands of peach trees lost their fruit in Spartanburg County to the south of us. Such a late killing frost has not been known for forty years.

In contrast to the untimely cold there is the fact that in the afternoon of January 19, 1943, there was a distant roll of thunder in the mountains, bees clambered over the yellow jasmine in the dooryards, and in the evening moths and a hatch of gnats came out to bother, while frogs set up a merry jingle in the river bottoms. At 11:15 that night the thermometer read sixty degrees.

In an effort to see whether it is possible to forecast changes in the weather from changes in barometric pressure I have kept consistent day-to-day records for months at a time. The results are disappointing. Often at the end of a rainy period the barometer takes a drop which is coincidental with a clearing gale from the northwest. Again at the end of a period of clear weather in which the barometer has held steady for days there will be a rise after a change to rain has already begun. It seems to me that wind shifts and changes in humidity are more significant of what is to come in the mountains than barometric variations.

In summer our favorite run for a quick, spectacular trip in the heights was to hop in the car bright and early and spend the afternoon on the Bobby Jones Course at Highlands. In eighty miles we climbed 2,400 feet and passed from a spot where the mean temperature throughout the year is 60 degrees to a grassy plateau of lakes and streams and pointed peaks where the temperature averages only 48.7 degrees. The rainfall at the Tryon level rarely exceeds 60 inches per year, while at Highlands it has gone as high as 111.20 inches in a single solar cycle.

Along the way we get the story of this change in temperature and rainfall from observing the tree growth and mosses at the various levels. There are no white pines indigenous to Tryon. Laurel and rhododendron are as you see them in New England. A few Carolina hemlocks inhabit the deep coves where a new waif, the purple-flowered paulownia from Japan, is grabbing greedily at every inch of air space between the native hardwoods. Mosses on rocks and trees are normal size. Blueberries and huckleberries are almost unknown. Figs ripen luxuriously and mockingbirds sing in dooryards.

But long before you reach the halfway point marked change appears. At Flat Rock white pines begin to replace the common weed pines. On above Brevard at the village of Pisgah Forest, mountain laurel, that dainty "calico bush" of New England, grows tree high in the "pink beds" with massive burled roots which, I regret to report, are being uprooted with dynamite and derrick by pipe-makers of the North to replace war-banned *bruyère* no longer obtainable from Mediterranean shores. When you reach Cashiers near High Hampton the Carolina hemlocks are giant size and mighty spruce trees are "snaked" down the mountainsides for spars in ship building. Here each fence post and board is bearded with moss. It hangs from every dead branch and thrusts out from the north side of tree trunks as though some prankster had tacked long strips of sage-green Angora wool on them. Such is the effect of summer mists. Blueberries and huckleberries are plentiful, but no mockingbirds are inhabitants of the region.

It is evident from all this that the mountain area is really a summer playground so far as outsiders are concerned. An increasing surge of families coming to the mountain area in search of ideal conditions for all-year residence has set in among those who are responding to the back-to-the-soil movement, and rightly so. This is most evident in the French Broad Valley and the Mills River district, above Hendersonville, where people of means are discovering that dairy farms patterned after the pioneer Biltmore Dairies offer ideal conditions of climate and soil. But there are many other good localities, such as the Burnsville district, northeast of Asheville, where beef cattle thrive and the highest mountains of the whole galaxy surround it. Mt. Mitchell and Mt. Celo are due south of it and Roan Mountain is due north. While winters are much colder than at the Tryon level they are as nothing compared with those that settle down under dun skies around the Great Lakes or the cold of New York and New England. For spring comes to this three thousand-foot level a month earlier and fall lingers a month later, and the climate in between is bracing but not extreme.

Mountain communities have long ago given up the contest with such towns as Pinehurst and Aiken for winter tourist trade. The only exception is the Tryon district where for the past fifty years the fall-to-spring population has far exceeded that of the summer months. One person has told another about the mountain trails for riding and the "hunting country" where the long crescent of White Oak, Tryon, the Warriors, Melrose, Rocky Spur, and Hogback Mountains is in full view. Here the children and grandchildren of those who used to come for winter vacations from Wisconsin and all the states eastward are tucking cottages away in the hills and buying tracts of land for substantial farms. You hear city folks talk knowingly about farrowing sows and how much they made on their sweet potato crop.

If you would like to see all these people at their best and mingle with them and their native-born neighbors; if you would like to taste an old-time barbecue and dance the old square dances on the green in time to mountain music; if you would care to recall frontier days of ox teams and covered wagons or compete in the simple, homey contests about who has the best horse and buggy, or the best brace of foxhounds; or if you want to take part in a steeplechase or don your hunting pink and test your stamina over jumps and streams, up hill and down dale with those who love the hunt for its own sake and not because it is the fashionable thing—why then the right thing to do is happen along in early April. But if you wish to join the company of those nature lovers, writers, artists, riders, common businessmen, and poets who have been coming here since the days of Sidney Lanier, there is no particular season. The show begins in early fall when dogwood and holly trees are ripening berries for the holidays and lasts till the Judas trees and silver bells tell us it is time again for the spring barbecue.

But no matter where and when you come to these mountains, all who know them will assure you that the climax of the symphony which climate and altitude provide is to listen to the birds while you wander under flaming azalea on the pass up near the top of Pisgah Mountain or climb up to Craggy Gardens where the purple rhododendrons stretch in unbelievable profusion clear to the top of Craggy Mountain. This will be your reward if you stay through May and the first weeks of June.

CHAPTER EIGHT

THROUGH THE YEAR IN THE GREAT SMOKY MOUNTAINS NATIONAL PARK, MONTH BY MONTH

by Arthur Stupka

The Great Smoky Mountains National Park lies astride the boundary between the states of Tennessee and North Carolina, and its area of approximately seven hundred square miles is about equally divided between those two states. If we were to draw a line from the southern shore of Lake Erie, at a point fifty miles west of Cleveland, due south to the northern coast of the Gulf of Mexico, the Smokies would lie at the halfway mark. They also lie very near the halfway mark between the Mississippi River and the North Carolina coast. The Great Smoky Mountains represent a portion of the high middle chain of three parallel mountain systems which, running northeast and southwest from Pennsylvania to Georgia and Alabama, together make up the Southern Appalachian Mountains. The Cumberland Mountains, separated by the Great Valley of East Tennessee, lie to the westward; the Blue Ridge Mountains of Western North Carolina lie to the eastward. Practically this entire high divide, bounded on the east by the Big Pigeon River and on the west by the Little Tennessee River has been designated as the Great Smoky Mountains National Park, and as such will be preserved for the enjoyment of the American people for all time.

The high backbone of the Smokies reaches its maximum elevation on Clingmans Dome, 6,642 feet above sea level. Only Mt. Mitchell (6,683 feet), which lies seventy miles to the east, has a higher elevation. We can say, therefore, that the second-highest peak east of the Black Hills of South Dakota, is within the Great Smoky Mountains National Park. A macadam-surfaced motor road, following the main divide southwestward from Newfound Gap, ascends to within a half-mile of the summit of Clingmans Dome. For a distance of thirty-six consecutive miles, the main Smokies ridge remains above the 5,000-foot altitude. It is along this high crest that the Appalachian Trail, a hikers' pathway which extends from Mt. Katahdin, in Maine, to Mt. Oglethorpe, in northern Georgia (over 2,000 miles), winds its way. Within the National Park are sixteen peaks whose altitude is greater than 6,000 feet.

At the higher elevations in the Great Smoky Mountains National Park we find the most extensive stand of virgin red spruce in the Eastern United States, and the combined acreage of unspoiled hardwoods may be without equal. In the approximately 202,000 acres of primeval forest growth we find some 130 species of native trees, many of which become giants of their kind. The number of shrubs is likewise great, and certain species assume definite treelike proportions. Altogether more than 1,400 kinds of flowering plants are known to grow here, and these include extensive stands of some of the most colorful wild flowers in eastern America. Beginning in late winter when the alders and various herbaceous plants come into flower, the pageant of bloom continues well into the autumn when the asters, gentians, and other species finally yield to the frosts.

To a New Englander, the high-altitude forests of the Great Smoky Mountains National Park would appear very similar to those of Maine, New Hampshire, and Vermont. The aspen and the white birches are absent from the Southern Appalachian Mountains, but the red spruce, yellow birch, mountain ash, moosewood, red maple, mountain maple, Canadian hemlock, fire cherry, and others are common species. Many of the shrubs are likewise identical in these widely-separated regions, for we recognize the hobblebush, witch hazel, red elder, withe rod, trailing arbutus, chokeberry and wintergreen. Many are the herbaceous plants which are at home in both places—clintonia (the "bluebead lily" of the north woods; the "amber bell" of the southern highlands), painted trillium, partridgeberry, Indian pipe, lady's-slipper, Canada mayflower, white baneberry, and twisted-stalk. In the half-hour's drive from Cherokee, North Carolina, or Gatlinburg, Tennessee, to Newfound Gap in the Great Smoky Mountains National Park, one passes through a change in plant species which is not unlike the change encountered when one drives from northern Georgia or Alabama to northern New England. To an individual who finds the study of plants especially appealing, this remarkable transition is of particular interest and significance. With increasing altitude in the Great Smokies one encounters increasing precipitation and fog, lower temperatures, soils of higher acidity, a growing season of shorter duration, winds of higher velocity, and other changes. Aside from their greater amount of precipitation and their soils of higher acidity, the upper Smokies experience temperatures, fog conditions, and length of growing season which would approximate the environment along the Maine coast.

It is at the lower and middle elevations that the species of plants become so numerous in this Southern Appalachian highland. Here there are more kinds of native trees than in all of Europe. In addition to the already-mentioned 1,400 species of flowering plants, botanists have discovered 49 ferns and fern-allies, 325 mosses and liverworts, over 200 lichens, and 1,200 fungi. The chestnut, tulip tree, black cherry, Canadian hemlock, magnolia, white ash, American holly, southern buckeye, red oak, silver bell, and others grow to exceptionally large size.

Occasionally the forest is interrupted by a lower-growing light-green mass of plants which serve to give a smooth appearance to the rough ridgetops which they carpet. Such areas are known locally as "laurel slicks." They are, in reality, extremely dense tangled growths of rhododendrons (called "laurel" by the mountain people), with some amounts of mountain laurel, blueberry, smilax, and occasionally sand myrtle. But it is the rhododendrons which predominate; when they are in bloom, in June, the spectacle they present is gorgeous beyond description.

The great varieties of plants which grow in the Smokies occupy diversified habitats. Although no natural lakes or permanent ponds are to be found in this area, the 5,800-foot range of altitude which lies between the lowest and highest places in the park denotes a varied environment. Animal as well as plant life is present here in considerable variety. More than 50 kinds of fur-bearers, 200 birds, 75 reptiles and amphibians, 74 fishes, and a correspondingly large number of species of insects and other invertebrates are known from the park area. With the exception of a few large mammals, such as the elk, wood bison, mountain lion, timber wolf, and otter, all of which once inhabited this region, the animal life has suffered but little change since the coming of the first white man. White-tailed deer have been reduced greatly in numbers, but should increase in the coming years. Black bears may be as plentiful here today as they were a century and a half ago. Duck hawks, ravens, wild turkeys, and other birds which have become rare elsewhere in the eastern states find a haven in this area of extensive wilderness. Brook trout occupy the upper reaches of the streams and the rainbow has been introduced to the warmer waters. These important game species, with the black bass in a few streams near the park boundaries, furnish fine sport in an unspoiled environment. Scientists have reported the occurrence of more species of salamanders here than in any other area of similar extent. Zoologists have found in these mountains a large number of insects and spiders which proved to be new to science.

To this primeval wilderness came American pioneers in the eighteenth century, to experience the continuing struggle of man with an untamed environment and aboriginal enemies that characterized the American frontier. Elsewhere in the following century the frontier passed on, yielding to change and innovation. But here in these silent and majestic mountains, the conditions of "the old frontier, that put the hard fiber in the American spirit and the long muscles on the American back," persisted to give future generations " a sense of the land from which their forefathers hewed their homes."

In the more favored coves, clearings of the mountain pioneer still prevail against a jealous and ever-encroaching forest. In these places sturdy log structures, the timbers hewed with a skill now lost, remain as eloquent testimony to the manner of domestic life. Attendant structures, together with many varieties of handmade machinery utilizing the power of mountain streams, the profuse assortment of handmade household objects attesting to the ingenuity and resourcefulness of man, all fashioned from the simplest of native materials, are still available to tell their own story of the pioneer way of life. In these folk survivals, their kind unequaled elsewhere in variety, quantity, and originality, are preserved the physical and cultural material of a typically American pioneering experience.

In the Great Smoky Mountains, as in practically all national parks, the finest views, the loveliest flowers, the grandest forests, and the best wilderness adventures await us along the trails. What is seen from an automobile may be all and more than we had hoped for, but neither this nor any other national park area can be judged simply by driving along its highways. Bring along a pair of comfortable walking shoes, some heavy socks, and a determination to see the Great Smokies afoot. After you have gained the summit of Mt. LeConte, the jagged backbone of the Sawteeth, or the high grassy expanse of Andrews Bald, you too will agree that that's the way to go. At such places you can quote Emerson and say, "I am taught the poorness of our invention, the ugliness of towns and palaces."

Over six hundred miles of trails in the Great Smoky Mountains National Park will bring the hiker to mountaintops, waterfalls, virgin forests, and mountain meadows. In going to these places the song of a forest bird or the sight of a flower or other natural object will delight many a hiker. Our lives become enriched when we learn that the singer was a winter wren—a midget of a bird whose home is in the northern forests of spruce and fir and in the extension of that forest southward along the crest of the Southern Appalachian Mountains—that the flower was a red elder, in bloom over a month ago at the foot of the mountain. Recognizing this desire on the part of a great many visitors to become better acquainted with the superlative areas under its administration, the National Park Service has established a Branch of Natural History whose personnel, the park naturalists and ranger-naturalists, conduct a free program of guided trips to outstanding places within the various areas. In the Great Smoky Mountains National Park, this program extends from June through October, and everyone is cordially invited to participate. Some of the trips may be long and somewhat strenuous, whereas others cover less than three miles for the round trip. Bird walks appear on the naturalists' program in June and July, and illustrated talks covering various phases of the natural history of the Great Smokies are given in places where park visitors congregate.

"When is the best time to visit the Great Smoky Mountains National Park?" So often have I been asked this question that for the purposes of what remains of this chapter I have planned to draw upon notes in my journals which will serve to give one an idea of what to expect from January through December. Of course it must be understood that nature's moods are extremely variable; the April of the past year was, in certain respects, quite unlike the April of any other year, but we could count on such things, for example, as the arrival of the redstart, the departure of the hermit thrush, the blooming of several species of trilliums, the renewal of activity among black bears and lizards, and the first real assurances of spring in the upland forests of spruce and fir. Those things on which we cannot count, such as the flowering of the yellowwood trees, the setting of seed by the red spruce, and the appearance of large flocks of pine siskins and red crossbills, become of special interest when they do take place. So omnipotent are nature's rhythms that any vagaries she may have, if studied carefully enough and over a *sufficiently long period of time*, will turn out to be orderly enough in the long run.

JANUARY

Which one of us has not been told that the winters of a few decades ago were colder, longer, snowier, and in all respects more severe than those which we have experienced but lately? In a general way, this may be true. The glaciers of the Rockies and the Sierras are shrinking in size, and those of the far north are receding. Some geologists believe that it will be a long time yet before we reach the bottom of the curve beyond which we can expect an upswing toward the next glacial epoch. But now and then come winters which statistics show are just as rigorous as those of fifty and more years ago. Such was the January of 1940 in the Southern Appalachian region.

Beginning with January 25 of that year, the town of Gatlinburg, Tennessee, lying at the foot of Mt. LeConte, reported sub-zero readings on five consecutive days. None of the older residents with whom I talked could recall any winter period quite as cold. To think of any activity on the part of plant or animal life which might have some springtime significance was out of the question. Winter and Carolina wrens, along with certain other species of birds, suffered a severe reduction in numbers. Total precipitation for the month was light, but the amount of snow which fell set records in many of the southern states. Crop damage in the rich vegetable and citrus lands of central Florida was considerable, and the Tennessee Valley Authority revealed that ice conditions in the southeastern states surpassed anything on record. Frost penetration ranged from 15 inches to about 3 feet. Snow piled up to a depth of 38 inches at Newfound Gap in the Park, with drifts greater than five feet in places along the cross-mountain road. At Hiwassee Dam the Authority reported the ice so thick that concrete blocks weighing about 40 pounds were dropped from a height of 200 feet without cracking the ice. Hundreds of lambs were frozen to death in those parts of middle Tennessee where sheep-raising is extensive. Rainbow Falls, one of the very popular hiking objectives in the Park, became a great ice cone above which were suspended huge stalactites of ice. Late in the month, stopping at Newfound Gap to listen for the notes of birds, I heard numbers of sharp reports given off by the sudden cracking of trees. These were, in reality, explosions resulting from the freezing of the moisture-filled cells of the trees' cambium layers, the expansion pressure finally becoming so great that the trees burst. Occasionally such cracks may extend the full length of the main trunk. Years ago I had heard this same winter sound in northern New England, during an exceptionally severe spell of weather.

A winter such as we had early in 1940 represents one extreme, the January of 1937 may well represent the other. Gatlinburg's weather station revealed that only on about six days of that month did the mercury dip below the freezing point, with 21 degrees being the minimum reading. On the other hand, the daily maximum temperatures soared to 60 degrees or more on at least 15 days, with a maximum reading of 81 degrees. No snow fell in the mountains; in fact, not one of the 172 weather-recording stations which cover the states of Tennessee and North Carolina showed a measurable amount of snowfall for the entire month. Black bears, woodchucks, chipmunks, and bats left their hibernating quarters in the Great Smoky Mountains National Park. Some of the snakes and lizards resumed their activities. Excessive rains (amounting to more than double the normal January precipitation), coupled with the high temperatures, not only revived many species of frogs and salamanders but brought on egg-laying by tree frogs, peepers, newts, and spotted salamanders. Wood frogs actually completed their period of "song" and egg-laying before the close of the month. Numerous kinds of insects were on the wing, with honeybees droning about the row of hives which characterizes many a mountain farm. Streamside alders dangled their pollen-laden catkins in the breezes, while such trees as winged elm, slippery elm, American elm, red maple, wild plum, red cedar, and probably others came into bloom. The high-mountain forests of spruce and fir remained dormant, for spring comes late to the uplands of the Smokies, but in the lowlands the observant hiker could have listed perhaps a dozen kinds of wild flowers in bloom.

Somewhere between the exceptionally warm January of 1937 and the record-breaking cold one of 1940 you will find an answer to the question, "What are the Smokies like during the first month of the year?"

FEBRUARY

Whether the ground hog (called "whistle-pig" by the mountain people of the Smokies) does or does not see his shadow on Candlemas Day isn't important. In the first place, the animal is ordinarily asleep in its hibernaculum at that time; in the second place I have been told by a number of native folks that the prediction is to be made on the fourteenth day instead of the second day of this month; and in the third place the statistics have long ago proved all this to be a myth.

Whatever the promises of spring held forth by the preceding month, February must be reckoned with. Ordinarily, the first two or three weeks belong to the winter. Ice will cover the pools wherein the venturesome wood frogs laid their quivering masses of eggs, and the early blooms and young leaves succumb to the cold. Snow comes to whiten the mountains time and again, and the wintering cardinals, juncos, titmice, and sparrows continue to be the guests of considerate people who maintain feeding stations in the towns on the boundary of the Park. The harbingers of spring must stake their claims again and again before they have full title to the land. February may come and go with no perceptible let-up in winter's hold on our bit of earth, but sometimes there comes, late in the month, a break whose potentialities are unmistakable. The pale faces of the first hepaticas appear in the lower woodlands of the Smokies, the crowns of the winged elms become hazy-brown with bloom, and from the marshy places the liquid trill of tree frogs and the plaintive notes of peepers herald the return of spring. In all probability, winter's forces will return again, but from now on no prolonged freeze-up is likely to wipe out all that has been gained. The germ of life which is dotted throughout the wood frogs' gelatinous spawn will mark time if the fetters of winter reglaze the woodland pools, but the seed has been sown and will not be denied.

A few black bears may leave their winter quarters and make extended journeys through the forests of the Park. This may take place during any time of the winter, and such wanderings do not seem to be affected by heavy snows or periods of extreme cold. Rarely are such individuals observed, but their tracks in the snow or in the mud are unmistakable. The majority of these animals remain in hibernation, a time of prolonged deep sleep when the bear's heart beats slowly. Occasionally the sleeper is covered by only a flimsy tangle of branched or upturned tree roots. In the lowlands of the Park this period of inactivity usually extends from December until the following March or April, and it is during this time that the mother bear gives birth to her cubs. Naked, blind, and weighing less than a pound apiece when born, the cubs remain close to the mother until about April, at which time they begin to follow her about on their skinny legs while she searches for food. Occasionally triplets, and in rare instances, quadruplets are born. In our national parks, no animal is as popular with visitors as the bear, and cub bears usually attract more attention than do the older ones.

MARCH

It was a warm day in early March and I was out rambling through the Sugarlands Valley of the Park. (Many Park visitors are acquainted with this long and narrow area which is marked by Chimneys Campground at its upper end and the Administration Building at its lower reaches.) The spicebush and shrub yellowroot were in bloom near the stream and the first of the violets appeared in the woodlands. Anglewing, mourning cloak, and the little spring azure butterflies were on the wing, tiger beetles hurried before me in the old road, and fence lizards made for cover here and there. Suddenly the angry cries of a few crows attracted my attention, and, after making my way to the foot of the pine- and oak-covered slope from whence the disturbance came, I made out the form of a great horned owl in a tall pine near the very crest of the ridge. On either side of the big bird, two crows were stationed, but so absorbed were they in denouncing the owl that they either disregarded my approach or failed to see me. The target of what must have been the most slanderous of corvine language was very much on the alert, and I was confident that he showed concern about my presence. With ear-tufts held high and body stretched to the fullest, the owl was faced with a problem. To take wing would bring the wrath of four crows upon him, to remain at his post—

I stopped when approximately fifty yards from the birds and watched them through my binoculars. Now and then one or two of the crows would leave and dive at the owl as though attempting to force him to take wing, but even in these actions the angry ones seemed to respect the object of their thrusts. Outwardly the harassed one appeared rather unconcerned, although once, when one of the crows either struck him or came very close to doing so he straightened up to his full height and turned his head halfway around to watch the retreat of his tormentor. Again, when all indications were that the big bird was about to fly off, the crows set up such a cry that he settled down as though to wait it out. The crows then lapsed into silence, and thus remained for some moments until finally they took wing, one by one, for by this time they were aware of my espionage and perhaps considered me the greater of the two evils. Since the great horned owl is one of the earliest of the birds to nest, I made my way to the top of the ridge hoping, perchance, to come upon the structure, but before I had taken many steps the bird disappeared into the forest, and my quest proved fruitless. However, on making my way back to the valley, the unexpected discovery of the first trailing arbutus flowers of the year brought ample reward. For me these white and pinkish waxy blooms, as delightful in their fragrance as they are humble in their growth ("gravelweed," the mountain people call the plant), always serve to mark a significant period in the chronicle of the year.

In March the wild geese wing their way northward over the Smokies, and such warblers as the Louisiana water thrush, black-and-white warbler, yellow-throated warbler, and black-throated green warbler may put in their appearance. The rough-winged swallow, brown thrasher, mountain vireo, rusty blackbird, grackle, cowbird, and chipping sparrow are among others who are due to arrive in the Park before March gives way to April.

APRIL

March may come and go with many a disappointment to temper the promises which that month holds forth, but in April the forces of spring can no longer be denied, and by the end of this month the floodgates are opened wide. The surge is northward and upward simultaneously—northward from the Smokies into Kentucky and the Virginias and on into New England and Canada; upward from the forests of elms, sweet gum, ironwood, and sycamore to forests of yellow birch, mountain ash, spruce, and fir. And, interestingly enough, at about the time the earliest wild flowers appear in the forests of Maine, the flowering season is just getting under way in the spruce and fir zone in the Great Smoky Mountains National Park. A thousand times more rapid is this northward progression of the season, as compared to the upward advance.

Those of us who live at the foot of the Smokies expect to see snow covering the higher mountains on occasions in April. Late in the month it may fall on the spring beauties and trout lilies which herald the blooming season at altitudes above 5,000 feet, and the Carolina juncos ("snowbirds") may be incubating eggs under a snow-covered canopy of rootlets and dried plant remains. Ordinarily the "sarvice" tree becomes arrayed with heavy creamy-white bloom by the first part of April. Known elsewhere by such names as "shadbush," "serviceberry," "Juneberry," and others, it occupies a greater altitudinal range (900-6,400 feet) than any other tree in the Smokies. At its lower limits, I have known it to come into flower as early as March 10 (1938), whereas this very same plant did not bloom until April 10 in the cold late spring of 1941. As lovely in its form and flower-color as it is early, conspicuous, and wide-ranging, no other species is so faithful an indicator of the upward progress of the season. In the lowland forests of the Park there are a few trees whose early blooming comes before that of the "sarvice," but above altitudes of 5,000 feet it is a true harbinger of spring. The background of evergreen spruces and firs sets off its beauty in so striking a manner that we cannot help but regard it as the queen of the high-mountain forests. Whereas its blooming over much of the eastern states is concentrated within a period of two or three weeks, here in the Park there have been years when fully eleven weeks elapsed from its coming into flower along Abrams Creek or Little River to the time when its blooms still persisted on the slopes of Clingman's Dome.

Bird migration reaches its peak at the end of April when late-arriving species such as the blackpoll warbler, the cuckoos, the tanagers, and various flycatchers arrive in the Park. The duck hawk is nesting on precipitous cliffs, whippoorwills make the lower valleys ring with their persistent calling, broad-winged hawks are staking their claims as they soar high over the mountains, and ruffed grouse drum from favored logs in the forest. While I have heard the drumming of the grouse in every month of the year, the strutting performance seems to be confined largely to the April breeding season. With tail feathers spread and held erect, the male bird, his neck feathers ruffled and his body appearing abnormally large, struts before his lady-love. At frequent intervals his head is given a vigorous shake during which it may be dipped almost to the ground. What effect does it have on the lady? I don't know, but so absorbed does he become in this performance that on several occasions when his courtship took place in the center of the road I have had to stop my car to keep from running over him, or else slow down to a speed of less than five miles per hour.

MAY

If it is wild flowers you wish to see, then you should plan to be in the Great Smoky Mountains National Park from late April to late June. Some of the earliest ones, such as the hepatica and bloodroot, will be missed, while many of the summer and early autumn blooms are yet to come, but the trained and observant botanist would list the greatest variety of flowering plants in bloom at this time. (I hardly need mention that the picking of wild flowers is not permitted in any of our national parks; they are here for all to enjoy.) By early May, the flame azalea will be in luxuriant bloom in the lowlands; by the middle of the month the mountain laurel will be coming into flower; and as May is drawing to a close the first clusters of the rhododendron serve to draw many a hiker out on those trails where this gorgeous shrub has its best growth. In May the native magnolias display their large cream-colored blooms and the closely-related tulip tree ("poplar," as it is erroneously called) plays host to a myriad bees. Silverbell, flowering dogwood, black locust, fire cherry, yellow buckeye, and many trees with relatively less conspicuous flowers will be in bloom at this time. In addition to flame azalea, laurel, and rhododendron, other shrubs with showy flowers will include blackberry, purple-flowering raspberry, sand myrtle, elder, hobblebush, and dwarf pink locust. Trilliums, some of which began their period of flowering in March, continue to be well represented here at this time; of these, the large maroon-colored Vasey's trillium, the nodding white- or pink-colored Catesby's trillium, the dark-centered erect white trillium, and the painted trillium (considered by many the finest of all this family) are plentiful enough in their favored habitats.

By the latter part of May the mother grouse is abroad leading her precious brood of young chicks. The responsibility of motherhood has brought on a change in this ordinarily shy bird which must be seen to be fully appreciated. One day, in the spruce forest near Indian Gap, I caught sight of what appeared to be a surprisingly tame female grouse. Upon approaching to within fifteen or twenty feet of the bird, two small chicks suddenly broke from cover almost at my feet and, screaming at the top of their lungs, scrambled away. Puffing, as though enraged, with wings quivering, the parent bird advanced right up to my feet, hissing, clucking, blowing, even growling—at least, so it seemed. In the meanwhile the chicks disappeared, the mother grouse slowly retreated, and all became quiet except for the occasional clucking note she uttered. I left them to become reunited, for it had not been my intention to bring about a panic in the usually calm life of a grouse family. Once, while on horseback, I had all I could do for a moment to calm the animal I was riding when we suddenly came upon a mother grouse and her brood, and many a rider has told me of having had a similar experience.

JUNE

How often I have been asked the question, "When should I visit the Great Smoky Mountains National Park in order to find the rhododendrons at their best?" Many a vacation is planned to coincide with the peak of blossoming of these fine shrubs. First it should be stated that of the various rhododendrons in the Park, the one most people favor is the Catawba or rose-purple rhododendron. Ordinarily this begins blooming in late May at its lowest range (3,000-3,500 feet) in the area, and reaches a flowering peak around June 10-15. At the later date it is in full bloom in the vicinity of Alum Cave Bluffs and on the various trails on Mt. LeConte. Toward the close of June the hiker should still find excellent flowers at a place such as Andrew's Bald. This evergreen shrub grows best on high ridges where it is exposed to the sun, and many of the so-called "laurel slicks" which one sees to good advantage in the drive over the cross-mountain highway are dominated by this plant. The great white rhododendron, on the other hand, favors the more moist situations under the forest canopy. Its blooming period begins in June, but it is not until July and on into August that its flowering peak is reached. This most abundant of the various rhododendrons in the Park is one of the commonest shrubs over wide areas of the Southern Appalachian region. A third species, the dwarf or Carolina rhododendron, blooms during the latter half of June and on through July. Its leaves are about the same size and shape as the leaves of the mountain laurel and its flowers are magenta, or purple-pink. Open situations at high altitudes, usually on the face of a cliff or on a mountain summit, are its preferred habitat.

Botanically speaking, the azaleas are species of the genus *Rhododendron.* Several kinds are to be found here, but I will mention but three of them. The pinkster flower, blooming in April and early May, is restricted to the lower elevations (mostly below 2,000 feet) especially at the western end of the Park. The smooth azalea is a fragrant whitish-flowered (sometimes pink) species which blooms in June; it is not a common shrub here, growing at altitudes of from 1,500 to 5,000 feet. The flame azalea, called wild honeysuckle by the mountain people, is one of the finest wild shrubs in the Park. Many discriminating flower-lovers will put it first on their list of favorites. In these mountains it has an altitudinal range almost as great as the "sarvice" tree. Except for places such as Gregorys Bald and Andrews Bald, where much of it is concentrated, this shrub is not nearly as plentiful here as the laurel and evergreen rhododendron. William Bartram, pioneer plant explorer, described "this most celebrated species of Azalea," as being "in general the colour of the finest red-lead, orange and bright gold, as well as yellow and cream-coloured. These various splendid colours can be seen on separate branches of the same plant; and the clusters of blossoms cover the shrub in such incredible profusion on the hillsides that suddenly opening in view from the dark shades we are alarmed with apprehension of the woods being set on fire. This is certainly the most gay and brilliant flowering shrub yet known."

Those who wish to see one of the finest natural wild-flower displays in eastern America and who are capable and willing to hike ten miles (round trip) to Gregorys Bald, should plan to be in the Park on about the twentieth day of June. It is then that the flame azalea is near its blooming peak. Should you arrive a few days later, drive to the end of the highway on Clingmans Dome and hike down (two miles) to Andrews Bald. There the spectacle isn't on the scale of Gregory, but it's mighty fine at that.

In June the mountain laurel, passion-vine, galax, trumpet creeper, mountain oxalis, mountain camellia, and various wild orchids (twayblade, purple-fringed, green-fringed, spreading pogonia) are among the long list of plants blooming in the Park. And I should add that it is in June that the wild strawberries and blackberries are ripe, and that you can take with you all that you can eat.

JULY

By middle July the regular summer's lull in bird activity is well under way, and the singing period for most species comes to a close. However, the winter wren, considered by many the finest singer in the upland forests of the Smokies, continues his fine vocal performance during the early part of the month. Mr. Albert Ganier, veteran Tennessee ornithologist, describes the song as a "tinkling roundelay," and many a bird-lover has gone to great lengths in an attempt to convey the charm and magic of this delightful, wild, sparkling melody. Some years ago in the early summer, while camping out in the dense coniferous forest near Mt. Guyot, second-highest peak in the Park, a few of these brown midgets commenced their singing shortly after sunset and kept it up through the twilight period. As soon as one sounded the last note of his rippling refrain, another, who could not have been far away, began, and so it went round after round during which there was no break and no interruption or overlap by these musicians. In the meanwhile the western sky was darkening and a few stars appeared through the trees overhead, and finally, when night fell, the last of the stanzas ended in silence. Only the voice of the wind in the crowns of the spruces and firs remained to break the stillness. Early the next morning, before the sun arose in the east, the winter wrens were welcoming the coming day with their melodious trills.

Perhaps I am overlooking some reference to it, but so far I have found no mention of the antiphonal singing of the winter wren in the works on our eastern birds. Ornithologists have reported upon the antiphonal singing of certain species of wrens of Central America, but there, where both the male and female may be good singers, the performance appears to be harmonized between the sexes.

In July the sourwood tree displays its fragrant cream-colored fingers of bloom—the source of a particularly fine honey. The ill-fated American chestnut comes into flower at the higher altitudes where it appears to be making a last stand against the devastating blight. The wild Turk's-cap lily, which may attain a height of seven or eight feet, reaches its blooming peak during the second or third week of the month; hundreds of these, growing in close proximity, are to be found along the section of the Appalachian Trail between Clingmans Dome and Silers Bald. Brilliant scarlet fruit-clusters adorn the red elder bushes at high altitudes, and the ripening "sarvice" fruits attract bears and birds alike. Late in the month the goldenrods begin to light their torches in the lowlands of the Park, and we are reminded that the year has already passed its crest.

AUGUST

Because the Park is visited by the greatest number of people in those months when our precipitation is heaviest, the region is often regarded as one of excessive rainfall. The records show July to be the wettest month, with August a close second. At the foot of the Smokies, on the Tennessee side, the annual precipitation has averaged about 53 inches; on the North Carolina side it is less. Generally speaking, the higher one ascends the mountains, the greater is the rainfall (and snowfall), so that the crest of this high divide may average 75-80 inches per year. This, of course, is one of the important factors accounting for the luxuriant vegetation which characterizes these mountains. Interestingly enough, the two wettest months (July and August) are followed by the three driest months (September, October, November), and those persons who spend their vacations here in the autumn rarely encounter much rainfall. As a result of the mid-August hurricane of 1940, which swept westward from the West Indies, the highest mountain in the Park received almost five and one-half inches of rain in a twenty-four-hour period; Mt. LeConte, the third highest peak, received a total well in excess of sixteen inches for that month. Many of the summer rains come in the early afternoon, and the hiker should be prepared for them at this season.

At the lower elevations the Hercules'-club, second only to witch-hazel as the latest-blooming tree, becomes crowned with its showy whitish flowers. Along the fence rows the wild clematis or "virgin's-bower" displays a profusion of creamy blooms, and in the fields the ironweed, evening primrose, cardinal flower, and goldenrods are arrayed in striking colors. Mushrooms of varied hues dot the forest floor, blueberries ripen, scarlet glossy fruits bring new beauty to the magnolias, and many trees and shrubs begin to take on their autumnal hues.

In the higher mountains the number and variety of wild flowers may well surprise the hiker. In open clearings, such as one frequently finds along the Appalachian Trail, a dozen species may be blooming within a small area, with many a gaudy butterfly flitting about adding its bit of life and color. Among these high-mountain wild flowers of August are the yellow or orange blooms of golden-glow, jewelweed, yellow-fringed orchids, and goldenrod; the purple of closed gentians and monkshood; the red or pink of bee balm, joe-pye weed, turtlehead, and Clingman's mint, and the white of Indian pipe, asters, saxifrage, grass-of-Parnassus, meadow rue, dodder, black cohosh, and white snakeroot.

Squirrels are harvesting a varied food supply at this time, and the hiker frequently comes upon evidences of such activity along the trails. At highest elevations fir and spruce cones are cut for

The world of peaks

Majestic Mt. LeConte from the hiking trail to Greenbrier Pinnacle

A low-hanging veil of haze all but obliterates the gorges below White Rock

Mt. Sterling is pointed out

their seeds; lower down, the maples, tulip, silverbell, beech, chestnut, magnolia, hemlock, and buckeyes are sought, while at the base of the mountains hickories, walnut, butternut, oaks, and pines are favored species.

In places the bears are digging for the soft whitish larvae in the ground nests of the yellow jackets. The penalty which they pay is, apparently, not too severe from the standpoint of a bear, for this is a favored food item for bruin in August. Although we may sympathize with the yellow jackets who survive this act of plunder and who now hover about the ruins, it is best to keep our distance, for the insects are now angry enough to take on all comers. Many a horseback rider has been confronted, suddenly, with the task of quieting a mild-mannered animal who inadvertently trespassed upon such a scene.

SEPTEMBER

Frosts have been known to occur in the higher mountains of the Smokies during every month of the year, but that is exceptional. Ordinarily the last frost comes in late April or in May, while the first will wither the ferns there in September. Thus the growing season at these high altitudes is shortened at both ends.

October finds the woodlands in their finest array of colors, but those who visit the Park at that time miss a species whose leaf color is truly remarkable. This is the hobblebush or witch hobble, an abundant high-mountain shrub whose large roundish leaves reach their color peak in September. The hiker will encounter this plant along all the trails which take him through forests of spruce and fir. Its orange-red fruit clusters are showy enough, yet these often go unnoticed against the richness and variety of leaf hues. Even the variegated sweet gum and sassafras of lowland areas do not afford such range—or am I prejudiced in favoring the hobblebush? For I have found it abundant on the slopes of Katahdin, Maine's highest peak, and on Cadillac, Acadia National Park's highest mountain, and have learned to associate it with those splendid northern forests which, in their southernmost extension, form the crowning glory of the Park.

By the end of September many a wild plant is ripening its fruits. Of these, the strawberry bush, called "hearts a-bustin' with love" by some of our mountain people, dangles its rich glossy crimson fruits from frosty-pink husks and becomes a favorite with many who discover it.

In the lowlands the September nights are vocal with the fiddling of katydids, crickets, and grasshoppers. The first of the wintering white-throated sparrows and ruby-crowned kinglets arrive, while others, such as the olive-backed thrushes and many warblers, stop here to rest and feed before continuing southward.

Although spring is the time when most of our amphibians lay their eggs, a few, notably the sluggish hellbender of our lower stream courses, deposits her string of large creamy-white eggs in September. I have handled specimens of this huge salamander, the largest in America, measuring more than two feet in length. It is brownish or grayish-brown in color, with heavy depressed head, prominent lateral skin folds, and flattened tail. Entirely aquatic in habits, the female deposits her eggs in a basin-shaped depression which the male has cleared for that purpose. He thereupon discharges the spermatozoa over them, much in the manner of various fishes, and proceeds to drive the female from the nest. This, then, becomes his charge, and he undoubtedly exercises a fairly effective guard against all comers—all but himself, for I have examined freshly-killed males whose stomachs contained a number of the eggs.

The first witch-hazel flowers may appear before the month has run its course—to bloom through frost and repeated frost, as though destined to carry the golden era of the year's bloom to the last hour of the aging year.

OCTOBER

Somber habiliments appear to be the lot of mankind in his old age, yet the mellowing year marks its period of decline with a pageantry of hues so varied that it is, as Walt Whitman said of the sundown, enough to make a colorist go delirious. Here in the forests of the Smokies, where well over a hundred kinds of native deciduous trees are to be found, the spectacle challenges description; the writer feels humbled and gropes for words.

The scientist attempts to explain that the coloring of the leaf is a chemical process and not the result of the first sharp frost. It is favored by gradual cooling which slows down and finally brings an end to the manufacture of chlorophyll—the dominant green which colors most plants. This material thereupon breaks up into the substances of which it is composed, exposing the yellow and gold in which hickories, tulip trees, birches, and other species become arrayed. The reds and purples of some of the maples and oaks and of sourwood, sumac, ash, black gum, sassafras, dogwood and others are the result of water-soluble pigments which occur in solution in the cell sap. Environmental factors favoring their development include an abundant supply of sugar, presence of sunlight, decrease in temperature, and reduction in the supply of moisture.

October's leaf-colors ordinarily reach their peak in the Park during the latter half of the month. Occasionally middle October will find the pageant at its best, whereas in other years the month is drawing to a close when it is at hand. Rains, high winds, and heavy frosts with subsequent defoliation all play a part. The high Smokies, dominated by evergreen spruces and firs, have a wintry aspect by the end of October.

Like the crow and the jay, to which he is related, the raven is much more in evidence in October than during the summer months.

Against the background of an October sky, I have seen as many as nine of these splendid wary birds together at one time. Occasionally they leave their favored haunts in the higher mountains and appear singly or in pairs at the lower altitudes. Such invasions, however, are often contested by the lowland crows who harass the bigger bird much as they do the various hawks and owls. A strong flier, the raven is capable of remarkable performances on the wing. Once, in March, while at Collins Gap, high up on the crest of the Smokies, I watched what may have been a mated pair come into view. Flying side by side, the two performed a series of thrilling acrobatics involving dipping, sailing, rolling (head foremost, as well as sideways), and plunging—all executed simultaneously and in the most finished manner. On occasions they uttered a few low notes. A third raven who came upon the scene was disregarded. Through all their evolutions there was nothing which might be interpreted as an act of animosity between them. For fully five minutes I had them in good view. Once they tumbled down together into the dense forest below. Finally I lost them when, in a series of power dives, they disappeared from sight far below.

NOVEMBER

October's cup appears to have more than its share of the waning year's beauty, and frequently this spills over, as it were, into the succeeding month. J. P. Mowbray thus describes this interval:

"There are some laggard days in November that have been left behind by the autumnal procession. They are wayward, dilatory, irrelevant days, and come in the rear of the retreating season, like indolent nymphs that, dressed for the nuptials, only arrived for the funeral, and could not abandon their voluptuous moods. They wear their bridal veils, and look at us reminiscently through clouds of mist. These beautiful, dreamy days appear to have been thrown off somewhere like fragments by the revolving August, and they come along like the Leonids, and as softly disappear. We call them the Indian summer." *

The winter wren, now having moved down to the foot of the mountains, may be involved in reminiscence when, on Indian summer mornings, he regales us with song. Meadow larks whistle in the fields, and the whitethroat wishes to remind us that he has but recently returned from "Sweet Canada, Canada, Canada." Paper hornets drone about the old deserted cabins where, along with the white-footed mice, they remain the sole occupants. Streamers of gossamer wave from every conceivable place of anchorage, the product of a multitude of spider-folk who weave their own parachutes and set sail on voyages which may carry them far from their place of birth. Violets bloom again, and such plants as goldenrods, asters, gentians, and witch hazel continue to be visited by numerous insects.

The mood may linger for days, or even weeks, until suddenly nature calls a halt. One morning we awake to find snow whitening the upper Smokies and a chill wind reminding us that this is November. Some of our American Indians are said to have called this eleventh month the "mad moon," since most any kind of weather is to be expected. Indeed there have been Novembers in these southern mountains which leaned heavily toward the side of winter, but rarely does the month come and go without the charm of Indian-summer days to atone for its every madness.

By the time November is two-thirds spent, practically all deciduous tree-leaves, excepting those of the beech and oak, have been harvested, and the tributary streams, now at their lowest water, may be fairly choked with this annual cargo. Outlined against the sky, in a leafless maple, hangs a big gray oval nest of the bald-faced hornets. Only yesterday, it seems, it was teeming with life. But death rides on the wings of the frost, and the number of insect-

* From *A Journey to Nature*, by J. P. Mowbray, copyright, 1901, 1939, by Doubleday, Doran & Company, Inc.

lives which it harvests may challenge the very toll of the leaves. Only the fertilized queen of the hornets is spared, retreating into a stump or rotting log to pass the winter nourishing the very spark of life itself.

DECEMBER

The constellation of the mighty hunter, Orion, with the Pleiades flying before him and the brilliant dog, Sirius, at his heels, now dominates the winter night. For many a wild animal, winter is the nighttime of the year. In the Great Smoky Mountains, the bears will seek their hibernating quarters before December has run its course, and chipmunks, bats, woodchucks, and jumping mice are usually asleep by this time. The skunk and the raccoon may be classed as hibernating animals in the northern part of their range, but here they are astir much of the winter. Snakes, lizards, turtles, salamanders, frogs, toads, and many insects and lesser forms meet the exigencies of the season which is now at hand by hibernating.

One day in December a crew of men working near the eastern boundary of the Park started notching a large dead chestnut tree preparatory to cutting it down. Suddenly a flying squirrel appeared at one of the several openings higher up, then another, and another, until finally a total of twenty-six of these large-eyed animals had been counted and made good their escape. In another part of the country one observer reports as many as forty flying squirrels occupying one tree. Since these squirrels are not known to hibernate, they undoubtedly benefit by sharing winter quarters with their neighbors. Two sleeping together will be warmer than one alone, three will be warmer than two, and so on.

One who visits the Park at this season may well be impressed by how green the Smokies appear. This is especially true at high altitudes where we not only find an evergreen spruce-fir forest, but where such broad-leafed evergreen shrubs as rhododendrons, mountain laurel, leucothoë, and sand myrtle are prevalent. As we make our way down the slopes, Canadian hemlock, five species of pines, American holly, and red cedar occur, with ferns, mistletoe, mosses, lichens, and the leaves of galax, wintergreen, arbutus, cross vine, and others contributing their bit of greenery.

CHAPTER NINE

THE GEOLOGIC STORY

by Henry S. Sharp

The Southern Appalachians are part of that well-defined natural region of the United States often vaguely referred to in romantic song and story as the Blue Ridge Mountains. With a very specific region in mind, geologists who have divided the United States into twenty-five natural "provinces," speak of the Blue Ridge province, which extends southwestward for about six hundred miles from a point near Gettysburg in southern Pennsylvania nearly to Atlanta, Georgia. The Blue Ridge province has had fully as much influence on the history and development of the United States as the names Atlanta and Gettysburg suggest, for it is a great mountainous upland, sometimes seventy miles wide, and acts as an important barrier between two lowland regions, the Piedmont on the east, and the Great Appalachian Valley on the west. The Roanoke River in Virginia separates two quite dissimilar parts of the Blue Ridge province. To the section north of the Roanoke, the term ridge may perhaps be appropriately applied, for the mountains there are long and narrow and frequently consist of nothing more than one or two parallel ridges. Furthermore, in this section, the mountains are obviously composed of more resistant rock than underlies the lower Piedmont to the east, and there is no "Blue Ridge Problem," as geologists have come to designate the question as to the origin of the difference in elevation between the Piedmont and the Blue Ridge province south of the Roanoke River.

The name Southern Appalachians is variously used, but it may be defined to apply solely to the section of the Blue Ridge province south of the Roanoke River, and in that sense it is used here. This part of the province is not at all ridge-like, as the first woodsman, adventuring westward and climbing to the top of the great escarpment by which the Southern Appalachians overlook the Carolina piedmont, may have discovered, to his disappointment. For once on top of this escarpment, one does not see the other side of the mountain sloping downward immediately before him, as by definition a well-behaved ridge should. The other side of this mountain is seventy miles away, and is separated from this side by wave on wave of green-clad mountains, a tumultuous sea of mountains in which the eye can grasp no order. These mountains were a much greater hindrance to westward migration than were the narrow mountains of the Blue Ridge province in Virginia, and the name Blue Ridge would probably never have been used here, if those who named it had known, and not imagined, what was on the other side of the escarpment, which they saw blue and hazy on the horizon as they advanced westward across the monotonous Piedmont. Or perhaps the name Blue Ridge was extended southward from Virginia where it was appropriate.

In addition to being used to designate the entire region from Pennsylvania to Georgia, Blue Ridge is also used to designate the great eastward-facing escarpment by which the Southern Appalachians overlook the Piedmont. The divide between Atlantic and Gulf drainage is usually located at the top of this escarpment, but occasionally may be somewhat farther to the west within the mountains, and when this is so, the divide is called the Blue Ridge. Except when the divide and the top of the escarpment coincide, the Blue Ridge is rarely a prominent topographic feature. Peaks upon the Blue Ridge are not markedly higher than surrounding peaks, and cannot always be picked out with ease either on a map or in the field. Sometimes peaks rising well above the usual height surmount it. Grandfather Mountain near Blowing Rock, North Carolina, is an example, and then the Ridge seems to justify its reputation. The Blue Ridge and most of the lesser divides in the eastern two-thirds of the Southern Appalachians are very irregular in plan, and if one made a map of all these ridge crests, he would find that they branched and interfingered like the limbs of an apple tree. This reflects the lack of structural trends in the underlying crystalline rock and is characteristic of the Blue Ridge region, that is, the eastern region of the Southern Appalachians, and of the Piedmont, too. The same type of rock, so far as can be determined, underlies the Blue Ridge and the Piedmont, and the "Blue Ridge Problem" is the problem of explaining the difference in elevation of these two regions, when they are both underlain by rock of the same resistance to erosion. It is generally accepted that the Blue Ridge was not lifted bodily above the Piedmont. Many hypotheses have been advanced, including one which says that the Piedmont was wave-planed, and that the escarpment is a dissected marine cliff.

The western one-third of the Southern Appalachians includes such famous groups of mountains as the Great Smokies. These mountains rival in height anything to be found farther east and are far more rugged and magnificent. Because of their geologic structure, and in contrast to the Blue Ridge type of range, the individual ranges generally run northeastward and parallel each other to a considerable extent.

The Southern Appalachians are real mountains; there are said to be 46 peaks and 41 miles of divide above 6,000 feet high and 288 more peaks and 300 more miles of divide above 5,000 feet high. When compared to many ranges of the western United States, these figures may seem humble. They are less so, however, when it is remembered that the Southern Appalachians rise from elevations only 1,200 or 1,500 feet above sea level, while many western mountains reaching 10,000 feet start at 5,000 or 6,000 feet elevation. It is true that cliffs and crags are rare, that the forms of the mountains are rounded and subdued, but the venerable finished beauty of these mountains tells a story beside which that of the Alps is like the raw roughness of a new-quarried block compared to a finished statue.

In the following pages no attempt has been made to give a complete story of the geology of these mountains. Since there are no fossils, references to that aspect of the subject is unnecessary. The structure and history of the bed rock is so complicated that few specialists understand it, and relatively little attention is given to bed-rock geology. Most visitors to the mountains are interested in scenery, and to the story of Southern Appalachian scenery most of this chapter is devoted.

THE EARLIEST MOUNTAINS AND THEIR DESTRUCTION

The geologist speaks of the oldest known rocks of the Southern Appalachians as metamorphic, meaning that great heat, pressure, and time has so changed them that their original character is destroyed, and it may be impossible to determine whether they were once igneous, that is formed by cooling from a molten condition, or were muds and sands deposited in an ancient sea. Such a metamorphic rock is the Carolina gneiss, named from its widespread occurrence in North and South Carolina. Asheville and a broad belt to northeast and southwest including Mt. Mitchell are located on this rock. In spite of its name, the Carolina gneiss is not everywhere a banded rock, as a true gneiss should be, but rather a group of varied types of metamorphic rocks. In places it is even granite, a type of igneous rock which can only be formed by intruding the crustal zone of the earth in a molten condition, solidifying, and being exposed to view after erosion has removed thousands of feet of overlying rock. In places, the Carolina includes marble which is derived only from the marine sedimentary rock, limestone; elsewhere it may be a schist, a metamorphic rock composed largely of shiny flakes of mica, and usually derived from the sedimentary rock, shale. The Carolina gneiss group of rocks ranks with the oldest of the earth, and because it is so old it has suffered almost every geological accident that can happen to a rock. Certainly it has been exposed to every geological vicissitude that has occurred in its quarter of the United States, and like an aged person who has experienced much trouble, seen many births and deaths, suffered the worries of several wars, and made out many income-tax returns, its life history has been very complicated, and much less easily comprehended and understood than that of its younger neighbors.

Long after the gneisses, schists, marbles, and granites of the Carolina formation had been completed deep below the surface of the earth, erosion removed the ancient mountains overlying them and exposed their complex structure to the light of day. But it was only a geologic moment before widespread volcanic eruption buried this ancient lowland beneath successive outpourings of lava, which now, too, are so changed by time and movement that they are scarcely recognizable. All this and much, much more happened in the Southern Appalachian region during that tremendously long geologic eon which in the geologic calendar is called the Cryptozoic, because knowledge of creatures living then is largely hidden from us. In these ancient rocks it is a waste of time to look for fossils, because few if any animals or plants living then had hard parts to be preserved, and even if they had, their fossil remains would almost certainly have been destroyed by the massive earth movements, which have frequently altered the rocks in which they might have been entombed beyond recognition.

Because these Southern Appalachian rocks were formed before the Cambrian period of earth history, the first in which fossils occur abundantly, they are commonly called pre-Cambrian. Except for a fringe of hard Cambrian rocks, forming such masses as the Great Smokies and other ranges along the western edge of the mountains in Tennessee and Virginia, pre-Cambrian rocks underlie almost all of the Southern Appalachians and much of the lower Piedmont region to the east. The intricate folding, breaking, and twisting which these pre-Cambrian rocks show is definite proof that the Southern Appalachians in earliest geologic times were the site of mountain-making disturbances, which may more than once have lifted skyward mountains even higher and more imposing than those of the modern "Land of the Sky." Had there been any mountain-lovers to explore those ancestral Southern Appalachians, they would have found their beauty far less alluring than the present mountains, for it is certain that they were clothed in no green garments of towering hardwoods and lovely rhododendrons; at most only lichens and similar lowly and simple plants clung to their naked rocks. Their aspect must have been nearly as bare and gaunt as the present ranges of the Nevada and Arizona deserts.

Judged by our puny scale, geologic time is incomprehensibly long, geologic processes imperceptibly slow. How long and how slow is suggested by an old Chinese proverb which says that once each century the wings of an angel brush a grain of sand from the top of the Himalayas until eventually those mighty peaks will be lowered to the plains, and yet this is but a second in eternity. Such a metaphor well expresses the length of time it took the slow processes of erosion to complete the next step in the geologic history, which was the wearing down of the pre-Cambrian Southern Appalachians nearly to sea level. Positive geologic evidence as to the height of these ancient mountains is lacking, but the internal structure of their deeply eroded roots indicates that they may have been tall enough to stand shoulder to shoulder with the Alps, the Rockies, and the Sierras, while there is every reason to believe that they outranked such peaks as Guyot and Mitchell. Whatever their height, we do know that the internal earthborne forces, which in this region had intermittently been raising highlands faster than the external forces of erosion could cut them down, gradually weakened, so that erosion eventually conquered and the highlands were worn down to a very even, gently rolling surface, not far above sea level. Such an erosional surface is called a peneplain, meaning almost a plain. Thus as a result of long processes of erosion the second stage in our landscape history of the Southern Appalachians could be represented by a straight line cutting across rocks of all kinds with slight respect for differences in hardness.

Soon after the formation of this peneplain some half billion years ago, Southern Appalachian history entered a new and better-known phase, called the Paleozoic era, because of its ancient types of life. In the Cambrian period, at the beginning of this era, the already low-lying land of eastern North America was bent downward in a long narrow zone extending from what is now Alabama to Newfoundland. This depression gradually formed a trough opening into the ocean at north and south, and as sinking of the Appalachian trough continued, marine waters entered each end and finally joined near the middle to make a strait two or three hundred miles wide and about two thousand miles long. Concurrently with the sinking which resulted in the strait, the land to the east began to be pushed and lifted upward, forming a great and mountainous island mass, also a couple of thousand miles long but of unknown width. The location of the eastern edge of this land mass, called Appalachia, is unknown, being beneath the Atlantic Ocean, but the western shore, although shifting to east or west as the sea advanced or retreated, was probably within the present Piedmont province.

Streams flowing westward from rising mountainous Appalachia had swift currents and carried tremendous volumes of sand and coarse gravel into the sea occupying the trough. Thousands of feet of sediment, composed predominantly of the resistant mineral, quartz, were thus accumulated. Today, the Great Smokies lying on the northwest edges of the Southern Appalachians owe their elevation and ruggedness to the superior resistance to erosion of their sandstones and conglomerate rocks, originally deposited in the Appalachian trough as deltas of sand and gravel. Among other mountains composed of these resistant Cambrian rocks are Stone, Bald, Holston, and Cohutta farther north. Although Cambrian rocks are largely restricted to the western one-third of the Southern Appalachians, wherever these rocks occur their great resistance is likely to cause mountains; Grandfather Mountain, 5,964 feet high, the highest point on the divide between Atlantic and Gulf drainage, is one such elevation on Cambrian sandstone.

Characteristically, streams flowing from newly-raised mountainous regions deliver coarse debris to the sea, but as the mountains are worn down, finer and finer material is carried seaward, the seas become clearer, and eventually the water near shore may become so free from land-derived sediments that chemical precipitation or vast accumulations of limy shells of marine organisms may permit the deposition of thick beds of limestones. By the end of the Cambrian period of earth history, and at the beginning of the succeeding Ordovician period, this stage had been reached in the Southern Appalachian region, and enormous thicknesses of blue limestone, composed chiefly of lime and carbon dioxide with a small proportion of magnesium, gradually accumulated above the earlier deposited Cambrian sandstones and conglomerates. The Ordovician period of earth history was one of widespread submergence in North America, and we know from the occurrence of these limestones in Cades and other coves of the Great Smoky region that the western edge, at least, of what is now the Southern Appalachians was then occupied by clear seas suitable for the deposition of limestone. In the seas of this time, and also of Cambrian time, varied shellfish and those curious early crustaceans, the trilobites (which many geologists would find almost as interesting to see alive as dinosaurs) flourished. The limestones of this geologic age have such great influence upon and so generally underlie the Great Appalachian Valley west of the mountains that they are appropriately called the Valley limestones.

Following deposition of the Valley limestones recurrent uplift and downwearing of Appalachia continued until the end of the Paleozoic era, when sedimentary material, largely derived from the land mass, had accumulated in the Appalachian trough to a thickness of some 40,000 feet. This later history of accumulation does not greatly concern the Southern Appalachians, although it was ended by the great mountain-making episode which began a new era in Southern Appalachian history.

At the close of the Paleozoic era eastern North America including Appalachia was subjected to a mountain-making revolution, which drove the sea from the Appalachian trough never to return and set up to rule in its place great ranges of new mountains. The Appalachian revolution resulted in the westward displacement of Appalachia and the simultaneous westward displacement and uplift of the sediments in the trough. Although the underlying cause of these movements is still a subject for debate, it is easy to understand from the evidence in the rocks that Appalachia moved or was pushed against the accumulation of sediments, so that these in turn were pressed against the unmoving central region of the continent. Like a rug pushed across the floor until it is stopped by a wall, the sediments were folded into great up-and-down folds termed anticlines and synclines. Eventually the increasing pressure caused breaks in the earth's crust along which the older pre-Cambrian rocks of Appalachia were pushed westward up and over the younger Cambrian sandstones. The Cambrian beds were in similar fashion broken and pushed westward up over the younger Valley limestones. These breaks are called faults, and such faults and folds indicating pressure from the east characterize the Appalachian revolution, and are found along the entire former extent of the Appalachian trough from Alabama to Canada. It has been estimated that the sedimentary beds of the Appalachian trough were thrown into folds, whose crests made mountains perhaps 30,000 to 40,000 feet high. As a result of the folding and faulting of this region, the zone formerly occupied by the Appalachian trough may have been made about one hundred miles more narrow.

The faults originating at this time served to separate the resistant pre-Cambrian rocks and Cambrian sandstones from the weak Valley limestones. East of and above the faults were the resistant rocks, while west of and below the faults were the limestones. As will be indicated later, differences in rapidity of erosion of the rocks on the two sides of these faults have ever since determined the location of the boundary between the Southern Appalachians on the east and the Appalachian Valley on the west.

SOME GEOLOGIC QUESTIONS

The topography of the end-of-Paleozoic mountain ranges cannot be reconstructed with any degree of certainty, for all the surface features developed then have been destroyed by later erosion. Appalachia, however, probably stood very high, perhaps reaching elevations comparable to those in the sedimentary mountains to the west. For a time much of the area now occupied by the Southern Appalachians may have been covered by a blanket of Cambrian sandstones and younger beds, which lapped over the western edge of Appalachia. But the considerable height of the mountains would cause extremely rapid erosion, quickly removing much of the Cambrian cover and exposing the pre-Cambrian rocks in much the same positions they occupy today. Erosion of the entire region apparently continued until it was reduced to a new peneplain which, however, is not today found anywhere within the area of the Southern Appalachians. There is no evidence to show that any further deposition of sediments occurred within the mountain region after Paleozoic time, although it is possible that younger sedimentary rocks were deposited and were later removed by erosion. Such deposits were made in the Piedmont and Coastal Plain regions to the east, however, and since the presence of these materials in adjacent areas may have had important effects on the history of the mountains, their places in the broad regional history are briefly mentioned here.

The peneplain developed as the result of erosion of the Appalachian uplift was destined for early burial, as is indicated by its occurrence at numerous places in eastern North America covered by sedimentary rocks belonging to the Triassic, the first geologic period following the Paleozoic. These rocks, which often contain dinosaur footprints, are characteristically red sandstones and shales and appear to have been deposited in a long basin or series of disconnected basins extending from Nova Scotia to South Carolina. Even before deposition ceased the Triassic beds were broken by great north-trending faults, which dropped them steeply downward into the older rocks upon which they had been deposited. Following this period of faulting, the region was again deeply eroded to a peneplain, but because they had been lowered below the level of erosion large areas of Triassic rocks still remained east of the Southern Appalachians.

While some important areas of Triassic material still remain, it is important to realize that at that time a much larger proportion of Virginia and the Carolinas than at present was probably underlain by these relatively nonresistant rocks. As will be indicated later, their former presence may in part explain the origin of the great escarpment separating the Blue Ridge from the lower Piedmont to the east.

FALL ZONE AND DRAINAGE

The erosional surface following the Triassic was buried, along its eastern margins at least, by the series of Cretaceous beds which are now restricted to the Coastal Plain east of the Piedmont. Because the falls and rapids characteristic of the fall-line of the eastern

United States are probably related in origin to this erosional surface it has become known as the Fall Zone peneplain. Cretaceous beds do not now occur west of a line passing through such fall-line cities as Washington, Richmond, Columbia, and Augusta, but their considerable thickness at these points gives reason to believe that they formerly extended farther inland. How much farther is one of the most fascinating enigmas of American geology. To the writer it does not seem likely that the Cretaceous beds extended the one hundred miles farther west which would be the average distance necessary to have them attain to the eastern edge of what is now the Southern Appalachians. There is very strong reason to believe that they did not extend entirely across the area now occupied by the mountains.

The question of the former extent of these Cretaceous beds is here chiefly of interest because of its bearing upon the origin of the drainage not only of the Southern Appalachians but of the entire Appalachian region. Brief study of any good map will show that the drainage of the northern and southern parts of the Blue Ridge province are very different. In the Southern Appalachian part of the Blue Ridge province, no streams succeed in flowing entirely across the mountain belt in either direction. A few streams, such as the New River in Virginia, and the French Broad, Little Tennessee, and Hiwassee rivers in North Carolina and Tennessee, have their sources far over on the eastern edge of the mountains and flow entirely across the mountain belt as tributaries to Mississippi-Gulf drainage. Thus, in the Southern Appalachians, the main divide to which the name Blue Ridge is given is very asymmetrically placed far to the east, often overlooking the Piedmont, and the headwaters of these streams actually rise east of the highest parts of the mountains and flow westward through them.

From the Roanoke River northward, on the other hand, all major streams of the Appalachian area rise well west of the Blue Ridge province and flow eastward through it. This course is followed respectively from south to north by the Roanoke, the James, and the Potomac rivers, while still farther to the north beyond the Blue Ridge province such great streams as the Susquehanna, the Delaware, and the Hudson flow southeastward with marked disregard for mountain barriers of resistant rock.

There are several ways by which a stream may gain a seemingly inexplicable course by which it flows from an open valley on one side of a mountain range to an equally open valley on the opposite side of the range by way of a narrow rocky gorge. One way is to have the stream flowing in its course before the mountain came into existence, and, as the mountain is slowly raised across its path, the stream continues to cut downward, maintaining its course. Streams successful in maintaining themselves in such a way are older than or antecedent to the mountains and are called antecedent streams. It is not impossible that the streams flowing westward out of the Southern Appalachians are modified antecedents, which in spite of all more recent movements continue roughly to follow northwestward courses which they gained as a result of the great mountain-making at the close of the Paleozoic era. Farther north, however, the transverse eastward courses of the Roanoke, James, and Potomac rivers through the mountains cannot be so explained, for if these streams developed simply in accordance with the western slope of rising Appalachia at the end of the Paleozoic they should now flow westward. It is probable that the original drainage in the Appalachian region was everywhere westward away from rising and thrusting Appalachian. If so, there are at least two ways by which the problem of the reversal of these streams into an eastern course may be solved.

According to one of these explanations, the Cretaceous beds of the Coastal Plain, which were deposited upon the even surface of the Fall Zone peneplain, extended inland to a line well beyond the position of the present gorges of the Roanoke, James, and Potomac rivers. The inland extension of these marine deposits naturally destroyed all earlier drainage patterns, and as the sea withdrew the surface of the deposits then exposed sloped gently eastward. On this gently sloping surface streams began to flow eastward, and in time, they cut downward through the Cretaceous cover and found themselves flowing transversely across underlying older rocks of varying resistance. As continued erosion completely removed the Cretaceous cover, differential erosion cut broad valleys in the weaker bands of underlying rocks, while only narrow gorges were cut in the resistant rocks, which were left standing high as mountain ridges. Thus the streams flow, apparently with little discrimination, from broad valleys into mountains, in courses which they have inherited from an entirely different set of geologic conditions. Such streams are younger than the mountain structures through which they flow, and since they have been let down upon them from above are called superimposed. Such a history would explain the courses of the Roanoke, the James, and the Potomac through the Blue Ridge, whereas the absence of any transverse eastward-flowing streams in the Southern Appalachians south of the Roanoke might be taken to indicate that the Cretaceous beds of the Coastal Plain never extended over this part of the mountains.

There is a second point of view concerning the origin of Southern Appalachian drainage, which holds that for much of the time since the Paleozoic uplift of these mountains the major divide between Atlantic and Gulf drainage has been situated within them, as it still is south of the Roanoke. According to this point of view streams from the Roanoke northward flowing to the Atlantic, had shorter courses to sea level than streams flowing to the Gulf. Due to this and perhaps also to a regional tilting of the land toward the east, the average slope per mile of their channels would be steeper, giving eastward-flowing streams greater erosive ability than the streams on the opposite side of the divide. This enabled the heads of the eastward-flowing streams to extend themselves westward, much in the way that gullies sometimes encroach upon the sod land of a meadow, until the headwater sources of these streams were pushed west of the mountain belt, and the streams flowed entirely across the range which once constituted the divide.

If this explanation is tenable, one may well ask why there are no eastward-flowing streams crossing the Southern Appalachians south of the Roanoke River. There are a couple of reasonable explanations for this. For one thing, it should be noted that south of the Roanoke, streams flowing to the Gulf and to the Atlantic now vary comparatively little in length. This means that the average slope of their channels is similar, and there is less tendency for eastward-flowing streams to push the divide westward out of the mountain region. More important, perhaps, the mountain belt from the Roanoke northward is seldom more than ten miles wide, whereas south of the Roanoke, the Southern Appalachians may reach a width of eighty miles. Thus it is so difficult and time-consuming for the eastern streams to push their headwaters through the Southern Appalachians that to date they have not been able to accomplish it. South of the Roanoke the divide is still within the mountains, although there are many evidences that eastward-flowing streams are overcoming westward-flowing and causing a westward shift of divide. Some of these drainage modifications will be described later, but it now becomes desirable to return from this excursion into drainage development to further consideration of Southern Appalachian erosional history.

THE FORMING OF THE BLUE RIDGE PENEPLAIN

Following the deposition of Cretaceous beds upon the Fall Zone peneplain, the Appalachian region was again uplifted, and then reduced to a new peneplain, remnants of which have been recognized all over eastern North America from Canada to Georgia. Although this erosional surface is known under a variety of names, it may well be called here the Blue Ridge upland or simply the Blue Ridge peneplain. The cycle of erosion which resulted in this peneplain endured so long that rocks and regions of very varied resistance were alike reduced to the same nearly featureless land. It is believed then that at the completion of this stage of Appalachian history, there would have been relatively little difference in elevation and relief between the regions later to become the Appalachian Valley, the Southern Appalachians, and the Piedmont. All the broad expanse of pre-Cambrian and Cambrian rocks which was later to become the Southern Appalachians was then a rolling lowland surface, for the most part having elevations which probably did not exceed 1,000 feet and may indeed have been no more than 500 feet. Above this rather monotonous land, there were marked elevations where residual masses of rock had successfully resisted the efforts of erosion to reduce them to the general level. Such masses left standing above a peneplain either because of their resistance to erosion or because of their position on a drainage divide at the heads of streams where erosion is less severe are known as monadnocks, after their type example, Mt. Monadnock in southern New Hampshire. Stone Mountain, the site of the great Confederate Memorial near Atlanta, Georgia, and Monticello, in Virginia, are excellent examples of relatively small monadnocks above the lower Piedmont peneplain. All the great named mountains of the Southern Appalachians were monadnocks above the Blue Ridge peneplain, and an accurate estimate of their elevation above the peneplain when it stood only a few hundred feet above sea level is easily obtained. Grandfather Mountain in the picturesque Blowing Rock–Lenoir region of North Carolina is an example of such a monadnock, owing its great mass and height to the superior resistance of the Cambrian conglomerate and sandstone composing it. As shown on the Cranberry, North Carolina, map, the top of Grandfather is 5,964 feet in elevation in a region where the Blue Ridge peneplain remnants stand about 3,800 to 4,000 feet above sea level, so it is easy to see that Grandfather Mountain loomed about 2,000 feet above the Blue Ridge peneplain before the latter was uplifted. How high above sea level the top of Grandfather then was cannot be ascertained, because the elevation of the old peneplain cannot be exactly determined. Grandfather Mountain is the highest point on the Blue Ridge divide here separating the Southern Appalachians from the Piedmont. The fact that this great monadnock happens to surmount the escarpment where the latter at elevations of 4,000 feet towers above the Piedmont to the east by 2,500 feet or more adds greatly to the impressiveness of the Southern Appalachian mountain front as viewed from the Catawba River valley in the Piedmont around Morgantown.

The Blue Ridge peneplain is now, of course, raised far above its position of origin and has to a large extent been destroyed by later erosion. This partly destroyed surface can, however, be restored with some confidence by connecting the tops of equally high peaks in a region or by noting the accordant skyline and broad flat or rolling upland elevations in an area where larger remnants of the peneplain remain. For two reasons it may be impossible to determine precisely the elevation of the Blue Ridge peneplain in some parts of the Southern Appalachians: it may be almost completely destroyed by later stream dissection, or it may have been so poorly developed originally that it cannot be recognized. In the second case, one might say that the region is all monadnock and no peneplain. In spite of these possible difficulties and imperfections, the Blue Ridge peneplain is by far the most important surface of reference in the mountains, and all other topographic features may be discussed as prominences above or valleys below it.

One of the best places in all the Southern Appalachians to see the Blue Ridge peneplain is at Caesars Head, North Carolina, on the Blue Ridge escarpment about two miles north of the South Carolina border. The peneplain here is at an elevation of approximately 3,200 feet, and one looking westward sees a textbook example of an uplifted and partly dissected peneplain. For mile after mile the hilltops and ridge crests seem to reach the same general level with the intervening stream valleys obscured and hidden. For twenty miles the even monotony of this view is not interrupted, until rather low on the horizon appear some rounded blue monadnocks, the highest of which is the Great Hogback, something over 4,700 feet in elevation and surmounting the upland by about 1,500 feet. In this region of about 100 square miles, roughly bounded by the French Broad River on the northwest and the Blue Ridge escarpment on the southeast, the peneplain was apparently better developed and is better preserved than anywhere else in the Southern Appalachians.

A third area in which the Blue Ridge peneplain may be seen to advantage is along the Blue Ridge escarpment on the divide between James and Yadkin River drainage south of Hillsville, Virginia, and north of Mt. Airy, North Carolina. Here the level of the uplifted surface appears to be about 3,100 feet, and it is not surmounted by any imposing monadnocks, although to the west of the immediate top of the escarpment the peneplain has been greatly dissected by streams.

The reader will have noticed that in the three regions described, the Blue Ridge peneplain ascends from elevations of 3,200 feet in the south at Caesars Head to 4,000 feet in the Blowing Rock area and then, farther north, descends to 3,100 feet around Hillsville. While these are considerable differences in elevation, the distances between the three points involved are so great that the average slope works out to about ten feet per mile. Whether this slope is initial in the sense that the peneplain had so much slope originally, or whether it is due to uneven uplift is difficult to determine. Peneplains ascend upstream, as Frank Wright of Denison University has shown, and the Blowing Rock area, on a divide from which streams radiate outward in all directions, being at the headwaters of the stream ought to be higher than any point farther down them. Still ten feet per mile is to be regarded as a high initial slope for a peneplain, and some of this may be due to uneven uplift.

There are many places within the Southern Appalachians where the peneplain was never, or only poorly, developed. One of these is southwest of Asheville where Tennessee Ridge and its northerly continuation, Pisgah Ridge, with their intricate pattern of subsidiary spurs, ridges, and peaks reach elevations of five and six thousand feet and completely obscure the peneplain over a wide area west of the upper French Broad River. Another and better-known region is northeast of Asheville, where (as shown on the Mt. Mitchell quadrangle) Mt. Mitchell and numerous other peaks of the Black Mountain Range exceed 6,000 feet in elevation. Among these famous peaks are Clingman Peak, 6,642 feet, the Black Brothers, 6,690 and 6,620, Balsam Cone, 6,645, and Mt. Mitchell, 6,684, the highest elevation in the eastern United States. The failure of erosion to reduce these mountains to the peneplain level may perhaps be attributed to their central location well within the more resistant rock areas. The peneplain is also absent in the Great Smoky and other ranges on the northwest edge of the Southern Appalachians adjacent to the weak limestones of the Appalachian Valley. Here the failure of erosion to reduce such rugged and inspiring peaks of the Great Smokies as Mt. Guyot and Clingmans Dome to the general level is certainly to be assigned to their composition of resistant Cambrian sandstone, now metamorphosed to quartzite, about as resistant a rock as is known.

By now it should be obvious that none of the higher mountains of the Southern Appalachians owe their prominence to localized uplift. In every instance, and this is generally true of all elevations in the eastern United States, regional erosion could not or did not wear down the rock of the monadnocks as rapidly and effectively as surrounding areas, and this differential erosion eventually brought about all the great differences in elevation that may be seen in the Southern Appalachians. The surface of the monadnocks and of the peneplain they surmount merge gradually into each other, and having been formed together, are of the same geologic age, apparently dating from middle Tertiary time, which is only the day before yesterday, geologically speaking. At the end of the long cycle of erosion which resulted in the Blue Ridge peneplain strong slopes were the exception, and the products of rock decay could no longer be carried away by sluggish streams and rain wash working upon the almost level surfaces. As a result very thick covers of residual soil derived from rock weathering gradually accumulated, making outcrops of fresh rock in the Southern Appalachians relatively rare.

UPLIFT AND THE CUTTING OF THE GREAT VALLEY AND PIEDMONT

The Blue Ridge cycle of erosion was ended by regional uplift which affected not only the Southern Appalachian area but all of eastern North America. This uplift was apparently in the nature of a broad updoming or upwarping increasing slowly in amount from little or nothing at the Atlantic Ocean and the Mississippi until along an axis corresponding approximately with the trend of the Southern Appalachians, it may have reached as much as two or three thousand, perhaps as much as 3,500 feet in places. This being true it is obvious that one half or more of the present height of the mountains is due to this uplift and not to earlier uplifts and mountain-making movements, the effects of which have been so largely obliterated by erosion. In the Southern Appalachian region the crest-line of the upwarped areas appears to have been slightly to the east of the present mountain belt.

While the raised landscape endured for a while without showing any changes due to uplift, nothing in the more recent history of the mountains has had such far-reaching effects upon their topography. It is not too much to say that without this regional movement there would today be no mountains. It was not that individual mountains were exalted, but that all the forces of destruction were rejuvenated and with renewed vigor quickly found differences in rock resistance and wore the weak areas down to lowlands while the strong areas were left in high relief. Thus developed the Piedmont lowland to the east, and the Great Appalachian Valley to the west of the Southern Appalachian Mountains.

When this uplift began the divide between streams flowing directly to the Atlantic and to the Mississippi was probably located somewhat to the east of the present Southern Appalachians. Since it was much farther from this divide to the ocean by way of the Mississippi River than by the direct route, and since the streams on the two sides of the divide had their sources at about the same elevation, it is clear that the eastward-flowing streams had steeper gradients, that is, a greater average drop in feet per mile than the westward-flowing Mississippi tributaries. This meant that the eastward-flowing streams had much swifter currents, and therefore much greater erosive or down-cutting ability than the more slowly-flowing streams on the opposite side of the divide.

To this primary advantage held by the eastward-flowing streams was added a second important advantage, for not only were they more powerful eroding agents, but they flowed eastward across a land which to a considerable extent was underlain by relatively weak rocks. Thus it appears probable that in flowing from the divide to the Atlantic, these streams crossed broad areas of downfolded or downfaulted Triassic rocks, mostly red sandstones and shales, which were deposited in the Piedmont region, as mentioned earlier, during the early part of the Age of Dinosaurs. These weak Triassic beds are now almost completely removed from the area east of the Southern Appalachians, but they still occur in Virginia and in North Carolina as far south as the South Carolina line. In fact, they extend just a short distance into South Carolina, and there is little doubt that they once had a much greater extent in the Carolina and Virginia Piedmont. It was the presence of the Triassic weak rocks east of the Southern Appalachians which provided an important additional cause for the rapid lowering of the land to a new level by the Atlantic streams. It has often been said that the great difference in level between the Piedmont and the Southern Appalachians could not be explained by differential erosion, since the rocks of the two areas are apparently of the same resistance, but this difficulty is overcome, when it is seen that weaker rocks present in the Piedmont region have been almost completely removed in the process of making that lower surface. The presence of weak coastal plain beds of Cretaceous and Tertiary age to the east of the Piedmont near the mouths of the Atlantic stream probably contributed further to the rapidity with which stream erosion lowered the country east of the Blue Ridge divide. Places where the ancient rocks beneath the Triassic stood higher, would have been areas of greater resistance to erosion, and here would be likely places for monadnocks standing above the new lowland surface to survive. Eventually the area east of the mountains was reduced to a younger and lower erosional surface of less relief than the Blue Ridge peneplain, and because this newer surface is broadly developed and widely preserved in the Piedmont, it may be called the Piedmont peneplain.

While the Piedmont peneplain was being developed by the Atlantic streams east of the divide, the streams tributary to the Mississippi were also occupied in attempting to erode a newer and lower peneplain than that of the Blue Ridge. In this they were only partly successful, for these streams worked under two geologic handicaps which did not affect their opposites east of the divide. As has been mentioned, their courses from source to sea level were much longer than the eastern streams, which means that their average drop in feet per mile was much less than that of the Atlantic streams. Downcutting in the headward parts of a Mississippi stream would therefore be greatly retarded in comparison with an Atlantic stream, and as a result, the former might have accomplished no more than the incision of a sharp narrow valley, while the Atlantic stream, after having cut its narrow deep valley might have been able to widen it to a great broad plain, which merging with that of other streams became a widespread regional peneplain.

The second handicap under which westward-flowing streams within the Southern Appalachians operated and still operate was the presence of great thicknesses of Cambrian sandstones and quartzites, making up about the western one-third of the mountains. Through these very resistant rocks such westward-flowing streams as the Pigeon, French Broad, and Little Tennessee were forced to make their way, notching these rugged mountains by a series of majestic gorges two to four thousand feet deep. The great resistance of these rocks has prevented the streams from doing more than cut narrow passes for themselves, and the gorges show no evidence that at any point in their erosion the streams were able to open out flat-floored valleys which might be considered the beginning of a peneplain. The retardation of stream erosion caused by these resistant belts of quartzose rocks slowed the process of downcutting in all parts of the streams east of the gorges, for not until these were cut downward was it possible for the headwater parts of these streams to renew their erosion and cut downward below the Blue Ridge peneplain on which until now they had been flowing. For the two reasons stated, and because of generally high average resistance to erosion of the crystalline rocks of the Southern Appalachians, streams have in general been able to do little more than cut narrow valleys for themselves, and large areas of the Blue Ridge peneplain are still preserved. This is in great contrast to the region of the Piedmont, where for the opposite reasons streams have been successful in completely destroying the Blue Ridge peneplain and in lowering the country to the Piedmont peneplain level.

There are only a few places in the Southern Appalachians where westward-flowing streams are believed to have opened out local lowlands corresponding in time of formation to the Piedmont peneplain. These are strips and patches of smoother country, usually hundreds or thousands of feet below the ruggedly dissected higher country of the Blue Ridge peneplain. They are not as smooth and even as originally, for regional uplift since their formation has set streams to work dissecting the surface which they earlier had formed. The best developed of these regions of subdued topography is in the region round about Asheville, known as the Asheville Basin (well depicted on the Asheville, Saluda, and Pisgah topographic maps of the United States Geological Survey). The Asheville Basin is very irregular in outline, and while it is well developed around Asheville, its characteristic subdued topography, suitable for farming, is perhaps even better seen twenty miles southeast of Asheville around Hendersonville, North Carolina. An extension of the Basin can also be traced up the French Broad River southwest of Asheville to the vicinity of Brevard. The elevation of the basin floor at Asheville is around 2,100 to 2,200 feet, and it increases gradually upstream (southward) along the French Broad River and more rapidly upstream along tributaries of the French Broad. At Asheville the French Broad River occupies a narrow valley cut about 200 feet below the basin floor, which may be called the Asheville peneplain. As one follows the river and its tributaries upstream to the edges of the Basin, the depth of the valley below the Asheville peneplain becomes less and less until the streams are flowing upon or practically upon the peneplain. Where the French Broad leaves the Basin to flow through quartzite, its valley is cut 400 feet below the Asheville peneplain. As already stated, no evidence of the Asheville peneplain is seen in the gorges below the Basin, either because the resistance of the rocks prevented its formation there, or because its narrow development has been destroyed by the same downcutting of the streams which has dissected the Asheville level.

The Asheville Basin is drained almost entirely by the French Broad River and its tributaries, but it is important to note that eastward-flowing Atlantic streams are encroaching upon French Broad territory east and southeast of Hendersonville as part of the continuous and strenuous struggle for territory everywhere taking place between streams on opposite sides of the Blue Ridge divide. In this area the Blue Ridge escarpment is much lower than ordinary, for the reason that the Piedmont streams have largely destroyed the remnants of the Blue Ridge peneplain, which once undoubtedly made a belt of higher country between the Piedmont and Asheville peneplains. Southeast of Hendersonville, therefore, the escarpment is only about 1,300 feet high, being made by the break between the Asheville peneplain at about 2,500 feet, and the inner edge of the piedmont peneplain at about 1,200 feet. In other areas where the Blue Ridge peneplain at elevations of three or four thousand feet is preserved directly above the Piedmont, the escarpment may reach 2,500 feet or more in height, or in those rare cases where a monadnock on the Blue Ridge peneplain looks down upon the piedmont from the top of the escarpment, the latter may reach heights of 4,500 feet. Grandfather Mountain, already described, is an example of a monadnock causing such exceptional height of the Blue Ridge escarpment.

Along a number of other streams of the Southern Appalachians local peneplains similar to the Asheville occur. They have been described along the Tuckasegee, the Little Tennessee, the Ocoee, and the Hiwassee. They occur also along the headwaters of the Nolichucky, and in Virginia Frank J. Wright has been able to trace a continuous surface upstream along the New River from elevations of about 2,400 feet in the Appalachian Valley to 2,700 feet in the Southern Appalachian Mountains around Hillsville. Farther south it has been impossible to trace a continuous surface from the mountains to the valley, because it never was well developed in the quartzite ridges of the Great Smokies. There local peneplains are found at different elevations along different streams, depending upon their distances from the sea, the size of the stream, and the resistance of the rock. Each was developed as a result of a partial

Contentment in the mountains

Blossom time in the mountains

Desperate agriculture

Dude ranch in Waynesville, North Carolina

cycle of erosion which allowed a certain master stream and its tributaries to lower the region under its control well toward the level of the sea before a later uplift caused renewed downcutting.

These local peneplains are to be regarded as essentially contemporaneous in origin with each other and with the Piedmont peneplain. While they were being formed, stream erosion was also accomplishing great things within the Great Smokies and the Great Valley region to the west. The Great Valley extending from Central Alabama to the Hudson River is very largely underlain by limestones and shales. There are no very resistant rocks, and soon after the Blue Ridge peneplain was uplifted that part of it which had been developed upon these rocks was destroyed, and a new and lower surface of slight relief, which may be termed the Valley peneplain, had formed. In the Knoxville region this peneplain, which is contemporaneous with the Piedmont and Asheville peneplains, is about 1,000 to 1,200 feet in elevation, and one looking southeastward from it to the massive peaks of the Great Smokies sees mountains of majestic grandeur, comparable to many ranges of the west, rising 5,000 feet or more above the valley level. This difference in elevation between valley floor and mountaintop, as may well again be emphasized, is entirely due to differential erosion on valley limestone and shale and on mountain quartzite and quartz conglomerate, and the history here given indicates that the Southern Appalachians owe their prominence to the superior resistance of their rocks over those of the Piedmont and Great Valley. There would have been no mountains to admire, if uplift of the Blue Ridge peneplain had not allowed stream etching to bring the hard rock areas into relief.

In the Great Smokies at this time were formed the series of coves such as Cade Cove, Tuskaleechee Cove, and Wear Cove, which seem like small editions of the fertile Great Valley isolated in the midst of a rugged wilderness. To a considerable extent this is what they are, for they are underlain by limestone and their relatively flat floors with characteristic sinkholes are covered with a pattern of farmlands like that of the Great Valley. Their geologic story, however, is more complicated than that of the valley, for they occur within the area of quartzite rocks although underlain by limestone. It will be remembered that at the close of the Paleozoic era the Appalachian Revolution resulted in the Cambrian sandstones and quartzites being pushed for miles westward across the broken edges of the younger limestone beds which were originally deposited above them. The break along which this occurred is the Blue Ridge fault, and in places the fault itself, instead of being a simple eastward-sloping plane, was arched upward. Where this upward-arching occurred, the limestone beneath the quartzite stood higher than elsewhere. Following the uplift of the Blue Ridge peneplain, streams cutting downward through the quartzite reached the up-arched limestone, which being less resistant was rapidly eroded to a mountain-surrounded basin, a cove, while downstream from the limestone areas the streams still flowing in resistant rock were in the same length of time only able to erode narrow valleys. Places of this sort where erosion has exposed to view the younger rocks beneath a fault plane are known to geologists as *fenster*, the German word for window, and ten occur along the western edge of the mountains in the Great Smoky region. It is interesting to consider that all the material removed in the etching of the coves has been carried downstream through the narrow gorges by which they are drained.

LAST STEPS IN SHAPING THE LANDSCAPE

With the completion of the Piedmont, Valley, and Asheville peneplains the erosional history of the Southern Appalachians is almost concluded. The cycle of erosion which resulted in the contemporaneous formation of these three surfaces did not endure as long as the older Blue Ridge cycle, or the Southern Appalachians would have been almost completely lowered to the level of these peneplains. It was interrupted by an uplift that rejuvenated the lazily meandering streams which quickly incised themselves below the surface of the peneplains in narrow, steep-walled valleys. This last uplift occurred so recently that there has been little time for the streams to broaden their valley bottom or to destroy the peneplain remnants, which remain between the valleys as broad flat upland areas with generally accordant hilltops. The evenness of the Piedmont peneplain can best be seen from the top or sides of some monadnock above it, such as Monticello in Virginia, where the skyline is so even that it resembles a horizon at sea.

During the long slow process of peneplanation, all but those rocks most resistant to chemical and physical atmospheric attack were very deeply weathered, so that throughout the Southern Appalachians a thick cover of soil, formed by rock decay, buries the bedrock. The streams have never been able to remove this residual soil as fast as it was formed, and outcrops of fresh rock are therefore very uncommon.

The deep residual soil cover of the Southern Appalachians is in great contrast to the mountains of New England, where rock exposures are very common. This contrast is due directly to the fact that the Southern Appalachians were never glaciated, while the great ice sheets which flowed down over New England completely removed the residual soil cover which had accumulated slowly during geologic ages, exposing fresh rock, which is only partly covered by stony soil transported by the ice from farther north.

In addition to the contrast in soils between the mountains of the north and of the Southern Appalachians, the difference in glacial histories of the two highland areas also explains the striking difference in the number of natural lakes they possess. Streams of the Southern Appalachians were not subjected to damming by glacial deposits nor were new lake basins scooped out along their courses by ice erosion, and as a result, to paraphrase the famous essay on the snakes of Ireland, there are no lakes in the Southern

Appalachians. This, it must be admitted, is a sad deficiency in comparison to the hundreds and thousands of lakes in the northern mountains, practically all of which trace their origin to glaciation. Lack of glaciation and not lack of height also explains the great difference between the gently rounded, beautifully contoured slopes of the Southern Appalachians and the sharp peaks and saw-tooth ridges of such intensely glaciated mountains as the Rockies and the Alps. It is such geologic factors that lend to each highland region its individual personality, distinguishing it from all others and endearing it to its admirers.

Before concluding this history of the Southern Appalachians some further reference should be made to the long-continued contest between Atlantic and Gulf streams along the Blue Ridge divide. This contest, which began as far back as the uplift of the Blue Ridge peneplain, has caused the divide to shift constantly westward, so that the Gulf streams have lost much territory to the Atlantic streams. Some geomorphologists estimate that the present divide may be five or ten miles west of its original position, due to encroachment by the more active Atlantic streams. The biblical saying, "To him that hath, shall be given," applies particularly to stream contests of this sort, for the drainage basin and hence the volume of the successful streams are being constantly enlarged at the expense of the losers, and as a result the contest becomes ever more unequal. In places the headwaters of streams on the two sides of the divide flow directly away from each other; the shift is very slow and merely an inch-by-inch working of one stream into the territory of another. Elsewhere a Gulf stream may flow parallel to the divide, and an Atlantic stream encroaching upon it may cut right into its valley, beheading it and making a spectacular capture of a large area. Some of these captures can be predicted for the future from present stream relations, others can be seen to have occurred in the past. One of the former, a few miles northeast of and visible from the top of Mt. Mitchell, was described by W. M.

Davis, who, to indicate its imminence, said that he felt like sitting down to wait for its conclusion. This contest is between Crabtree Creek and Bee Rock Creek of Gulf and Atlantic drainage respectively. The former flows in a relatively open gentle valley, while on the opposite side of a divide just an eighth of a mile away, Bee Rock falls 1,500 feet in two miles. It is obvious that Bee Rock Creek is pushing its head into the valley of Crabtree Creek and will soon divert the head of the latter to Atlantic drainage.

On the Georgia-South Carolina boundary is an example of a capture already accomplished. Here the Chattooga River flows southwest into the Tugaloo, which then flows southeastward to the Atlantic Ocean by way of the Savannah River. Southwest of the junction of the Chattooga and the Tugaloo and flowing on a line continuing the Chattooga is the Chattahoochee, a stream delivering its waters to the Gulf by way of the Apalachicola River. It is generally believed that the Chattooga once flowed into the Chattahoochee but was tapped and diverted into its new course by the Tugaloo. If so, there is a suggestion that contrary to "The Song of the Chattahoochee," the river does not go on forever.

CHAPTER TEN

HOW SHALL I PLAN MY TRIP?

by Edward S. Drake

Until after the beginning of the twentieth century the beauty and charm of the Southern Appalachians were known to few outsiders. The chief reason for this was the inaccessibility of the entire region. Only in recent years have roads been improved. The best information on the condition of the mountain roads and the rigors of travel in the early nineteenth century can be found in the diaries of some of the people who used them. Bishop Francis Asbury, who made several preaching trips through the mountains between 1800 and 1813, left interesting accounts of his travels.

On November 6, 1800, he wrote: "My roan hoarse, led by Mr. O'Howen reeled and fell over, taking the chaise with him. I beheld the poor beast and the carriage, bottom up, lodged against a sapling which alone prevented them both from being precipitated into the river."

November 9, 1800: "We must bid farewell to the chaise; this mode of conveyance by no means suits the roads of this wilderness; we were obliged to keep one behind the carriage with a strap to hold by to prevent accidents almost continually."

October 1, 1806: "I rode, I walked, I sweat, I trembled and my old knees failed."

All of this was written about what may be called the main roads. But they were gradually improved until the outbreak of the War Between the States. During that conflict labor and money to maintain roads were lacking, and when peace came the states were too impoverished to rebuild them. From the cities, macadamized roads, extending a few miles into the surrounding country, were built, but the highway system all through the mountains was not such as would attract tourists. Moreover, Northern people could not believe that a trip anywhere in the South would be enjoyable in the summer. Consequently most of the visitors to the mountains were people from the lowlands of the Carolinas and Georgia, seeking relief from the summer heat or cures at some of the springs.

Though the railroads did much to advertise the attractions of the southern highlands and started a small amount of tourist travel to them, the automobile should have more credit than any other factor for opening the region and attracting people from all over the country. The states sharing in the possession of the Southern Appalachians were quick to sense the value of opening the mountain country to automobile travel, and today good roads can be found everywhere through the mountains.

Automobile tourists from any part of the United States going to Great Smoky Mountains National Park and the many scenic attractions a short distance outside its boundaries may choose from several routes. Visitors from the Midwest and Northwest, going to the Park for the first time, will probably use U.S. 25W from Corbin, Kentucky, principally because a trip to Norris Dam and the adjacent T.V.A. development can be made with very little additional mileage.

At the southern edge of Corbin, U.S. 25W makes a right-angle turn to the southwest. Eleven miles farther it turns south and joins Kentucky Route 90; over this road it is only eleven miles to Cumberland Falls. Here the Cumberland River has a sheer drop of 68 feet, with an expanse of 125 feet. In 1930, T. Coleman duPont presented the falls and 500 acres of surrounding land to the state of Kentucky for a park. There is a pretty, winding trail along the river, with many ferns and flowers, and overhanging trees. For some reason I like this trail after a shower and before the sun comes out. Then it is eerie and mysterious, the wet branches hang lower, the ferns seem a darker green and the colors of the flowers are softer. That part of the park near the falls is maintained, but there is no unnatural development except the necessary parking space. There is a lodge to accommodate those who wish to stay overnight.

It is best to go back to U.S. 25W and continue south. Shortly after crossing the Tennessee line the road enters a deep gorge, enclosed on both sides by very high rock cliffs. A tumbling stream below the road, crossed by swinging footbridges and a railroad on the other side, add to the interest. In many places the rock is pierced with short tunnels to accommodate the tracks. There is much laurel and rhododendron along the river and hanging to the cliffs. When these are in bloom the gorge is a rare sight.

At Lake City, seventy-four miles south of Corbin, a sign directs those who wish to visit Norris Dam to turn left on the Norris Freeway, a splendid concrete road with easy grades and curves. It is five miles to the dam. The Freeway crosses the dam, but before crossing be sure to stop in the ample parking place provided for automobiles and walk down to the pier behind the dam. Hundreds of power- and sailboats are at the pier or anchored in the lake and one realizes that, besides providing power, the dam has made possible a huge play area for the public. On the farther side of the dam and below it is another parking space from which the vast size of the dam can best be realized. Four miles beyond the dam is the town of Norris, owned by T.V.A. It is a pleasant place, with attractive houses built among the trees. Twelve miles south of the village the Freeway ends at a junction with Tennessee Route 33, over which it is nine miles to Knoxville.

THE KNOXVILLE-GATLINBURG REGION

From Knoxville there are two routes to the western entrance to the Great Smoky Mountains National Park. To get to the park as quickly as possible, the shortest and best road is Tennessee Route 71. From Knoxville to Sevierville there is a twenty-five mile stretch of excellent concrete, a very fast road, and many fine views of the mountains. On the thirteen miles from Sevierville to Gatlinburg, a valley road overhung by mountains, there are several sharp turns, mostly at the ends of bridges, some of which are narrow.

With more time available, the longer trip via Tennessee Route 73 through Maryville has greater scenic attractions. This route is about eighteen miles longer than the route through Sevierville. From downtown Knoxville go west on Cumberland Avenue past the University of Tennessee. A few blocks farther, at the University Experiment Farm, Route 73 turns left. Fifteen miles from the city is Alcoa, site of the enormous plant of the American Aluminum Company, and a short distance beyond is Maryville. On the right, at Kinzel Springs, sixteen miles from Maryville, is a gravel road to Cades Cove, the locale of *The Prophet of the Great Smoky Mountains* and other books by Miss Mary Murfree who wrote under the name of Charles Egbert Craddock.

The cove is a level tract, two miles wide and six miles long, entirely surrounded by mountains. It is drained by a creek which flows through a gorge so narrow that no road has been built along it, and the only approach is by the road from Kinzel Springs, which goes over two mountains. The cove is now included in the Park, but for well over a hundred years it was an isolated farming community having little contact with the outside world, although a few families accommodated summer boarders in the last years before the Park was established. But in the latter part of the nineteenth century the people of the cove had rarely gone out of it, and there were few visitors. Their speech and their ways of living were of the eighteenth century, and Miss Murfree's books give insight to language and customs that have disappeared except in the most isolated parts of the southern highlands. From the cove there are fine views of Thunderhead Mountain (5,530 feet) and others of the high Smokies.

Five miles from Kinzel Springs the route enters the gorge of the Little River and continues for several miles between almost perpendicular rock walls. This is some of the most rugged scenery in the Park, and one of the reasons for coming by way of Maryville is that the route from Knoxville to Gatlinburg via Tennessee Route 71 avoids driving from Gatlinburg through the gorge and returning the same way.

After leaving the gorge the road winds in easy curves up to Fightin' Creek Gap. Just before reaching the gap a trail to the left leads to Laurel Creek Falls, 1.4 miles off the highway. Though it is not one of the most spectacular falls in the mountains, it is a favorite with those who enjoy a not too strenuous hike. A roadside sign marks the trail.

At Fightin' Creek Gap a curve is rounded and one of the most awe-inspiring scenes in the Smokies appears so suddenly that one's breath is almost taken away. Five miles off Mt. LeConte rises from the valley of the Little Pigeon River near Gatlinburg. The top of Mt. LeConte is more than 5,000 feet above the valley and nearly the entire slope of the mountain is in sight. The thrill one experiences from having this scene suddenly burst into view is worth the extra eighteen miles traveled over the longer route from Knoxville.

Two and one-half miles beyond the Gap is the junction with Tennessee Route 71, where it curves to the right to start the ascent to Newfound Gap. Straight ahead on 71, two and one-half miles, is Gatlinburg, with excellent hotels, cabin camps, and tourist homes. Many people stop at Gatlinburg overnight, take the road to Newfound Gap and Clingmans Dome, and go on into North Carolina, or return home thinking they have seen the Park; some people coming from the other direction stop for lunch or a night's rest and leave with the same opinion. Several days should be spent here, to see the many interesting and beautiful spots that can be so easily reached with Gatlinburg as headquarters.

Before describing a few places worth visiting around Gatlinburg, let me say something for those who have seen the Norris Dam and wish to take a different route to the Park from Corbin. They should veer left at the north edge of Corbin onto U.S. 25E, which avoids the business section of the city. There is nothing unusual along this route until Middlesboro, fifty miles from Corbin, is passed. Here a splendid wide road with easy grades and curves winds up to Cumberland Gap, a place of great historic interest and scenic beauty. Through this gap came the Wilderness Road, blazed by Daniel Boone along an old Indian and buffalo trail, and over it thousands of the early settlers from the eastern seaboard traveled to their new homes in Kentucky. During the War Between the States several skirmishes took place here and the Gap changed hands several times.

At the summit, 25E leaves Kentucky and enters Virginia. Less than a mile farther the Tennessee line is crossed. At several places on the down grade there are excellent views of the town of Cumberland Gap, which seems to be directly below.

About twenty-two miles from the Gap the road crosses Clinch River, which has been widened by backwater from Norris Dam. A few miles farther, after going through a pretty little valley with a tumbling brook, Clinch Mountain looms to the northeast. On this road are many wide views of mountains and valleys, also several sharp curves.

At the summit is Bean Gap and a parking place from which one looks down into a peaceful valley far below and across to range after range of mountains in the distance. On the down grade two hairpin curves should be approached with care.

From Morristown a nineteen-mile stretch of new, almost straight concrete comes to a junction with U.S. 70. This is rolling country and from almost every hilltop the Smoky Mountains loom up directly ahead. At the junction with U.S. 70 we turn right. Three miles farther we turn left onto Tennessee Route 35, a pretty, winding drive through a narrow valley enclosed by low conical hills which leave room only for the road and a small brook. The valley gradually widens, and seventeen miles from the junction with U.S. 70 the road meets the Little Pigeon River, which it follows for four miles. At the east end of Sevierville is a junction with Tennessee Route 71 where a very sharp left turn is made around a filling station. From here it is thirteen miles to Gatlinburg.

Two trails from Gatlinburg lead to the top of Mt. LeConte—a steep hiking path which has been in use for many years, and a new bridle trail. The new path is better than the old, but it is nine miles long and in that distance climbs from 1,550 to 6,593 feet. Needless to say it should not be attempted as a hike by those unaccustomed to strenuous exercise. Horses and guides can be engaged in the village. At the summit are rough accommodations for tourists wishing to stay overnight.

The trip of nine miles from Gatlinburg to Greenbriar Cove can be made by automobile over an unimproved road. The cove is one of the largest wilderness areas in the Park.

As the Park and its attractions are described elsewhere in this book, I shall not list the many trips that can be taken from Gatlinburg, but I cannot refrain from urging everyone to hike over the road and trail which follow Roaring Fork. Walk a mile, two miles, or farther if you can, and there will be something of interest all the way. There are cascades and quiet pools, wild flowers and birds, and shops where all sorts of things are made by hand, where the workers will be glad to chat and show you their handicraft, and, of course, will be glad to make a sale if you are disposed to buy.

But the other side of the mountains has many attractions, and after having seen as much in and around Gatlinburg as your time will allow, you will probably take Tennessee Route 71 to Newfound Gap. In fifteen miles the road climbs nearly 4,000 feet, but

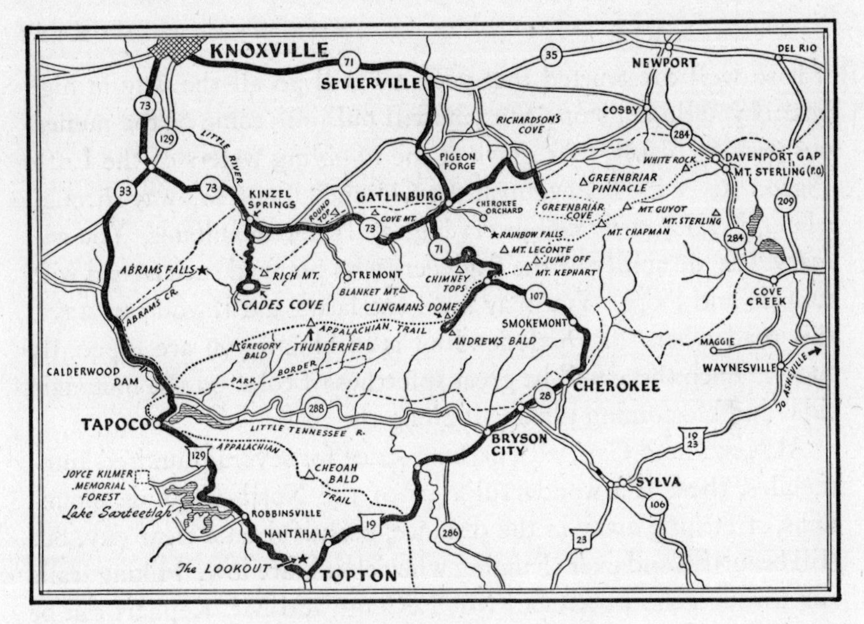

KNOXVILLE-GATLINBURG REGION

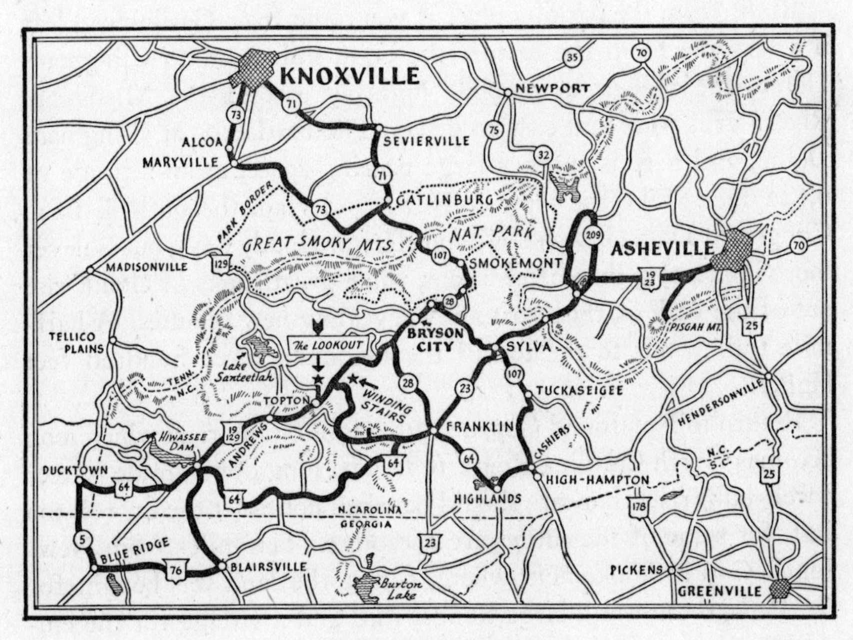

BRYSON CITY REGION

it is so well constructed that your car will go all the way in high gear if you do not stop. But you will pull into some of the numerous parking places, look down at the tumbling waters of the Little Pigeon River far below, up at the Chimney Tops, or away through a lateral valley enclosed by very high and steep mountains. You will marvel at the ability of the engineers who planned such a road with tunnels and loops. You may see some bears and if you can travel this road when the rhododendron is in bloom you are especially lucky. Then there will be great splotches of color on the mountain sides and blossoming plants all along the road.

At Newfound Gap, with parking space for several hundred automobiles, there is a wonderful view of the North Carolina mountains, stretching away in the distance, beautiful on a clear day, but still beautiful and ever changing when clouds are low. Hiking trails run through the woods and Mt. LeConte and Mt. Kephart can be reached over them.

Right from the parking place if you come from Gatlinburg, left if you come from the east, is the eight-mile road to Clingmans Dome, the highest automobile highway east of the Mississippi River. It is wide and easy to drive. The road ends at Clingmans Dome, and here is another large parking space, at an altitude of 6,642 feet. Like the view at Newfound Gap, the outlook from Clingmans Dome is wonderful on clear or cloudy days, but is never more interesting than after a rain, when great banks of clouds rise out of the valleys, then float away revealing new beauties. A half-mile trail winds to the top of the mountain three hundred feet higher.

Return to Newfound Gap and turn right on the road which soon becomes North Carolina Route 107. The long down-grade is over a well-built road, but care should be taken not to let the car roll too fast, for some of the curves are deceptive. Ten miles from Newfound Gap is Smokemont where, before the land was bought for the Park, there was a large lumber mill and a village for the employees. About seven miles farther, on the right, is the Cherokee Indian School. You are now in the largest Indian Reservation east of Wisconsin. Just beyond the school Route 107 makes a sharp left turn onto a concrete bridge over the Oconaluftee River, which you have been following. Along the road on both sides of the bridge are a number of stores which sell articles made by the Indians. This is the village of Cherokee, the commercial center of the reservation.

Six miles from Cherokee, Route 107 ends at a junction with U.S. 19, which is the road to Asheville. But there is much beautiful scenery in this part of the mountains, and Bryson City, where there are accommodations to suit all purses, is a good place to make one's headquarters for a few days. It is ten miles from Cherokee and is reached by turning right onto North Carolina Route 28 at the Oconaluftee River Bridge.

I never ride over the splendid roads between Bryson City and Newfound Gap without recalling the first time I made the trip. It was in the summer of 1922 and I was accompanied by two friends, one of whom was the late Horace Kephart, author of *Our Southern Highlanders* and of *Camping and Woodcraft*, with which every Boy Scout is familiar. We left Bryson City late in the afternoon and drove to Smokemont at the end of the highway for supper and lodging at the very good clubhouse operated by the lumber company for its office employees. The superintendent gave us permission to ride the work train on the railroad the company maintained to haul logs down the mountains. After breakfast next morning we mounted an open flat car which was one of several pushed by the engine. This was very well for a mile or so, until we came to a place where the railroad had to change direction. There was no room for a curve, so the change was made by means of a switchback, a sort of Y-shaped arrangement. We were shoved out on the shank of the Y, then pulled over a switch to the arm opposite the one over which we had come. Thus we zigzagged up the mountain, enveloped in black smoke when the puffing locomotive pulled us, sitting in bright sunshine when we were pushed.

About ten o'clock we came to the railhead, having traveled nine miles to make an airline distance of three and having gained 1,300 feet in altitude, detraining at 3,500 feet. The lumber company had started construction to extend the railroad to Newfound Gap and had completed several miles of grading to a place where the altitude was 4,500 feet.

After making arrangements with the train crew to be back at four o'clock we started up the new grade, which was easy hiking, and met a small construction gang composed of mountain men. One of them knew Kephart and introduced him to the others. One man spoke up: "Oh, yes, this is the man who wrote the book." In *Our Southern Highlanders* and in his stories for magazines, Kephart wrote about the mountain people in a sympathetic and understanding way that pleased them. (I knew another author who wrote about the highlanders, but his stories laid so much stress on feuds, the making of moonshine liquor, and the primitive ways of living that they felt they were classed as outlaws and were being held up to ridicule. After a few of his stories were published some of his friends warned him that it would be well for him to stay out of the back country; at least he would not be welcomed.)

It was after one o'clock when we reached Newfound Gap. We had used the best route available in those days but, omitting the night spent in Smokemont, it had taken us seven hours to travel the distance that now can be made in forty-five minutes' driving over the new road.

Our objective was a mountain locally known by several names. It was three miles from the gap and there had been a definite trail, marked at frequent intervals by blazed trees. But we found the path overgrown with bushes and obstructed in many places by fallen trees. Usually it was impossible to go around a fallen tree because of the dense underbrush. I remember as we climbed over one very large bole, "Kep," as his friends called him, remarked that he thought he was doing very well for a man who would be sixty in a few weeks.

Just as we started up the last grade a light fog suddenly enveloped us. We realized that if it became dense we should find it difficult to keep on the trail, and so after reaching the top of the mountain we started the return immediately. Cold drops of water fell from the trees and when we arrived at the end of the railroad we were so wet and cold that we sat on the cinder-covered floor of the locomotive in front of the firebox door to warm and dry ourselves. When we arrived at Smokemont, our clothes and our faces were black with smoke and cinders, but we had the satisfaction of having reached a mountain top that, according to the superintendent of the lumber mill, had been visited by very few white men, and not often by Indians.

After Kephart's death the mountain we had climbed was officially named Mt. Kephart in his honor.

Bryson City is a small county seat, partly in the narrow valley of the Tuckasegee River and partly on the low hills which come close to the business section of the town. On one trip to the Northwest I drove west of Pierre, South Dakota, then south, traversing an Indian reservation for twenty-five miles. On another trip I spent a day and a half crossing Oklahoma. But in neither South Dakota nor Oklahoma did I see an Indian. Rarely can you walk down the main street of Bryson City and not see several, and on Saturday or a county-court day you may see twenty-five or thirty.

From Bryson City there are several trips that can be made in one day or less, and I am going to borrow an idea from the state guide books of the Federal Writers' Project of the Federal Works Agency. Some of the shorter trips can be combined with other short ones or parts of the longer ones and by using the numbering system it will be easier to make references when suggesting combinations.

TRIPS IN THE BRYSON CITY REGION

Trip Number One will be west from Bryson City, starting on U.S. 19. For a couple of miles the road follows the south bank of the Tuckasegee River and then curves left into the Alarka Mountains. Thirteen miles from the city it descends a long, easy grade and enters Nantahala Gorge and for six miles is hemmed in by very high rock walls. At times the cliffs hang over the highway. At Nantahala Station, twenty miles from Bryson, a road to the left crosses the river on an iron bridge and immediately starts up a steep, crooked grade. This is called the Winding Stair Scenic Road; it will be mentioned later.

Almost straight ahead but a trifle to the right is a yellow splotch high on the side of a mountain. This is Point Lookout, our next objective, less than four miles away by airline, six by the highway, but with careful driving it will take twenty-five minutes to reach it. Four miles from Nantahala is a junction with U.S. 129; the road comes from the right over a wooden bridge above a railroad. Turn here and proceed two miles to Point Lookout at Tulula Gap. U.S. 129 curves back so that it parallels but climbs high above U.S. 19. At "The Lookout," as it is called locally, are a small parking place and a covered pavilion. Straight ahead is the gorge through which you have come, and Nantahala Station, three miles distant and 1,000 feet lower than the pavilion, can be seen plainly. A little to the right on the other side of the gorge the Winding Stairs Scenic Road climbs a mountain and if your eyes are keen you will discover, near the top, a waterfall looking like a piece of white ribbon against the rocks. Good field glasses are very useful at Point Lookout.

To follow Trip One as planned means a return to U.S. 19, but let us see what lies ahead on U.S. 129. It may be useful to people who, having come into the mountains from the east, have not seen Newfound Gap and the country around Knoxville. For their benefit we might call this *Alternate Trip One.*

Eleven miles from Point Lookout is Lake Santeetlah, an artificial lake of 3,000 acres; for ten miles the road follows the irregular shore line. The lake water is impounded by a dam and piped nine miles to Lake Cheoah, where there is a power plant. At one place the large pipe line is carried over the road. At Lake Cheoah the highway passes below a dam and in front of the powerhouse, a pretty, ivy-covered building.

Six and one-half miles farther is Deals Gap, at the Tennessee-North Carolina line, and a junction with North Carolina Route 288, which extends from the Gap to Bryson City. But let me give a word of warning to anyone who sees this road on a map and thinks it may be a short cut to Bryson City. It is fifty miles of very narrow and crooked road that becomes rutty and muddy in wet weather, and the western third is not improved.

Nine miles after crossing the state line U.S. 129 is high above the Little Tennessee River. To the left can be seen another dam, which holds back the waters of Lake Calderwood, in a long, narrow valley between mountains.

U.S. 129 is paved and wide enough for cars to pass, but the many sharp curves should be approached carefully, and drivers should always keep to the right side of the road, especially on curves.

Maryville is thirty-eight miles from the state line—Knoxville sixteen miles farther. At Maryville is a junction with Tennessee Route 73, leading to Gatlinburg. A favorite trip with Tennessee and North Carolina people who are driving visitors about the mountains is the circle tour, which includes Gatlinburg, Bryson City, Nantahala Gorge, Point Lookout, and Maryville. This circle is a drive of approximately 200 miles, including a trip from Newfound Gap to Clingmans Dome. This may not seem like a day's trip, but if you drive the crooked roads carefully, stop for lunch and at the many places where beauty demands more than a glimpse from a moving automobile, you can use all of the time between breakfast and dinner.

Continuing Trip One from Point Lookout, go to the junction with U.S. 19 and turn right, passing a railroad station named Topton. The road descends into a wide and level valley of good farm land. To the right, thirteen miles from Topton, great piles of white marble can be seen. There are many quarries in this neighborhood. Near some of them it is interesting to see log cabins with white marble chimneys and blocks of the same material supporting the cabins.

At Murphy, twenty-four miles from Topton, is a junction with U.S. 64. The Tennessee-North Carolina state line is twenty-three miles from Murphy and four miles beyond is Ducktown, Tennessee, at the edge of a copper-mining district. For years the smelters poured out their fumes, which destroyed every bit of vegetation, and erosion of the soil naturally followed. Four miles south on Tennessee Route 68 is Copperhill, the commercial center for the mining country. From the road the scene is one of utter desolation. Even the soil has taken the copper color and there is not a tree or even a blade of grass.

In 1789, the Legislature of North Carolina ceded to the Federal Government its western lands, now the state of Tennessee. The act stated that the boundary should follow the crest of the highest mountains between the southern line of Virginia and the northern line of Georgia. The copper mines are in Tennessee but east of the highest mountains in that section. There is a tradition that the surveyors who ran this part of the line in 1821 had been supplied with whisky by the guides who accompanied them. But when they reached a point near the Hiwassee River they had not had any whisky for some time and, hearing about a still directly south of them, near the Georgia boundary, they ran their line straight for it. Thus North Carolina lost the valuable copper deposits.

To avoid returning to Murphy over the same road, you can continue on Route 68 which, just outside of Copperhill, crosses another state line and becomes Georgia State Highway 5. Twelve miles south is Blue Ridge and a junction with U.S. 76. Driving east on this road it is twenty-eight miles to Blairsville and a connection with U.S. 19, by which it is twenty-two miles to Murphy and seventy-one to Bryson City. As outlined, taking in Point Lookout, the copper country, and the dip down into Georgia, Trip One covers about two hundred miles. Between Bryson City and Murphy, U.S. 19 is used both going and returning.

If one does not care to see the copper country, the trip can be varied by turning onto U.S. 64 at Murphy and following it eastward through a sparsely-settled country for sixty miles. At the western edge of Franklin is a junction with North Carolina Route 28 over which it is twenty-seven miles to Bryson City. This is a round trip of one hundred and forty miles.

U.S. 64 is a pretty drive, but along it there are no places of outstanding scenic interest, although near Franklin Wayah Bald is only thirteen miles from the highway, on a forest service road. But I am outlining a special trip to this mountain because it should be visited on a clear day and can be reached when one feels in the mood for a short drive.

Trip Number Two starts from Bryson City on the same road as Trip One. For six miles the highway is both U.S. 19 and North Carolina Route 28; the latter number is followed to Franklin, where a right turn is made onto U.S. 64. Five miles west of Franklin the highway joins a graveled National Forest Service road, where another right turn is made. Nine miles farther another service road branches off, again to the right. Over this it is four miles to Wayah Bald. In the highlands when you hear a mountain called a "bald" you will know that it has no trees on its summit.

The forest service road goes to the summit of Wayah Bald, where from a stone observation tower superb mountain views extend in all directions. You will do well to take a lunch and stay the day because, with the traveling of the sun, the light falls on different places and the scenes are constantly changing. In the late spring or early summer, depending on the weather, azalea blossoms are thick around Wayah Bald. Again you are fortunate if a shower has fallen somewhere in the distance. Then great masses of clouds, looking like bunches of cotton, rise out of the forest.

The return trip offers several alternative routes, but for a real experience in mountain driving you can return to the main forest road and turn right. From here it is twenty-three miles to Nantahala Station and a junction with U.S. 19, twenty-five miles from Bryson City. The last three miles of the forest road is the Winding Stair Scenic Road, which has been mentioned before. It is steep and very crooked, and none too wide for a timid passenger, but not dangerous if you have a careful driver. However, if you have not been over this road before, I strongly recommend that you use it going down instead of going up, for then you are on the inside of the road, instead of on the edge, looking into a deep gorge.

If you do not want to drive the Winding Stair Scenic Road you can return to Franklin, going through the city on combined U.S. Routes 64 and 23. One mile east of the city, where the roads fork, keep straight ahead on U.S. 23 to Dillsboro, where a left turn on U.S. 19 will take you to Bryson City, eighteen miles from Dillsboro.

On *Trip Number Three* a number of beautiful waterfalls should be seen. From Bryson City this trip goes east on U.S. 19 eighteen miles to Dillsboro, where a right turn is made onto U.S. 23. From Dillsboro a twenty-mile drive brings you to a junction with U.S. 64, a short distance outside the city of Franklin, which you do not enter. North Carolina Route 28 is eight miles shorter between Bryson City and Franklin, and if you have not driven over it on Trips One or Two it would be as well to use it now. If you do so, you will go into Franklin, turn left on combined U.S. 23 and U.S. 64 and drive through the town to the junction mentioned above, where U.S. 64 turns right. After you pass through the business section, watch out for a steep down grade with a curve to the left at the bottom. Franklin has an altitude of 2,113 feet and is one of the oldest summer resorts in these mountains, having been frequented by people from South Carolina, Georgia, and Florida for many years.

For a few miles U.S. 64 goes through a farming community and then starts a gradual ascent to the highlands. Before long the road is on the side of a cliff two hundred and fifty feet above the Cullasaja River. The highway is wide enough for two cars to pass, but there are many curves, some of them blind. In such places, however, sturdy stone walls line the side next to the gorge.

Ten miles after leaving U.S. 23 you will notice a series of cascades in the river, and five miles farther is Dry Falls, said to have received its name because it is possible to walk behind the falls and not get wet. Here are a parking place, a small shelter house, and steps and a trail down to the waterfall. It might be noted here that nearly all of this trip is in the Nantahala National Forest, and that the conveniences at Dry Falls were installed by the United States Forest Service.

In the woods across the road from the parking place are great clumps of galax. This plant furnishes the round bronze leaves used for Christmas decorations and for funeral wreaths. But in the summer the leaves are green; perhaps you will be lucky enough to see it when each plant has a spike of fine, white blossoms.

A mile beyond Dry Falls a new experience awaits you. Bridal Veil Falls, with a considerable flow of water in any but the dryest season, breaks from an overhanging cliff and drops into the gorge, leaving space for the highway between the face of the cliff and the falling water.

Four miles beyond Bridal Veil Falls is the village of Highlands, at an altitude of 3,835 feet. This, like Franklin, is an old-established summer resort for Southerners, and since the era of automobiles and good roads, has been discovered by Northerners, who return year after year. There are good hotels, inns, tea rooms, and good shops where mountain handicrafts are sold. The days are seldom hot and blankets can be used almost every night. U.S. 64

angles to the left in the center of the village, but if you enjoy a hike up an easy grade, park your car and walk up the gravel road straight ahead. You will see rhododendron and laurel in lush growth that comes from ample moisture, galax with immense leaves, and other flowers in profusion.

I remember a colorful expression that I learned in South Carolina one summer, years before there were paved roads in this part of the mountains. We were headed for Atlanta, but thinking it would be uncomfortably hot there, decided to try to reach Highlands for supper. In a village we asked a man to give us directions. He replied, "Well, you all can get to Pickens all right, but after that the roads are kind a-scatterin'!" Now Highlands can be reached by excellent paved roads from any direction.

A mile outside the village is an eighteen-hole golf course, which has special rates for visitors.

Eight miles northeast of Highlands U.S. 64 curves left around a cliff disclosing another view comparable to that at Fightin' Creek Gap near Gatlinburg. On the left side of the road is a parking place, and if you stop I'm sure you will stay for some time. Several hundred feet below a valley stretches far into the distance, and near by, on the right, is Whiteside Mountain with a sheer rock cliff rising 1,800 feet above the valley.

The road winds down into the valley and in four miles comes to Cashiers and a junction with North Carolina Route 107. Two miles to the right on this road is the estate of General Wade Hampton, an officer in the Confederate Army, Governor of South Carolina, and United States Senator. The estate contains 1,800 acres on which are a resort hotel, a golf course, and several small lakes. Horses are available for those who wish to ride.

Straight ahead six miles from Cashiers on U.S. 64 is Toxaway Falls. This can be seen from the road but to get a good view one should go down into the gorge. Except for a fifteen-foot drop one-third of the way down, the water slides one hundred and twenty-five feet over a dome-shaped rock.

U.S. 64 leads to Brevard and Hendersonville, where one may take U.S. 25 to Asheville. From Brevard U.S. 276, a very crooked concrete road ascends Caesars Head and goes down the other side into South Carolina. After the summit is passed the rolling land of upper South Carolina stretches as far as the eye can see, and after a few more miles on this road fields of cotton grow.

The country is pretty all the way from Franklin to Hendersonville, but, with the exception of Toxaway Falls, the best part of the scenery is between Franklin and Cashiers, and so I advise you to go north from Cashiers on North Carolina Route 107 from the junction with U.S. 64.

Onion Skin Falls is nine miles north of Cashiers. This, like Toxaway, is not a sheer drop; the water slides over the rock.

In *The Scenic Resources of the Tennessee Valley* it is said that "the High Falls of the Tuckasegee rank among the three or four most impressive and beautiful cataracts in the Tennessee Valley region." This fall cannot be seen from the highway. One half-mile north of Onion Skin Falls, a prominent trail to the left leads up over a low ridge and one half-mile down to the base of the High Falls. The water plunges straight down sixty feet, striking a ledge of rock which splits it into two additional falls of twenty-five feet.

Beyond Onion Skin Falls a long down grade leads to the valley of the Tuckasegee River, which is followed to Bryson City. Twenty-eight miles from Cashiers is Cullowhee, and the pretty campus of Western Carolina Teachers College. Four miles farther is Sylva, and it is twenty miles to Bryson City on U.S. 19. The round trip via Franklin, Cashiers, and Sylva is about one hundred and fifteen miles.

At Fontana, about forty miles west of Bryson City, a huge dam is being built on the Little Tennessee River. It will be four hundred and fifty feet high, the highest dam east of the Rocky Mountains and the fourth largest concrete dam in the United States. The lake which it will form will extend to the western limits of Bryson City. Much of Route 288 will be submerged and the road will be abandoned or relocated.

Trips One, Two, and Three do not include all of the interesting scenery in this section of the mountains, but I think they omit none of the outstanding features.

Trip Number Four is to Asheville, seventy miles east of Bryson City on U.S. 19, where several days can be interestingly spent. The highway follows the Southern Railroad all the way. Shortly after passing the hamlet of Addie you begin the long climb up to Balsam Gap on a wide concrete road with no very sharp curves. You lose sight of the railroad and when you come upon it at the Gap wonder how it made the climb. At an altitude of 3,315 feet, this is claimed to be the highest standard-gage railroad east of the Mississippi.

A long, straight stretch of down grade leads from the gap; a mile and a half below it on the left is the Morrison State Fish Hatchery. Out of doors, in concrete pools, are trout of all sizes. A small menagerie in cages is scattered around the ample grounds and many prairie dogs, uncaged, scamper into their holes when people come near.

Thirty-five miles from Bryson City is Waynesville, another old resort town with good accommodations for visitors. From Waynesville an interesting circle drive of approximately thirty-two miles can be made, which I like very much because it goes into the back-country. As part of the route is not hard-surfaced it would be inadvisable to drive it after a heavy rain. Leaving Waynesville, go north on North Carolina Route 284. Eleven miles from the city, just outside the hamlet of Cove Creek, a gravel road joins the highway on the right. It goes through eight miles of peaceful mountain farming country and forest to meet North Carolina Route 209, a paved road, over which it is twelve miles to a junction with U.S. 19, at Lake Junaluska, four miles northeast of Waynesville.

Canton, eight miles east of the lake, has one of the largest paper pulp mills in the world.

Nine miles east of Canton is a junction with North Carolina Route 112. If you have had an early start it is possible to go south to Mt. Pisgah over this road and still get into Asheville before night. Pisgah, altitude 5,791 feet, is the outstanding mountain in this region and almost every visitor to Asheville makes this trip. A whole day is not too much time to devote to it.

From the junction nine miles east of Canton seventeen miles' driving bring you to Pisgah Forest Inn. It is said that five states can be seen from the summit of Mt. Pisgah in clear weather. A profusion of bloom through the spring and a gorgeous display of colored foliage in the autumn make the region notable. It is possible to go beyond Pisgah and circle into Asheville by way of Hendersonville, but this necessitates driving over seven miles of unpaved road on the south side of the mountain. Therefore I advise a return to the junction with U.S. 19, from which place it is eight miles to Asheville.

TRIPS IN THE ASHEVILLE REGION

In and around the city are many interesting short trips and several long ones. Go north on Charlotte Street and drive around the Grove Park district to see the pretty homes built in spacious yards with many flowers. Turn right from Charlotte Street onto Macon Avenue and visit the Grove Park Inn. In each end of the enormous lounge is a fireplace high enough to admit a tall person. Each fireplace is built of granite boulders, some of them so large that you wonder how they were put in place. The front porch looks out over a golf course and Mt. Pisgah looms prominently in the distance. The inn is truly one of the architectural marvels of the South. During certain hours of the day it is closed to all but registered guests, so that it would be well to inquire about visiting hours.

A short distance beyond the entrance to the hotel grounds, Macon

Avenue ends. From this place a toll road leads to the top of Sunset Mountain, a five-mile drive. The summit is 900 feet above Asheville and the city and the surrounding country are spread out below like a map.

The Elk Mountain Scenic Tour is a seventeen-mile drive along mountaintops. It can be reached by going north on Charlotte Street to a left turn onto Kimberly Avenue and following North Carolina Route 694, which circles around and comes into the city from the east.

Biltmore and Biltmore Forest are pretty residential districts on the south side of the Swannanoa River. Biltmore Avenue leads to them. Biltmore was laid out as a model English-type village in 1889. Biltmore Forest is newer and more modern in architecture.

Thirty miles northeast of Asheville are the Craggy Gardens, where there is a wonderful display of rhododendron flowers in June. The growth is so dense that the blossoms form an almost solid expanse of purple, ten miles long and almost a mile wide. To reach the gardens by good roads go out Merriman Avenue, following U.S. 19 and U.S. 23 to Stocksville, and North Carolina Route 197 to Barnardsville. From Barnardsville the Craggy Gardens Highway leads to a parking place overlooking the gardens. One can reach the gardens more directly by a parkway continuing from Route 694, but road conditions should be investigated before taking the shorter route.

These short trips have not been numbered, and they have been described with less detail than the others because information about them is easily obtained at the hotels and tourist bureaus in Asheville.

Trip Number Five will be a round trip of about eighty miles, but so many things are to be seen along the way that a full day should be allotted to it.

From downtown Asheville follow U.S. 74 through the long tunnel under Beaucatcher Mountain. At fourteen miles the road begins the long ascent to Hickory Nut Gap by a series of corkscrew

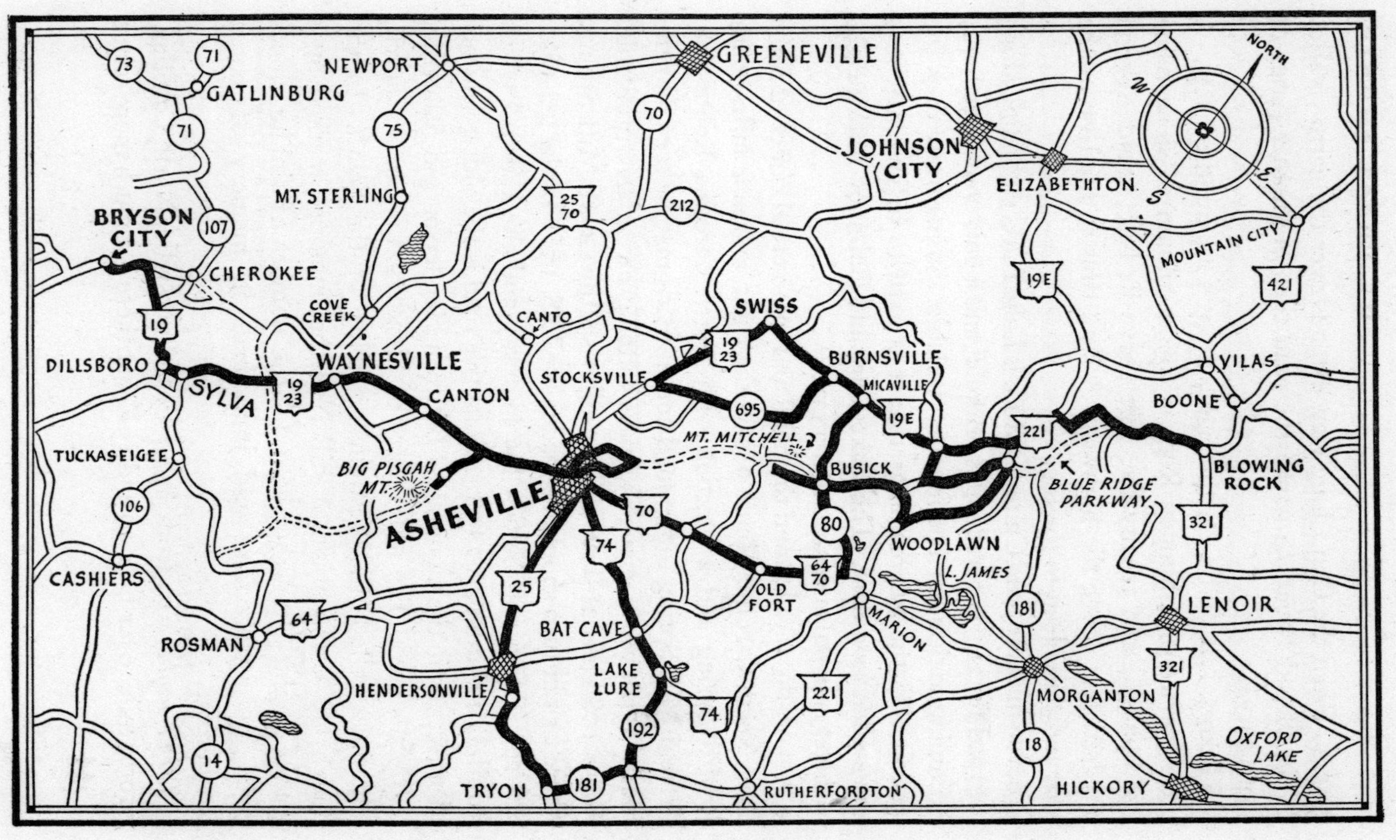

ASHEVILLE AND MT. MITCHELL REGION

curves. From the Gap a long view extends over the narrow valley of the Broad River, to which the road dips in another series of sharp curves.

Hickory Nut Falls, on the right, drops four hundred feet. A little farther on Chimney Rock, a round column of stone rising two hundred and twenty-five feet above its base, stands several hundred feet above the highway. A road runs to the base of the rock and stairs lead to the top.

Seven miles beyond Chimney Rock is Lake Lure, extending along the road for nearly three miles. A hotel and a golf course are here; swimming and motor boating are available. So naturally does the lake fit into the surroundings that it is hard to believe that it is impounded by a dam. The Lake Lure and Chimney Rock neighborhood is popular vacation territory.

A short distance beyond the hotel and commercial center of Lake Lure North Carolina Route 9 is on the right, and nine miles south is Mill Spring and a junction with North Carolina Route 108. Around Mill Spring some small cotton fields may be seen, but the climate is not warm enough to make cotton growing very profitable. Route 108 ends at Tryon, nine miles southwest of Mill Spring, where a right turn should be made onto U.S. 176. In the ten miles between Tryon and Saluda the highway and the railroad which parallels it climb 1,000 feet. Along this road is the oldest summer resort section in the mountains. Between Henderson and Asheville, U.S. 25 is used. Ten miles north of Henderson is Christ Church, sometimes called the Westminster Abbey of the South. In the churchyard is the grave of Bill Nye the humorist, marked by a granite boulder, together with a large number of similar stones given by organizations and individuals in memory of noted Southerners.

Trip Number Six, from Asheville to Burnsville, North Carolina, is forty miles over U.S. 19 and 19E, but there is a much more scenic route twenty-one miles longer. Route 70 leaves Asheville through the Beaucatcher Tunnel. Fifteen miles east of the city is the entrance to a toll road which goes almost to the top of Mt. Mitchell, the highest mountain east of the Mississippi River. Traffic goes up in the morning and down in the afternoon. Eighteen and a half miles further, at Camp Alice, a trail runs one mile and a half to the summit of Mt. Mitchell.

At Ridgecrest, two miles beyond the entrance to the toll road, Route 70 starts the ascent of the Blue Ridge. Just over the summit of the Ridge is Point Lookout, with a parking space, refreshment room, and a shop selling mountain handicrafts. A view of the Royal Gorge, many hundred feet below, is seen from the porch of the shop. From Point Lookout twists a long down grade with many sharp curves. Fifteen miles east is a junction with North Carolina Route 80. Between the junction and Micaville, twenty-six miles to the north, lies some of the finest scenery in these mountains. Three miles from the junction is Lake Tahoma, and a little farther on the road starts the climb, with several sharp curves, to Buck Creek Gap. At the Gap (another fine view), Route 80 is crossed by the Blue Ridge Parkway, a continuation of the Virginia Skyline Drive.

To the left a seven-mile stretch of the Blue Ridge Parkway goes to a point below the summit of Mt. Mitchell. It is a wide road with a good gravel surface, with many extensive views over rugged mountainous country.

All the way from Buck Creek Gap to Micaville, fourteen miles, Route 80 parallels the Black Mountain Range of which Mt. Mitchell is the southern peak and Mt. Celo the northern. On a clear day the stone tower on the summit of Mt. Mitchell can be seen from several points on the road.

Burnsville, five miles to the west of Micaville on U.S. 19E, is an excellent place from which to tour the country to the northeast of Asheville.

TRIPS IN THE MT. MITCHELL REGION

Trip Number Seven returns east from Burnsville, fifteen miles to Spruce Pine, where a right turn is made on North Carolina Route 26. Six miles from Spruce Pine is a junction with the Blue Ridge Parkway. Northeast from Spruce Pine a thirteen-mile paved section connects with U.S. 221, one mile from the village of Linville Falls, which receives its name from one of the prettiest cataracts in this region. A short trail leads from the village to the gorge in which the falls are located. There Linville River makes a sheer drop of forty feet, between high rock walls.

In the fourteen miles between Linville Falls and a junction with North Carolina Route 26, U.S. 221 drops 2,000 feet. Turn right from U.S. 221 onto Route 26, which in the nine miles to Little Switzerland gains back the 2,000 feet of altitude. From the road wide views extend to the east and two prominent mountains, Hawksbill and Table Rock, are outlined against the sky.

A short distance beyond Little Switzerland at the junction with the Blue Ridge Parkway, a left turn was made on the way to Linville Falls. Another left turn at this point will take you to Buck Creek Gap over thirteen miles of good gravel. From the Gap the return can be made to Burnsville as described in Trip Six.

If you want a short interesting trip into an isolated section, go to the east end of Burnsville and turn right on North Carolina Route 197, a good gravel road. Along the way are several grist mills operated by water power. Almost every miller will be glad to have you come in and visit, and he will show you how the mill operates. The corn meal manufactured in these mills is not bolted and it is not necessary to add wheat flour to it when making corn bread or pancakes. Therefore you get the full corn flavor. Buy some of it, or better still, purchase some shelled corn in town and have it ground at the mill. Instead of paying cash for the work, ask the miller to take his toll of the corn as he does for his neighbors; you will have experienced something that the highland people do at least once each week, for meal to be good must be freshly ground.

Twelve miles from Burnsville is Pensacola, and here one of three courses can be taken. You can return to Burnsville as you came; you can continue on Route 197 over fifteen miles of gravel and seven miles of pavement to a junction with U.S. 19, thirty-six miles from Burnsville, or you can go two and a half miles over what is known as the Tom Wilson Road to Eskota. At this place is an entrance to another toll road up Mt. Mitchell.

The driver unaccustomed to mountain roads would do well to take the toll road up Mt. Mitchell, mentioned in Trip Six, fifteen miles east of Asheville. It is wide enough for only one car, but traffic is allowed in only one direction at a time, and when the last car starts up or down, a patrol car follows and anyone having trouble is assisted.

Before leaving the Burnsville region let me speak of the glitter which you will see on the gravel roads and in the cultivated fields. It is caused by particles of mica and if you happen to get in a windstorm, you will have it on your clothes and even in your hair. Mica, feldspar, kaolin, and chrome iron are obtained in this vicinity and there is asbestos too, but the mine has not been operated for several years.

Trip Number Eight, for its first twenty-three miles, will take us east from Burnsville on U.S. 19E to a junction with North Carolina Route 194, a paved road to the right. Four miles further the road meets U.S. 221, and for seven miles the highway bears both numbers; you follow U.S. 221 when it makes a right turn. Two miles on is Pineola and three miles beyond, Linville. Along the road are nurseries that specialize in mountain shrubs.

For a mile you drive between rows of evergreens with branches that meet over the road, giving the effect of a tunnel; you cross an arm of a lake which is on a private estate, pass a golf course and enter the park-like resort village of Linville.

In 1886 a narrow-gage railroad was built from Johnson City, Tennessee, to take out the lumber from this part of North Carolina. It was not long until passenger service was installed, giving easy access to the summer resorts already in existence, and Northerners began to come in considerable numbers.

A ride on the narrow-gage was an adventure. The coaches were too narrow to accommodate two rows of double seats and so, to balance the weight, one-half the car had double seats on the right side and single ones on the left, the arrangement being reversed in the other half. The engine labored up the steep, crooked grade in the Doe River Gorge and took four hours to make a sixty-six-mile run.

In wide, sweeping curves U.S. 221 climbs out of Linville onto a spur of Grandfather Mountain and for twenty miles is above 3,500 feet in altitude. One mile out of the village the great rock forming the summit of Grandfather can be seen on the left and half a mile farther is a mile-long toll road to a parking space from which it is only half a mile to the summit over a foot trail.

Grandfather is one of the easiest mountains to climb in this whole region and the view from the top is one of the most far-reaching. The Black Mountain Range, of which Mt. Mitchell is one of the peaks, can be seen on a clear day.

In late June or early July there is so much rhododendron and azalea blooming along U.S. 221 that the trip over the road seems like a drive through a garden.

Twenty miles east of Linville is the village of Blowing Rock, which receives its name from a cliff overlooking the narrow valley of the Johns River, more than 2,000 feet below. There is an almost constant flow of air up from the valley and light articles thrown from the cliff are returned by the draft.

Nine miles north of Blowing Rock is Boone and the end of this trip. Whenever I drive into Boone I think of Miss Margaret Morley and how, in her book, *The Carolina Mountains,* she bemoaned the passing of the old way of living. She recalled that when she first visited Boone it was thirty miles from a railroad and there was peace and quiet; now she could hear the tinkle of a telephone bell. "With what pangs of regret one has watched the passing of the primitive life of the mountains, and—those old days when everybody was uncomfortable and everybody happy." I wonder what Miss Morley would say now, if she could see Boone and scores of other mountain towns, with their wide paved streets, picture shows, and modern stores.

Twelve miles east of Boone, on U.S. 421, is a junction with another section of the Blue Ridge Parkway, which is completed to a point on U.S. 11 close to Roanoke, Virginia. This is a good way for those going northeast to reach the Sky Line Drive. Those who have come to the mountains from this direction will no doubt be on their way to the Great Smoky Mountains National Park and thence into Tennessee. People from the Midwest can return on U.S. 11 from Knoxville. Those who do not wish to go via the Sky Line Drive will find a good route over U.S. 221 and U.S. 21 from Boone. From the south there are so many routes into the mountains that I shall not list them.

For those who do not care to drive, there is excellent railroad service from any part of the country to Knoxville and Asheville. In normal times from each of these cities bus tours operate on schedules. The busses go through the Park, over Newfound Gap and return by a different route. On overnight trips all arrangements for accommodations are made by the company operating this service.

Only a very small number of many interesting places have been mentioned, but I have attempted to include the most prominent and most accessible ones. If you come once you will return again and again and you will hear about other places, many of them as beautiful as those I have mentioned.

So these are the southern mountains, "these be the mountains that comfort me." Here are the hills, which once loved, call the traveler again and again. The Rockies are dramatic, the Sierras are loved with passion, but the Great Smokies and the Blue Ridge fit into the scheme of life like a good and understanding friend. Yet, like an interesting friend, they are not learned in a day nor perhaps in a lifetime. They have many facets and many moods. There is nothing obvious about them as there is with a desert range. Their secrets are hidden in misty glens. One does not easily find the rhododendron garden on the peak. Only the informed know where the best view is to be found.

And, not least, there are the mountain folk. Perhaps no other American people are so perfectly fitted to an environment. In this new land we have a way of destroying the character of locale by altering the provincial environment to our cosmopolitan desires. But the mountain folk have taken on the color of the forest and mountain until they are blended inconspicuously and perfectly into the scene. Sky, mountain, forest, and man in these southern mountains make a perfect whole. There is no discordant note. Out of this very harmony one gains not only a sense of the art of nature, but a love of land which cannot be measured except by a pull, a provincial gravity, which surely and certainly draws one to return.

Editor

AN APPENDIX
OF FURTHER READING

On History

Adair, James (Samuel Cole Williams, ed.). *Adair's History of the American Indians.* Johnson City, 1930.

Alvord, Clarence W., and Bidgood, Lee. *The First Exploration of the Trans-Allegheny Region by the Virginians. 1650-1674.* Cleveland: Clark, 1912.

Arthur, John Preston. *Western North Carolina.* Raleigh, North Carolina, 1914.

Asbury, Francis (E. S. Tipple, ed.). *The Heart of Asbury's Journal.* New York: Methodist Book Concern, 1904.

Bakeless, John E. *Daniel Boone.* New York: Morrow, 1939.

Bartram, William. *Travels of William Bartram.* New York: Macy-Masius, 1928.

Becker: *Gold Fields of the Southern Appalachians.* Sixteenth Annual Report. U. S. Geological Survey. 1895.

Draper, L. C. *King's Mountain and Its Heroes.* Cincinnati: Thomson, 1881.

Driver, Carl S. *John Sevier, Pioneer of the Old Southwest.* Chapel Hill: University of North Carolina Press, 1932.

Ford, Henry J. *The Scotch-Irish in America.* Princeton, N. J.: University Press, 1915.

Gilmore, James R. (Edmund Kirke, pseud.). *The Rear-Guard of the Revolution.* New York: Appleton, 1886.

James, Marquis. *The Raven.* A biography of Sam Houston. Indianapolis: Bobbs-Merrill, 1929.

Jameson, J. Franklin (ed.). *Original Narratives of Early American History: Spanish Explorers in the Southern States, 1528-43.* New York: Scribner, 1906.

Henderson, Archibald. *Conquest of the Old Southwest.* New York: Century, 1920.

Mooney, James. *Myths of the Cherokee.* Bureau of American Ethnology. Nineteenth Annual Report. Washington, D. C., 1900.

Pusey, William A. *The Wilderness Road to Kentucky.* New York: Doran, 1921.

Sondley, Foster A. *History of Buncombe County.* Asheville, North Carolina, 1933.

Williams, S. C. *History of the Lost State of Franklin.* Johnson City, Tenn.: Watauga Press, 1924.

On the Mountain Folk

Campbell, John C. *The Southern Highlander and his Homeland.* New York: Russell Sage, 1921.

Chapman, Maristan. *Hoe Place.* New York: Viking Press, 1929.

Craddock, Charles E. (pseud. of Mary N. Murfree). *Prophet of the Great Smoky Mountains.* Boston: Houghton Mifflin, 1885.

———. *The Despot of Broomsedge Cove.* Boston: Houghton Mifflin, 1889.

Dargan, Olive Tilford. *Highland Annals.* New York; Scribner, 1925.

Hannum, Alberta Pierson. *The Hills Step Lightly.* New York: Morrow, 1934.

———. *The Gods and One.* New York: Duell, Sloan & Pearce, 1941.

———. *Thursday April.* New York: Harper, 1931.

Kephart, Horace. *Our Southern Highlanders.* New York: Macmillan, 1926.

Murdock, Louise S. *Almetta of Gabriel's Run.* New York: Meridian Press, 1917.

Sheppard, Muriel E. *Cabins in the Laurel.* Chapel Hill: University of North Carolina Press, 1935.

On Forests

Coker, W. C., and Totten, H. L. *Trees of the Southeastern States.* Chapel Hill: University of North Carolina Press, 1937.

Green, Charlotte Hilton. *Trees of the South.* Chapel Hill: University of North Carolina Press, 1939.

Mathews, F. Schuyler. *Field Book of American Trees and Shrubs.* New York: Putnam, 1915.

Pinchot, Gifford, and Ashe, W. W. *Timber Trees of North Carolina.* North Carolina State Geological Survey. *Bulletin 6.* 1897.

Sargent, Charles S. *Manual of the Trees of North America.* Boston: Houghton Mifflin, 1933.

Wells, B. W. *Natural Gardens of North Carolina.* Chapel Hill: University of North Carolina Press, 1932.

Articles in Scientific Magazines, on Forest Ecology

Davis, John H., Jr. "Vegetation of the Black Mountains of North Carolina: an Ecological Study." Elisha Mitchell Scientific Society *Journal*, vol. 45, pages 291-318. 1930.

"Forest Cover Types of the Eastern United States": Report of the Committee on Forest Types, Society of American Foresters. *Journal of Forestry*, vol. 30, pages 1-48. 1932.

Oosting, Henry J. "An Ecological Analysis of the Plan Communities of Piedmont, North Carolina." *American Midland Naturalist*, vol. 28, pages 1-126.

Lumbering and Forest Conditions

Bowman, Isaiah. *Forest Physiography*. New York: Wiley, 1911.

Frothingham, E. H. "Timber Growing and Logging Practice in the Southern Appalachian Region." U. S. Department of Agriculture *Technical Bulletin* 250. 1931.

Glenn, Leonidas Chalmers. *Denudation and Erosion in the Southern Appalachians.* U. S. Geological Survey *Professional Paper* 72. 1911.

Holmes, J. S. *Forest Conditions in Western North Carolina.* North Carolina Geological and Economic Survey *Bulletin*, vol. 23. 1911.

Pinchot, Gifford, and Ashe, W. W. *Timber Trees of North Carolina.* North Carolina State Geological Survey *Bulletin* 6. 1897.

On Flowers

Identification:

Fink, Bruce. *The Lichen Flora of the United States.* Ann Arbor: University of Michigan, 1935.

Grout, Abel J. *Mosses With a Hand-lens and Microscope.* The Author, New Brighton, N. Y. 1924.

Krieger, L. C. C. *The Mushroom Handbook.* New York: Macmillan, 1936.

Lounsberry, Alice. *Southern Wild Flowers and Trees.* New York: Stokes, 1901.

Small, John Kunkel. *Ferns of the Southeastern States.* New York: Science Press, 1938.

———. *Manual of the Southeastern Flora.* New York: Science Press, 1933.

Wells, Bertram W. *The Natural Gardens of North Carolina.* Chapel Hill: University of North Carolina Press, 1932.

Plant Distribution and Evolution

Berry, Edward W. *Tree Ancestors.* Baltimore: Williams & Wilkins Co., 1923.

Cain, Stanley A. "Certain floristic affinities of the trees and shrubs of the Great Smoky Mountains and vicinity." Butler University *Botanical Studies*, vol. 1, pages 129-156. 1930.

———. "The Tertiary character of the cove hardwood forest of the Great Smoky Mountains National Park." Torrey Botanical Club *Bulletin*, vol. 70, pages 213-235. 1943.

Coker, W. C. "The distribution of *Rhododendron catawbiense* with remarks on a new form." Elisha Mitchell Scientific Society *Journal*, vol. 35, pages 76-82. 1919.

Core, Earl L. "Plant migrations and vegetational history of the southern Appalachian region." *Lilloa*, vol. 3, pages 5-29. 1938.

Gray, Asa. "Diagnostic characters of new species . . . with observations upon the relations of the Japanese flora to that of North America . . . etc." American Academy of Arts and Sciences *Memoirs*, series iv, vol. 6, pages 377-452. 1859.

———. "Forest geography and archaeology." *American Journal of Science* (series iii), vol. 16, pages 85-95, 183-196. 1878.

Ecology

Cain, Stanley A. "An ecological study of the heath balds of the Great Smoky Mountains." Butler University *Botanical Studies*, vol. 1, pages 177-208. 1930.

Cain, Stanley A., and Sharp, Aaron S. "Bryophytic unions of certain forest types of the Great Smoky Mountains." *American Midland Naturalist*, vol. 20, pages 249-301. 1938.

Davis, John H., Jr. "Vegetation of the Black Mountains of North Carolina: an ecological study." Elisha Mitchell Scientific Society *Journal*, vol. 45, pages 291-318. 1930.

McDougall, W. B. "Mycorhizas from North Carolina and Eastern Tennessee." *American Journal of Botany*, vol. 15, pages 141-148. 1928.

Plant Hunting and Shortia

Bartram, William. *Travels of William Bartram*. New York: Macy-Masius, 1928.

Gray, Asa. "Notes of a botanical excursion to the mountains of North Carolina, etc., with some remarks on the botany of the higher Allegheny Mountains." *American Journal of Science* (series i), vol. 42, pages 1-49. 1842.

Jenkins, Charles F. "Asa Gray and his quest for *Shortia galacifolia*." *Arnoldia*, vol. 2, pages 13-28. 1942.

Jennison, Harry Milliken. "A sketch of the flora of Great Smoky Mountains National Park." Tennessee Academy of Sciences *Journal*, vol. 14, pages 266-298. 1939.

Michaux, F. A. "Journal of André Michaux, 1787-1796." With an introduction and notes by Charles Sprague Sargent. American Philosophical Society *Proceedings*, vol. 26, pages 1-145. 1899. In French.

Plant Lore, Herbs, Dyes, Ginseng

Eaton, Allen H. *Handicrafts of the Southern Highlands.* New York: Russell Sage Foundation, 1937. See this for dye plants.

Goodrich, Frances L. *Mountain Homespun.* New Haven: Yale University Press, 1931. Good on dye plants and herbs.

Kains, M. G. *Ginseng, Its Cultivation, etc.* New York: Judd, 1908.

Lounsberry, Alice. *Southern Wild Flowers and Trees.* New York: Stokes, 1901.

Mooney, James. "Sacred Formulas of the Cherokees." Bureau of American Ethnology, *74th Annual Report,* 1891, pages 301-39.

Sievers, A. F. "American Medicinal plants of Commercial importance." U. S. Department of Agriculture *Miscellaneous Publication* No. 77, pages 1-74. 1930.

Yoakley, Ina C. "Wild plant industry of the southern Appalachians." *Economic Geography,* vol. 8, pages 358-368. 1932.

On Crafts

Eaton, Allen H. *Handicrafts of the Southern Highlands.* New York: Russell Sage Foundation, 1937.

Morley, Margaret. *The Carolina Mountains.* Boston: Houghton Mifflin, 1913, pages 193-197 and 226-231.

Sheppard, Muriel E. *Cabins in the Laurel.* (Chapter on Fireside Industries.)

W.P.A. *Guide: North Carolina,* a Guide to the Old North State. Chapel Hill: University of North Carolina Press, 1939.

On Ballad and Folk Song Collections

Child, Francis J. (ed.). *The English and Scottish Popular Ballads.* Ten parts, five large volumes. Containing 305 ballads with full explanatory text and every extant version of each ballad. Boston: Houghton Mifflin, 1882-98.

———. *The English and Scottish Popular Ballads* (Student's Cambridge Edition). A one-volume reduction of Professor Child's work referred to above, edited by Helen Child Sargent and George Lyman Kittredge. Boston: Houghton Mifflin, 1904.

Sharp, Cecil, and Campbell, Olive D. *English Folk Songs from the Southern Appalachians.* New York: Oxford University Press. 1932. (Two volumes.)

Cox, John Harrington. *Folk-songs of the South,* Cambridge: Harvard University Press, 1925.

Scarborough, Dorothy. *A Song-Catcher in the Southern Mountains.* New York: Columbia University Press, 1937.

Mackenzie, William R. *Ballads and Sea Songs from Nova Scotia.* Cambridge: Harvard University Press, 1928.

Smith, Reed. *South Carolina Ballads.* Cambridge: Harvard University Press, 1928.

Gummere, Francis B. *Old English Ballads.* Boston: Ginn, 1894.

Sandburg, Carl. *American Songbag.* New York: Harcourt, Brace, 1927.

Brewster, Paul G. *Ballads and Songs of Indiana.* Bloomington: Indiana University Press, 1940.

Jackson, George Pullen. *White Spirituals in the Southern Uplands.* Chapel Hill: University of North Carolina Press, 1933.

The Songs Themselves

Niles, John Jacob. *Songs of the Hill Folk.*

———. *Ten Christmas Carols.*

———. *More Songs of the Hill Folk.*

———. *Ballads, Carols and Tragic Legends.*

———. *Ballads, Love Songs and Tragic Legends.*

All the above published by G. Schirmer, Inc., New York, New York. Many of the carols and folk songs are also arranged for a cappella singing and published in octavo form, same publisher; also recorded, Victor albums M-604, M-718, M-824.

Wyman, Loraine, and Brockway, Howard. *Lonesome Tunes: Folk Songs from the Kentucky Mountains.* New York: Gray, 1916.

McGill, Josephine. *Folk-songs of the Kentucky Mountains.* New York: Boosey, 1917.

Richardson, Alfred M. *Mediaeval Modes.* New York: Gray, 1933.

On the National Park

"Great Smoky Mountains National Park" (information circular), National Park Service, U. S. Department of the Interior, Washington, D. C.

Jennison, H. M. "Flora of the Great Smokies." *Journal* of the Tennessee Academy of Science, vol. 14 (3), 1939.

Komarek, Edwin V., and Komarek, Roy. "Mammals of the Great Smoky Mountains." *Bulletin* of the Chicago Academy of Science, vol. 5, no. 6, 1938.

Kellogg, Remington. "Annotated List of Tennessee Mammals." *Proceedings*, U. S. National Museum, Vol. 86, No. 3051, Washington, 1939.

King, Willis. "A Survey of the Herpetology of Great Smoky Mountains National Park." *The American Midland Naturalist*, vol. 21, no. 3, pages 531-582, May, 1939.

Arthur, John Preston. *History of Watauga County*. Richmond, Virginia: Waddey, 1915.

Preston, Thomas W. *Historical Sketches of the Holston Valleys*. Kingsport, Tenn., 1926.

On Hiking

Guide to the Appalachian Trail in the Southern Appalachians. (Appalachian Trail Conference Publication No. 8.) Second edition, 450 pages, app., 4 maps. 1942.

Guide to Paths in the Blue Ridge. Third edition, 865 pages, 15 maps. 1941.

Hiking on the Appalachian Trail in Georgia. 30 pages, 3"x5" map. 1941. The Georgia Appalachian Trail Club. Procurable from The Appalachian Trail Conference, Inc., Washington, D. C., or from the Georgia Appalachian Trail Club, Chamber of Commerce, Atlanta, Georgia.

On Motoring

Federal Writers Guides, Tennessee, North Carolina, South Carolina, Georgia, and Kentucky.

Official Highway Maps of the same states

Morley, Margaret W. *The Carolina Mountains*. Boston: Houghton Mifflin, 1913.

Sondley, F. A. *History of Buncombe County*.

Map of The Nantahala National Forest, U. S. Department of Agriculture.

Map of The Great Smoky Mountains National Park (for checking mileage only).

INDEX

INDEX

corvine

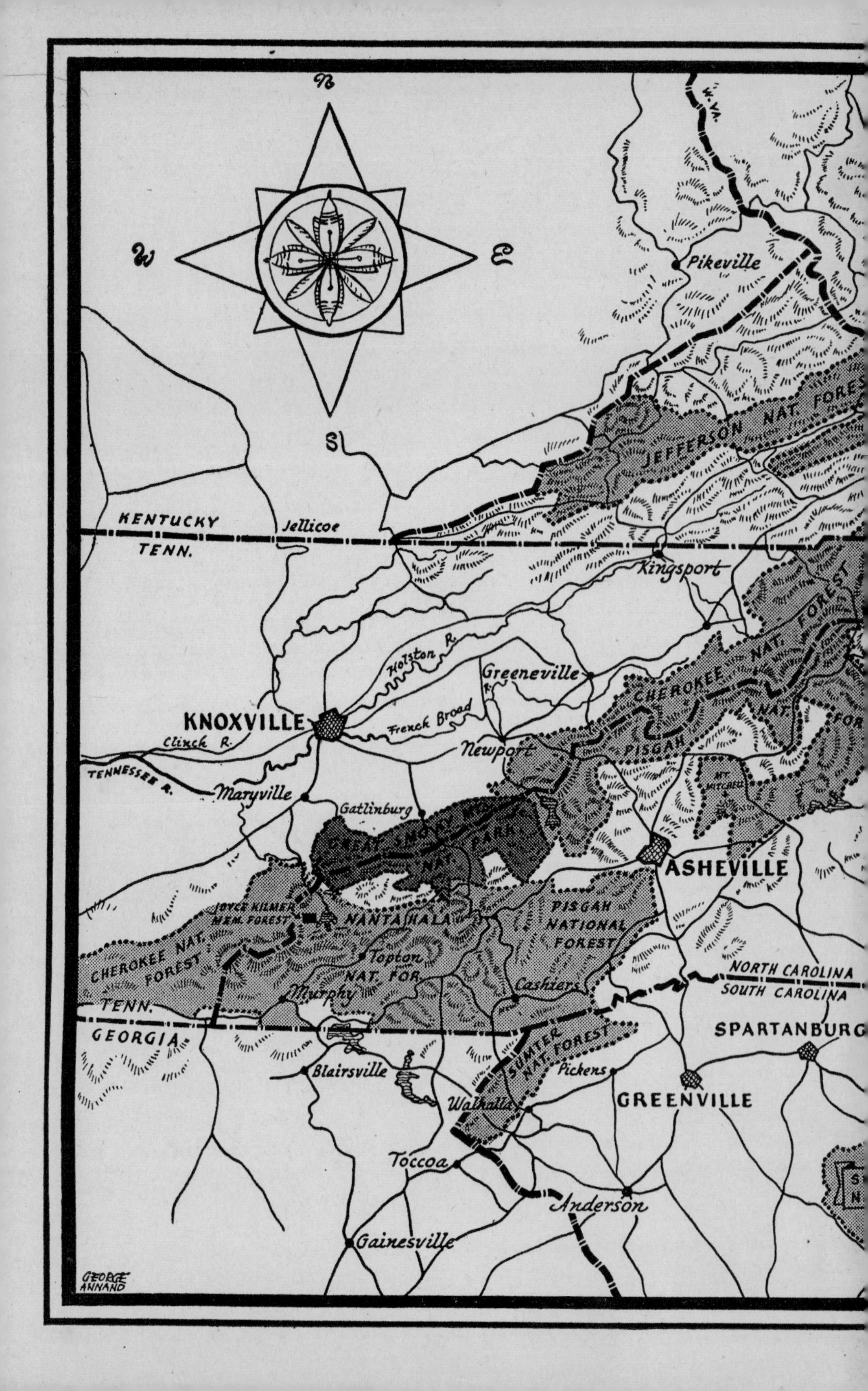
N
W
E
S
W. VA.
Pikeville
JEFFERSON NAT. FOREST
KENTUCKY
TENN.
Jellicoe
Kingsport
CHEROKEE NAT. FOREST
Holston R.
Greeneville
KNOXVILLE
French Broad
Clinch R.
Newport
PISGAH NAT. FOR
TENNESSEE R.
Maryville
Gatlinburg
MT. MITCHELL
GREAT SMOKY MTS. NAT. PARK
ASHEVILLE
JOYCE KILMER MEM. FOREST
NANTAHALA NAT. FOR.
PISGAH NATIONAL FOREST
Topton
CHEROKEE NAT. FOREST
Murphy
Cashiers
NORTH CAROLINA
SOUTH CAROLINA
TENN.
GEORGIA
SPARTANBURG
SUMTER NAT. FOREST
Pickens
Blairsville
GREENVILLE
Walhalla
Toccoa
Anderson
Gainesville
GEORGE ANNAND